# JACK'S STORY...
# TO THE RAINBOW BRIDGE
# AND BACK AGAIN

BY SUSAN MARANO

# JACK'S STORY

### To the Rainbow Bridge
### and Back Again

## SUSAN MARANO

ISBN 978-1-968944-01-8 *(paperback)*
ISBN 978-1-968944-02-5 *(kindle)*

To my Dad—

You bought me my first puppy when I was four years old, and in that small act, you awakened something timeless in me—a soul-deep connection to animals that has shaped the course of my life. Thank you for planting that seed of love and compassion, and for teaching me to live by your words:

"Good, Better, Best. The good become better, the better become best, and the best don't rest."

Your faith in me, and your quiet encouragement of my gift to communicate with animals, have been the steady light guiding my path.

# CONTENTS

# FOREWORD

Those of you who have animal family members will most likely know what it is like to have loved and grieved deeply when that special being dies. It just doesn't seem fair, but our precious animal friends have shorter lives than we do. That's just the way it is. We bring them into our lives knowing they will not be with us for our full life span, and we choose to do it because loving an animal companion, even for a brief time, fills us with laughter, gratitude, fun and a feeling of complete unconditional love.

I have had the privilege of communicating with animals since I was a child. I can hear them, and they can hear me. It's called telepathic communication. I spent 25 years in corporate America. For the last 13 years, communicating with animals has been my full-time passion. I help people have conversations with their animal companions who are alive and in spirit. Topics of conversation can range from behavioral, or health-related concerns to understanding their wishes regarding death, dying, and euthanasia.

The animals that I have spoken with over the years have profoundly expanded my view of life and death. Each opportunity to converse with an animal, especially with those in the process of dying or already in spirit, has helped me to know that life is everlasting. Our animal companions do not fear death; they know that leaving their physical bodies is a transition back into their original essence. Many share similar stories about their transition experiences. They want us to know that once they return to spirit, they remain connected to us and continue to watch over us. Many of them also choose to return to us by incarnating into a new physical body. That is how I met Susan Marano and Jack.

Susan came to me after her "heart dog" Jack, crossed over into spirit. She felt that Jack wanted to return to her again in a new physical body and wanted Jack to tell her how she could find him. When I connected to Jack, he was very excited to communicate the details of his return. He shared an image of himself wearing a top hat, shades of green and a shamrock. It was clear he was communicating that he would be born to a litter of puppies arriving on St. Patrick's Day. He wanted Susan to recognize him easily so the two could be reunited. And that is exactly what happened.

You see, animals routinely return from spirit and reunite with their human family members. Sometimes they are very specific about how they return and other times they just show up on our doorsteps. In our family, we have five out of our seven dogs, which have been with us before. It was through the gift of animal communication or telepathy that we were able to have awareness of this. We were able to learn what they were thinking and feeling before they transitioned back into spirit and then hear their messages after they crossed over.

Animals have also told me that when someone we love crosses over into spirit, we feel emptiness and loss very deeply. Because we are feeling the absence of our loved one, it is difficult to feel their spirit near us. Our attention is on their absence and the hole that is left in our lives. By feeling their absence, we are focused on the opposite of their presence, even if it is the presence of their energy or their spirit. It is like looking for the setting sun in the sky where the sun rises. When we are drawn to the feelings of absence, it is difficult to feel their presence. But they assure me that they are always close by and watching over us.

I hope that those of you that have experienced the loss of a dear animal companion will gain deeper insight from Susan & Jack's story. I also hope it will bring comfort in knowing that we never truly lose those we love; they are always nearby, connected to us, heart to heart and soul to soul.

Wishing you peace, joy and—of course—tail waggles,

— Debbie Johnstone
*Angels and Animal*

# INTRODUCTION

For as long as I can remember, I had a deep love for animals—all animals. So much so, that I wanted to be a veterinarian until I realized that I could never euthanize a dog. It wasn't until years later that I thought about it logically and realized that I would never have had to euthanize a healthy animal, nevertheless my heart would not be able to stand the circumstances of abuse or euthanasia. Maybe I will attain that dream in my next lifetime. I can't imagine life on earth without animals. They are precious and equal and should be treated as such.

Animals are truly intelligent beings with their own languages and cultures. They, like us, are a combination of both body and spirit. Most people struggle with the spiritual aspect of animals. However, I believe that each animal is a spiritual being with a purpose and a mission to accomplish while on this Earth, just like us, humans. And some, in fact, most, have a soul contract with their human guardians that they are meant to carry out on Earth. Think of it as a "Life Assignment". Trust me when I say that I was unaware of any of this until I had to release my Jackson Bean "Jack", my soulmate of many millennia, from this Earth.

What do I mean by this? Great Question, we had a "Soul Contract"! A Soul contract is a spiritual agreement or arrangement made between souls - whether in human or animal form - before they incarnate into physical bodies. It is believed that souls enter these contracts to learn and grow through various experiences and lessons in life. These contracts are made to facilitate the soul's evolution, personal growth, and spiritual development. Your soul contract with your pet is your agreement or connection that you entered together before you both entered your physical bodies. Before entering a physical body, both the human and the pet's souls agree to come together in a specific lifetime to support and learn from each other. This contract is based on love, companionship and mutual growth.

The soul contract with your pet can also involve various aspects, such as providing unconditional love, companionship and emotional support to one another. Additionally, a pet's presence in the human's life can bring joy, comfort, and healing. The contract can also be for the pet's ascension and to learn lessons for their own life assignment and higher self work before they complete their journey with their human.

My soul contract with Jack was—and still is—that beautiful, meaningful connection that has allowed Jack and myself to experience love, growth, and gratitude as we've navigated through the last twenty-one and a half years. Every detail that transpired was for our greater good. In fact, it was through his passing that the most important lessons were to be learned by both me and Jack, in the spirit realm. I would not have realized my life assignment or my ability to telepathically connect with animals had it not been prearranged in our soul contract. I am grateful for the paradigm shift that has occurred and for the people who nourished my soul and spirit during that time.

I have traveled the road of gratitude and embraced what has transpired with Jack's passing and his reincarnation as my pet again in this life. I would not be the person I am today if it hadn't been for the "contract" Jack, and I shared through many incarnations. It all happened exactly as we agreed to it. No matter how hard his passing was for me—and believe me, it was crippling—it unfolded the way it was planned.

My intention in writing this book is to bring awareness to the interspecies connection on both a soul and spiritual level for those who seek it. Having done much research and reading after Jack's transition, my grief and desire to find my soulmate again led me to the afterlife and to seek the answers I needed about reincarnation. I had the privilege of being in the presence of five amazing animal communicators, as well as my very own special personal intuition, who each gave me a message from Jack. Each message carried the same premise: a message of deep unrequited love and a desire to return to continue our journey together when the time was right.

I hope my story will empower you and help people who are searching, in any way. My desire is to help you understand your pet's energy before, during, and after their transition to a spirit form, and to be able to seek out the channels to assist you in their next incarnation. When a pet and its guardian decide it's time to return, a good, ethical animal communicator can assist you in connecting with the life force energy that is physically present after the incarnation into a new physical body takes place. When an animal transitions, that energy joins back up with its soul energy. I hope you will enjoy my story, along with the stories of those whose pets have "come home again." I hope my grief—and the grief shared by those in this book—helps you realize the very real possibilities of reincarnation. Always remember: grief is not a place to unpack and move in, but to pass through in your own unique way.

Namaste.

— Love & Light,
Susan & Jack

## 1

# FROM HEARTACHE TO WHOLENESS AGAIN

*"The Heart was made to be broken."*

—OSCAR WILDE

September 14, 2012, dawned as the day that would etch itself indelibly into my being—the most harrowing day I had ever faced. The events of that morning, irrespective of their outcome, would forever remain a poignant and heart-wrenching chapter in the narrative of my life.

The previous day, Thursday, September 13, 2012 unfolded as any typical day. My morning ritual commenced with letting the dogs out, followed by brewing a fresh pot of coffee. I meandered through the house in the comforting company of my beloved fur babies, ensuring they received their morning treats and a generous dose of love and affection.

However, a small, unusual detail caught my attention: Jack's lethargy. As I opened the door to let them out of their room, I observed Jack's sluggish rise. His stretch and walk to the door were notably slower than usual. Perhaps, I mused, he simply had a restless night—after all, aren't we all familiar with such discomforts? Shrugging off the concern, I dressed and stepped out to embrace another day at the helm of a local wellness and weight loss clinic, unaware of how profoundly the following day would alter my life.

Over the last few weeks, I have been feeling overly attached to my babies. I usually go to work and straight to the gym for an hour or so before heading home, a routine I've been doing for the last 20 years. However, in the last few weeks, I had felt the need to skip the gym and just head straight home, eager to be with my furry family.

Every day, coming home is a joy because of my three pets. Buffy, "the Momma dog" 12.5 years old, her daughter Brandi, 9.5, my black beauty, and Jackson Bean, also 9.5, fill my home with love. Seeing them is the best part of my day. They are not just pets—they are family.

They came to greet me, but I noticed Jack was moving a bit slower than usual. He squatted to do his business—a habit he picked up from being raised with his mother and sister; he was never one to raise his leg. This time, though, nothing seemed to happen. I didn't think much of it initially, since the wee-wee pad inside was wet, and I assumed all was well.

Back inside, I prepared their meals: bowls filled with their favorite duck and potato, enhanced with a bit of gravy. They devoured it in under a minute, tails wagging happily. We then headed outside again into the warm Florida night. It felt like the perfect end to the day, or so it seemed, as everyone did their business in the fading dusk. Everything appeared peaceful in our little paradise. Tomorrow, life would change on a dime.

Freshly showered and ready for some quality snuggling, I joined all three of my kids in bed. Buffy is at the end of the bed, always content to do her own thing. Brandi is always struggling for an extra bit of love, as Jack has always been the favored one. Jack climbed onto my lap and stretched out. Lying on his back along the length of my legs, he closed his eyes, and I grew a bit concerned. I picked him up and cradled him in my arms, recalling how earlier I had to lift him onto the bed, when usually he would be there waiting for me. Looking into his eyes, he started giving me kisses, just like so many times before. Except this time, it would be the last night we would spend together as we knew it.

## 2

# IN THE BEGINNING

*"No matter how hard the past is, you
can always begin again."*

—BUDDHA

Since the day I helped deliver Buffy's litter of six puppies on November 6th, 2000, they have learned to love their crate, much like their own bedroom. By the tender age of six weeks, I had already taught all six of them to sit, give a paw, high five, and lie down. Three boys and three girls, three black and three beige—I was in heaven! There is nothing more rewarding than having six healthy, happy, and beautiful puppies in your home for the first fourteen weeks of their lives.

At the time, I was working as a Neonatal Intensive Care Nurse, and I had prepared myself with extensive reading on breeding, whelping, and the delivery process. This litter was perfect, each one uniquely beautiful.

The first three black puppies were born—two with white markings and one all black. That little one would become Brandi. Then came the beige ones. The largest of the litter, weighing 0.8 oz (about 22.68 g), was nicknamed Pudgie, a name that seemed to fit him perfectly. Next was Jack, whom we initially called Toby, after my beloved Maine Coon cat who thought he was a dog and had passed away 19 years earlier. Two hours after Toby (Jack) was born, the runt got stuck in the birth canal. We walked Buffy and did everything the ER vet advised over the phone. He warned me to be content with five healthy puppies, as the one stuck in the birth canal might be stillborn due to the lack of oxygen.

After another brisk walk in the cold November air of Old Bridge, New Jersey, Buffy began to pant and push. Number six was on the way! With her final yelp, success - the tiniest pup I could have ever imagined emerged. She was cold and white. My son Jerry, a tenth grader at the time, urged me to act, reminding me of my expertise as a neonatal nurse. He was right. I had read all the whelping books, and knew exactly what to do. I vigorously massaged the little puppy, but there was no response. Then, I gently shook her head between my forefinger and middle finger. A slight movement and a faint sound emerged.

There was only one thing left to do: I placed my mouth over her nose and mouth and gave gentle suction. Miraculously, she came to life! It was a truly special moment. We decided to name her Honey.

The days that followed were filled with joy, laughter, and a great deal of work! Even now, I wouldn't change a single moment of it. Witnessing Buffy teach her litter was nothing short of miraculous. At first, we harbored concerns about her maternal instincts, as she had always been our pampered baby, and even our vet had cautioned us that she might not be inclined to care for her young. Yet, despite her being accustomed to being the "baby," Buffy, amidst her constant grumbling every time she settled in the box to feed them, proved to be an exceptional mother. Now, at thirteen, as of this writing, she still "grumbles" at Brandi daily, a dynamic that has been their norm since birth.

Six Cocker Spaniel puppies and their mother—what a sight! My heart yearned to keep them all. The agreement was to keep just one, and my then-boyfriend was not too enthusiastic about the idea of two. But my feelings told a different story. He ran a retail soft serve ice cream store and employed several young girls, one of whom, Lisa, was destined to become Pudgie's new owner. Unbeknownst to me, he had already spoken to her about wanting a puppy, and she was thrilled. However, the thought of parting with Pudgie made me queasy.

By four weeks, all their eyes were open, and they were scooting around everywhere—except Pudgie, who dragged his back legs. Fearing a congenital anomaly, I called Dolores, the owner of the Stud/Kennel Service. She suggested he might be a "swimmer," a term used for puppies that fail to crawl or walk by four weeks. Thankfully, by the fifth week, Pudgie was lifting his little rear and walking with his siblings. The vet assured us he would outgrow this condition, attributing it to his larger size; after all, he was the heaviest of the litter. Lisa committed to taking Pudgie when he was old enough to leave his mother. I was comforted knowing he would have a loving family yet saddened that he wouldn't be mine forever.

As a registered nurse in New Jersey working with various agencies, I had the opportunity to meet a wide array of people. I never missed a chance to share stories about my puppies. While on a rotation at St. Elizabeth's Hospital in Elizabeth, NJ, specifically in the mother-baby unit, I met Ina. She instantly fell in love with the first photos of Buffy's litter, particularly drawn to "Toby" (later Jack). We agreed on a price, and she was prepared to take him when he was old enough. That night, however, I went home and cried.

My boyfriend, largely indifferent, simply wanted his house back in order. Later, a coworker informed me that Ina couldn't have pets in her condo. The last dog she owned, she had let out into the cold winter, faced with the ultimatum of losing her home. Consequently, I decided it was not the right choice for Jack—or for me. By then, I had already fallen deeply in love with this puppy. Our connection was unlike any I had ever known: so pure that it made me feel a heart center connection to the depths of my very soul.

Around this time, we took the puppies for their first shots, including the removal of dewclaws and the docking of their tails. We still had many memories to make together. We decided to keep Brandi; after all, she was the reason we bred Buffy. When I was a little girl, I had a black Cocker Spaniel named Trixie, a gift from my dad for my fourth birthday. She tragically died of heartworm when we moved to Florida in 1979; my mother, unfamiliar with heartworm living in NYC. Brandi was taken to the vet one day and there she died. I never got to see her again. I remember that day like it was yesterday. I was 16 years old, and I didn't even get to say goodbye to my best friend. She was 16 too. So, Brandi was our new beginning.

At a follow-up vet visit to check on their healing and for more shots, I had already decided to keep Toby—now renamed Jackson "Jack" Bean. Dr. Larry examined all the puppies and gave them a clean bill of health, except Jack. "This one is a dud," he said bluntly. I bristled at his comment about my Bean. He explained that Jack had an overbite which could require extensive dental work in the future, including the removal of lower canines to prevent damage to his palate. He noted the breeder's code that allows returning a puppy within three days for any medical or dental issues. I assured him that returning Jack was not an option. He was staying with me.

In time, Jack's palate adjusted, creating little holes to accommodate his lower canines. We never had an issue with his teeth and adored his quirky overbite.

The two other black Cocker Spaniels were perfect, true descendants of Chez Milrose Barrister III, a dog with champion bloodlines. Among them was Stripe, a male with a glossy black coat and a distinctive white stripe down his neck. I placed a highly selective ad to ensure excellent homes for the remaining puppies.

One evening, a local man called. He shared a heart-wrenching story. His father's dog, a black Cocker, had tragically passed away due to a medication error at the vet's office, leaving his father devastated. That same evening, the man's son visited and made a deposit for the puppy they would name "Blackjack." With each passing day, my heart grew heavier.

I confided in Ina that "Toby Jack" had a medical condition requiring costly monthly medication and that I had found someone affluent to take him. She understood, or so I let her believe. In truth, I lied. My boyfriend insisted we find a home for Jack as well, declaring he wouldn't tolerate three dogs. Inwardly, I vowed that Jack would stay; our bond was unbreakable. Silently I said to myself "I'll get rid of you before I get rid of my Jackson Bean." He was mine, and I was his, and the bond was already formed, a deep bond, which no one would break.

Molly was the next to go; she was also black with a little diamond-shaped white patch on her chest. A woman called me to inquire about her, saying: "my son's fiancée just called off the wedding, and in the same week, his company that he's been working with for many years is folding. I want to do something to pull him out of his depression." Molly did the trick. When it was time for her to come and get the puppy she named Molly, she explained that she had nothing for the puppy and asked if I could go to PetSmart with her to get a crate, some food, toys, and a bed. I agreed, so off we went. She paid for all the items, and we loaded them into the car. I lifted Molly into her new crate with her comfy furry bed placed inside.

The tears started to flow; even though I knew she would be making a big difference in someone's life, quite possibly every difference, it did not make it any easier. I cried all the way home. I kept in touch with David for years, and yes, Molly was an angel and had made all the difference in the world. He was heartbroken when she passed away at 16.

Finally, it was our little runt, Honey turn, what a character she was! My mother had committed to adopting her long before she was born, feeling it was time for a new puppy in their home.

Time flew by, and before we knew it, fourteen weeks had passed. The cocker crew mastered all the basic commands and received most of their puppy immunizations. They were now ready to venture into their new homes. We had arranged a trip to Florida to visit my parents and to bring Honey to her new family.

Just a week before our Florida journey, we dropped Pudgie off with Lisa and her family. Lisa, having recently lost her father to swiftly progressing cancer, found Pudgie's arrival a much-needed distraction.

Yet, with each puppy's departure, I couldn't help but feel my heart breaking, bit by tiny bit, as they each embarked on their new adventures.

With Blackjack settled and brightening the days of a grieving soul, Pudgie thriving in his new home with his new boy and girl, and Molly lifting David's spirits, only Brandi, Jackson Bean, and Honey remained. As we prepared for our Florida trip, we packed one Sherpa bag, squeezing all three tiny cockers inside and set off, eager for the sunshine. Unbeknownst to my boyfriend, I had no intention of finding a home for Jack in Florida, what a foolish thought on his part!

Upon our arrival in Florida, the puppies were an instant hit. My parents immediately fell in love with Honey, and the feeling was mutual. The thought of saying goodbye to Honey in two weeks weighed heavily on me. After all, I had saved her life, breathed life into her, and she had been the most dependent of them all. Parting with her would be anything but easy.

The next two weeks were blissful, filled with beach outings for the dogs and plenty of sun-soaked fun. If dogs had a way of remembering the good times, then those days would surely stay etched in their memories forever.

Our trip to Florida ended, and my boyfriend was unhappy about bringing Jack back home with us. Frankly, I didn't care. Jack was mine, and I was his, and I was resolute in keeping him, regardless of the cost. Eight years into this relationship, and I was no closer to a fairytale ending than I was to winning the Powerball lottery. My bond with Jackson Boy was unshakeable, and a mantra formed in my mind, repeating like a defiant drumbeat, "Get rid of Jack? No way! I'd leave you first."

It had taken this man seven years to tell me he loved me. And the deep connection, my "soul connection" with Jack was undeniable. I vowed nothing would change that...EVER! During this period, I began to seriously consider leaving him. His reluctance to fully commit to me and "us," coupled with his aversion to having three dogs weighed heavily on me. I've lived comfortably enough, but material desires have never been my driving force. Happiness, commitment, and love—these are where my heart truly lies.

## 3

# WE ALL GROW UP

*"Pets are the best teachers of responsibility
and unconditional love. They help us
grow into better human beings."*

—JANE GOODALL

The next three years passed in a blur. The puppies had grown into little dogs, each earning their PetSmart Training Certificates—a testament to their intelligence. But there's something quite remarkable about the pack mentality that they exhibited. Jack was very protective and apprehensive, and Brandy and Buffy followed the Alpha male's role. I felt that I did my best to socialize them, my idea and the correct way were two different things. Being in a very cold northern state, we spend most of our time inside. Many of the visitors were friends of our kids and us. That is not enough folks. You must bring them out around strangers and smells that they are not accustomed to. Lesson learned.

The relationship between my boyfriend and me had become increasingly strained. In September 2005, I reached a decisive moment. I packed up my dogs and my belongings, determined to make a significant change. I purchased three extra-large, airline-regulated crates, fervently hoping the weather would be ideal for my beloved pets, who had long outgrown their Sherpa-sized carriers.

Upon our arrival at the Sarasota-Bradenton Airport, I eagerly made my way to the cargo delivery area to reunite with my children. Their eyes, filled with joy and relief, greeted me as we embarked on our journey home. The house, vast and welcoming, with its sprawling backyard bathed in sunshine, awaited us. The years ahead, though a mix of highs and lows, were punctuated by the enduring memories of a 12-year relationship I had recently left behind. Those initial three years in Florida were challenging, but the loving gaze of my children, especially Jackson Bean, provided much-needed comfort and strength.

My son, armed with a newly minted degree in Culinary Arts from Le Cordon Bleu Academy in Orlando, returned home with his fiancée and their little dog, Kayla, infusing our lives with renewed energy and change. Despite not being fond of Florida's heat and humidity, significant life changes followed. Life changed a lot. I didn't like the heat, and the end of my relationship meant selling the house and other big changes. But we always had each other; my fur-babies were always my constant.

Dipping my toes back into the dating pool was daunting. The local men didn't quite measure up to my expectations, and I found more joy in the company of my fur babies. Life took another turn, and as my kids grew older, I eventually met someone who changed my perspective—a doctor whose presence was both comforting and exciting. Our connection was so strong that I envisioned a swift journey from dating to engagement, and perhaps even marriage. However, his allergy to dogs posed a unique challenge, leading us to creative solutions like taking the dogs on ocean trips where his allergies were less of a concern. Jack, our adventurous companion, eagerly became the first to join in these new adventures.

The weight of uncertainty pressed down on me regarding my relationship. My dogs are an inseparable part of my essence, and the thought of rehoming them was inconceivable.

I yearned deeply to find someone who would embrace not only me but also my cherished canine companions with equal affection. Though the good doctor and I had shared just over a year together, our paths seemed to be diverging, casting a shadow of doubt over our future. He was kind and caring, yet there's a profound difference between being treated well and finding a soulmate who aligns perfectly well with one's dreams and desires.

Everyone reassured me that my aspirations for love were normal, but there comes a time when you realize that running in place is no longer an option.

One afternoon, my friend Patricia called, urging me to turn on the radio. A song by the emerging artist Adele, "Chasing Pavements," was playing, and she felt it mirrored my situation with the good doctor. The lyrics resonated deeply, speaking of decisive moments and the crossroads of love: "I made up my mind, no need to think it over. If I'm wrong, I am right. Don't need to look no further, this ain't lust, I know this is love... should I give up or should I just keep chasing pavements, even if it leads nowhere?"

It was a clear call to cease "chasing pavements," to stop pursuing a path that led to uncertainty. With newfound resolve, I ended the relationship. There was no looking back this time. Our desires for the future differed too much. The final chapter I sought in my life's story was one of unbridled happiness, shared with my beloved dogs.

4

# STEPPINGSTONES

*"The journey of a thousand miles begins with a single step."*

—LAO TZU

Navigating my return to Florida, I found myself once again seeking solace in the tender gaze of three sets of eyes, belonging to hearts that have seen me through many a challenge. Among them, Jack possessed a unique presence. He had this peculiar way of sitting, his head tilted, nose lifted skyward as he gazed at me—not just looking, but peering into the very depths of my soul. I would beckon him over, yet he remained still, locked in that intense, soulful stare.

Whenever my son was around, I'd point out Jack's behavior, half-jokingly musing, "Look at him, just look at him. I swear he was my husband in another life." I would call him over and he would just sit and stare at me. No, he would actually stare right through to my soul. "If only I could find a man who loves me as Jack does, I'd be set for life." Little did I know how close to the truth I was. Tragically, Jack's life would be cut short by a hidden, insidious tumor, an ailment beyond my foresight.

In the wake of this loss, I would connect with an Author/Animal Communicator named Jacquelin Smith. It was she who confirmed my whimsical belief: Jack indeed had been my husband in a past life. The revelation was as comforting as it was astonishing.

I was aware, vaguely, of something called reincarnation. The concept had danced around the periphery of my understanding, like a firefly blinking in and out of the shadows—curious, mystical, but never quite real to me. I never gave it serious thought—not for people, and certainly not for animals. But life, in its quiet genius, has a way of peeling back the veil just enough for you to see. My maternal grandmother had been a psychic medium, a woman who carried wisdom in her bones and a knowing in her eyes. And while I had inherited what some might call "mother's intuition," I would soon learn that this gift ran deeper than I ever imagined. I wasn't just intuitive—I could hear, feel, sense the souls of animals in ways I couldn't yet explain. Jack was about to show me how profound that connection could be.

Even while Jack was still beside me, alive and deeply woven into every part of my daily life, I began to feel something stirring beneath the surface. A knowing, a pull, as though there was more to our story than companionship. It was a quiet, persistent whisper that led me to Jacqueline Smith, an author and renowned animal communicator.

She became a lighthouse in the fog, illuminating truths I hadn't dared to believe. On our very first call, she confirmed what had only been a whimsical, whispered thought in the corners of my mind: Jack had been my husband in a past life. And in this one, he came back to me—as my dog. My breath caught in my throat. It was both bewildering and soul-affirming, a moment that cracked me wide open.

Three months passed, and with them came layers of realization that would reshape how I saw love, loss, and connection. There is love in this world that transcends every boundary of logic, time, and form. There is the love we chase in people, the fleeting stories we write with romantic partners, and then there is the love that anchors our soul to its own divinity. I had been seeking a person to fill the void, unaware that the void was already being filled in the most extraordinary way. Jack's presence wasn't just comforting—it was purposeful. He was guiding me, teaching me, walking with me. What I thought I was missing in others, I already had in him.

Through Jack, I began to grasp the Universal Law of Perpetual Transmutation of Energy—that nothing ever truly dies, it only changes form. Love, when you sit with it long enough, starts to whisper its secrets. It tells you that soul contracts are real. That our companions— those sacred souls who find us in one life—will find a way to return, sometimes even before they've left. Jack's reincarnation wasn't just a miracle for me; it became a beacon for thousands. I created a Facebook community for grieving pet owners, and Jack's story became their solace. His journey into my life—this life—became proof that heartbreak might one day be transformed into hope.

What began as curiosity transformed into a spiritual awakening. Jack didn't need to leave for his impact to deepen. The love between us became the doorway to something bigger. The path we're on isn't ending—it's unfolding.

Three months slipped by, and with them came a profound realization. There exists true love, and then there are the stepping stones along life's journey. What I had recently experienced in my search for love, was merely a stepping stone. My true love was still right by my side and as time inched forward, I would find out how true this really was.

For the moment, I found contentment in my job, my life, and most importantly, in the unwavering love of my fur-babies. I made a bold decision to further enrich my professional life: pursuing a degree in cosmetology. Already armed with a registered nursing degree and with my family owning a salon, it seemed like a natural, advantageous step. The allure of additional income was compelling, especially as I was working full-time. The only shadow cast over this exciting endeavor was the thought of spending less time with my beloved dogs, seeing them for just a few hours each night and briefly before school. Yet, the practicalities of life beckoned. Their premium kibble and the monthly pet insurance for each dog, weren't going to pay for themselves. An extra source of income was not just desirable, it was necessary.

In 1000 hours, I would unlock another avenue for financial gain. Throughout the grueling 14 months of balancing work and school, my dogs remained my steadfast supporters. Buffy, Brandi, and Jack made me feel whole no matter what life was throwing at me. Their joyous greetings, every time I walked through the door, were the highlights of my days. One of my cherished rituals upon returning home—after attending to their needs, of course—was to lie on the floor and immerse myself in their affection. Picture a scene where a group of puppies lovingly surrounds a baby, showering them with licks. My dogs, still brimming with youthful enthusiasm, would engage in a similar, fervent licking session, eliciting peals of laughter from me.

In the company of my dogs, life felt complete and unconditionally loving. There was no judgment, no questions—just a pure, unwavering sense of being loved and needed.

This was our unbroken routine, a circle of love and joy that I had no intention of altering. Why fix what's not broken? In their presence, I found an incomparable sense of fulfillment and belonging.

Having settled into a splendid new home, graced with an expansive backyard complete with a charming swing, a luxurious hot tub, and an inviting deck, Jack and Brandi found a new favorite pastime: basking in the sun on that deck. Accustomed to the comforts of indoor living, they cherished these moments in the sunshine, but only when I joined them. The moment I stepped indoors, they would dutifully form a 'gravy train,' following me in perfect unison.

Each morning, as part of our ritual, they would eagerly dash out to the deck, leaping atop the hot tub cover in anticipation. They seemed to know that I would soon join them, initiating our daily exchange of affectionate "kisses." However, one morning, Jack, in his usual exuberance, raced to claim his spot atop the hot tub cover before Brandi. He darted around the corner so swiftly that I barely had time to shout, "Hey, the hot tub isn't covered!" In an instant—splash! Jack found himself unexpectedly submerged in the hot tub. I couldn't contain my laughter at the comical sight. Rushing to his rescue, I scooped him up, drenched as he soaked me in return. Yet, even in this unexpected bath, he didn't forget that it was time for our 'kissy' ritual.

Oh, the delightful life and times of Jackson Bean! His antics, his boundless love, they brought a radiance to my life, pure joy. I'm convinced that much of my happiness stemmed from his unwavering affection and the blissful moments we shared.

Returning home to my trio of fur babies, what a blessing! In the realm of Florida's medical field, where the pursuit of an ideal nursing job has been elusive, they were my unwavering source of joy.

After long days at a job that fails to spark my passion, the enthusiastic welcome of doggie kisses and adoring eyes never fails to uplift my spirits. Slowly, the grind of Corporate America had been wearing me down, leaving me increasingly burnt out. With no romantic relationship occupying my time, I found myself lost in contemplation during my solitary hours.

5

# BEING NEIGHBORLY

*"The best way to find yourself is to lose
yourself in the service of others."*

—MAHATMA GANDHI

At the time, I was employed by an industry leader in the Home Health
Care space. I recall a particularly brisk day in Florida, with temperatures
plummeting to about 36 degrees. As I was out marketing, I spotted a
frail elderly lady shuffling down the street. Dressed in a long winter
coat and a kerchief—reminiscent of what my grandmother would
wear—she was painstakingly navigating with a small two-wheeled
bag. Observing her struggle, I thought, *"If this were my grandmother,
I would hope someone would offer her a ride in such cold weather."*
Compelled by this thought, I pulled over, stopping her in her tracks.

"Hello, I'm Susan," I introduced myself, pointing to my name tag.
"I work for a home care company. It's quite chilly today; may I offer
you a ride?" Her response, in broken English, was a heartfelt, "Tank

you, Dalli, tank you." In her broken English Grecian accent. I assisted her with her grocery-laden bag, placing it in my car and helping her into the front seat. As she directed me to her home, a mere 15-minute walk away, it dawned on me that she lived just a block from my house.

Upon entering her modest home, I was instantly met by Chippy, her small, scruffy Shih Tzu, who greeted me. The elderly lady, now known to me as Despina Spyridakos, hospitably offered Greek pastries and soda. Her home, though in need of tender loving care, exuded warmth. Despina, a widow of 18 years, shared her affiliation with St. Barbara's Greek Orthodox Church and told me a bit about her life, in broken English.

Our conversation led me to offer her my number, insisting she call if she needed anything, especially given the cold weather. I could easily pick up groceries for her or accompany her on shopping trips. As I left, she thanked me, bending over to treat Chippy to a bowl of vanilla ice cream. Little did I know that Despina and Chippy would soon occupy a special place in my heart.

I began visiting Despina once or twice a week. Her solitude, in her late 80s with no family around, stirred deep empathy in me. Despite her loneliness, she always seemed in good spirits, taking Chippy on long walks, stopping every so often to give him water.

One day, I dropped by to check if she needed milk, but there was no answer. Worried, I called her later, only to be met with silence. The next day, still no response. Concerned, I reached out to Dean, a family friend and her attorney, who managed her finances. He informed me she had fallen, was hospitalized, and subsequently moved to a rehab center. I knew this was a grim turn for independent Despina, and Dean confirmed my fears: she was not faring well and was refusing to eat.

Determined to help, I visited her at the rehab center. Despina, sitting disinterestedly in a wheelchair, brightened upon seeing me. She pleaded to go home, expressing her dislike for the facility's food and yearning for some homemade Greek avgolemono soup. That evening, I learned to make the Avgolemono soup from scratch, returning the next day to feed her. Despite her momentary happiness, she grew sadder with each departure. After a heartfelt conversation with Dean, I rooted for Despina's return home, emphasizing that her strong will to be with Chippy should be honored.

That night, a call from Dean inquiring about home care services sparked a realization. This was the opportunity I had been searching for—a chance to break away from corporate life. I quickly called him back, offering to take on Despina's case as a private duty nurse. Dean agreed, seeing it as the perfect solution. Unbeknownst to me, this decision would pave the way for a profound change in my life and career.

Monday morning, I arrived at the facility to bring Despina home, there was a palpable sense of hope in the air. She was weak but visibly brightened at the thought of returning to her own bed, to her beloved Chippy. I couldn't help but relate, remembering the overwhelming joy and comfort my own dogs, Jackson Bean, Brandi, and Buffy, brought to me daily, easing the stresses of life.

The initial days at home were daunting. Despina spent more time in bed than out, and I feared the worst. On the third day, while tidying the fridge, I stumbled upon empty thyroid medication vials. Realizing these weren't listed on her current medications, I contacted her primary doctor. It turned out she hadn't refilled her prescription in over six months—a crucial oversight. With the medication resumed, Despina's energy returned. She began engaging in her at-home physical therapy with renewed vigor. Working long hours, I dedicated myself to her care, seeing her progress from frailty to walking 150 feet with her walker within just three weeks.

The sight of Despina happily walking Chippy again, even in the sweltering 90-degree heat, filled me with a deep sense of fulfillment. I had helped restore a vital part of her life. Weeks turned into months, and Despina's health steadily improved. She regained the weight she had lost in rehab, thriving on the Greek dishes I learned to prepare. The approaching holidays found her in good spirits.

As time moved forward, signs of dementia began to surface in Despina. Her walks with Chippy became less frequent, often just opening the door to let him out. One Saturday, my day off, I received a call from Cindy, Despina's neighbor, with alarming news that Chippy had been hit by a speeding car. Rushing over, I found him in severe pain. His pelvis was fractured. At the emergency clinic, they assured us he would recover, but it would be a long process.

When I informed Despina of Chippy's condition and the mounting costs, she insisted on paying for everything, but wanted him to come home. Yet complications arose—Chippy couldn't urinate on his own, and a home health aide reported that Despina, in her confused state, wished to have him put down. I knew this wasn't her true wish. I reached out to a Shih Tzu rescue, hoping they could aid in his recovery.

When I received the call that Chippy had finally urinated independently, I rushed to the clinic, only to be met with a heartbreaking sight. Chippy lay there, his soul's pain palpable with every labored breath. With every breath, he whimpered. My heart shattered. He was like my own. Faced with this grim reality, I made the agonizing decision to put Chippy to rest. It was a decision I had never imagined

I would have to make, reminding me painfully of my own beloved Jack. Looking into Chippy's eyes, I realized that over the past year and a half, he had become more than just a part-time companion. I had fallen deeply in love with him, and with his passing, a part of my heart shattered.

I implored the vet to please gently ease Chippy's passage from this world. As I cradled his paw and tenderly stroked his head, the vet administered a milky white substance into his already present catheter. His pained whimpers gradually subsided, eventually ceasing altogether. Until I had helped Jack transition, I hadn't known that all dogs pass with their eyes open. Sitting there, tears streaming down my face, I whispered apologies to Chippy. I confessed my ignorance of his deep suffering, regretting any moment he had spent in pain. I thanked him for being a wonderful companion to Despina, and for briefly gracing my life with his presence. In those final moments, I made a solemn vow to him—I promised to look after his beloved Mommy.

As I left the clinic, the weight of Chippy's absence hung heavily in my heart. The drive back to Despina's house was a blur, my mind grappling with the responsibility of breaking the news to her. Upon arriving, I found her anxiously awaiting our return. The look in her eyes—a mix of hope and worry—pierced me deeply. Taking a deep breath, I gently explained that Chippy had passed away, ensuring his comfort and peace in his final moments.

Despina's reaction was heart-wrenching. The clarity in her eyes faded as she grappled with the reality of her loss. Yet, in her confusion, there was a poignant acceptance, a silent acknowledgment of Chippy's unconditional love and the joy he had brought into her life.

In the following days, I dedicated myself to Despina's care with renewed fervor, honoring my promise to Chippy. Each day, as I helped her navigate the complexities of her daily routine, I felt Chippy's spirit guiding us, his memory a comforting presence in the house. The bond between Despina and Chippy, though physically severed, remained unbreakable in spirit. Their story—a testament to the profound impact pets have on our lives—continued to inspire me.

Through the bittersweet journey of caring for Despina and Chippy, I found a deeper understanding of love, loss, and the unspoken language of companionship. It was a poignant reminder that sometimes, the most profound connections we make are not with humans, but with the loyal pets who walk beside us, teaching us about unconditional love and the beauty of simple companionship.

Monday morning, and the first weekend without her Chippy, I was sure there would be questions! As I walked through the door, questions about Chippy swirled in the air. Despina's inquiries were laced with a growing sense of urgency. "Where is Chippy?" she asked, her voice tinged with worry. It was then that the undeniable signs of her decline began to emerge. Despina, always a fortress of physical strength, had once amusingly doused an unsuspecting aide with orange juice—a temporary aide who dared to disrupt the familiarity she so cherished.

Change, after all, is a hard pill for anyone to swallow, isn't it?

Her plea for Chippy was heartfelt, her eyes brimming with a mix of hope and desperation. As her nurse, I strived to explain the situation, but the reality of Chippy's absence was a concept too distant for her to grasp. Despina's yearning for a canine companion was palpable, a longing that filled the room. She begged me to go get Chippy. I felt her pain to my core. I missed him too. Despite her independence, managing well alone at night, the idea of bringing another dog into her life weighed heavily on me. The risk was too great, the thought of losing another beloved pet through an inadvertently opened door was a burden too heavy to bear. It would be irresponsible, I told myself. Yet, in the depths of my role, I had transcended the boundaries of a mere caretaker. I had become something more akin to a daughter, my heart aching in tandem with Despina's for both Chippy and her unfulfilled wishes.

Then, in a twist of fate, I found him—a dog named Jack. The irony of the name did not escape me as I stumbled upon his listing on Craigslist. Jack was an adorable sight, his eyes gleaming with the promise of companionship and joy. The fear gripped me, though; Craigslist, with its shadowy corners of "free" dog listings, was no place for such an innocent soul. But as I looked into those trusting eyes, I knew I had to take the chance. For Despina, for the memory of Chippy, and for the little cutie who needed a home as much as Despina needed him. The decision was fraught with risks, but sometimes, the most profound acts of love are those taken in the face of fear.

Jack, a Maltese, at merely three years old, was the epitome of charm and cuteness. The couple who had cared for him were moving and couldn't take him along, paving the way for his entry into Despina's life. The joy he brought her was a ray of sunshine piercing through the clouds that had gathered since Chippy's departure. Sometimes, in her moments of blissful forgetfulness, she would even call him Chippy. I noticed many similarities he shared with Chippy. I even believed that the similarities were no coincidence, and later I would learn that Chippy may have reincarnated into Lil Jack as a braided soul. Much more on this later!

We arranged for Jack's crate to be placed right beside Despina's bed, creating a comforting nightly ritual. As night fell and I prepared to leave, Jack would dutifully enter his crate, and Despina would drift into sleep, lulled by his presence. The lock I added to the crate was a necessary precaution, meant to prevent Despina from waking in the early hours and inadvertently putting Jack in harm's way. She protested, her independence clashing with my protective measures. She believed Jack was her dog, to be cared for on her terms, and my restrictions only fanned the flames of her frustration.

However, as time passed, Despina's health took another downturn. Returning from grocery shopping one day, my heart sank as I found Jack darting frantically across the street. The fear of losing him, much like we had lost Chippy, rushed through me as I scrambled to bring him to safety. It was then that I had to face a heart-wrenching decision.

Laura, the weekend caregiver, was a bright ray of kindness and had grown fond of little Jack. She offered to take him in, a solution that seemed both a blessing and a pang of guilt. It pained me to think of uprooting Jack once again, but Laura's offer presented a silver lining. With her, Jack would still be a part of Despina's life on weekends, a compromise that offered some solace.

The decision was made with a heavy heart. For Despina, Jack's departure was another wave of loss, yet his weekend visits with Laura provided a bridge, a connection to the joy he had brought. And for Jack, it was another chapter, a new home filled with love. In the tangled web of caregiving, love, and responsibility, we navigated the best we could, each decision a delicate balance between safeguarding and letting go.

Several weeks elapsed, and the need arose to hire another alternating, temporary aide who could fill in for another who would be away. The substitute, unfortunately, was not to Despina's liking. In a display of her spirited defiance, she would often slip out the side door of her bedroom, seeking refuge with the neighbors. It was a humorous escape, yet it left me with concern. This was, after all, the same woman upon whom Despina had once, amusingly, thrown a glass of orange juice on. I was looking for a replacement, but in the interim, I had to retain her services.

One Sunday night, as I was returning from a weekend getaway, Ashley, the aide, called with alarming news. Despina was despondent, unwilling to rise from bed, and appeared to be running a fever. I promised to come over with a fever reducer and arranged a visit to her primary doctor the following morning.

Almost home, another call from Ashley jolted me—she needed Despina's date of birth for the paramedics she had called. Racing to the hospital, I met Despina in the emergency room. The doctor revealed a distressing error, Ashley had given her an overdose of her anti-anxiety medication, struggling to manage her in her uncooperative state. Despina was admitted with a UTI but was discharged back into my care after three days. This time, however, my culinary skills and nursing expertise seemed to make no difference. Her once hearty appetite had vanished, and she rarely left her bed for more than an hour each day.

To bring some comfort, I set up a TV/VCR in her room, where we watched old movies she had recorded during her years living in New York City. My visits with my dogs during the week provided fleeting moments of interaction, but her interest waned quickly. It was clear to me that we were nearing the end. I expressed my desire to stay by her side, but her persistent refusal to leave her bed was a cause for concern.

A guardian was appointed to manage her affairs, and after two years of dedicated care, I began to seek new employment, my heart heavy with the knowledge that I could not reverse her decline this time. Despite everything, the bond between us was undeniable. She loved me, and I loved her deeply in return. The difficult decision to place her in a nursing home was made, and though I found another job, I visited her often. Sometimes she didn't recognize me, but there were fleeting moments when our eyes met, and I saw a glimmer of the Despina I knew—smiling, grateful, and strong.

Then, on January 29th, 2013, I received a call from Dean. I was busy, and couldn't answer, but somehow, I knew. It was the call to inform me that Despina had peacefully passed away, joining Chippy at the Rainbow Bridge. Despina would have turned 94 next month, but now, she celebrates in a realm beyond, free from earthly constraints. And I, blessed with memories and the silent promise of another guardian angel watching over me, continue carrying her spirit in my heart.

## 6

# THE JOURNEY

*"The best way to find yourself is to lose
yourself in the service of others."*

—MAHATMA GANDHI

Moving on from anything that has profoundly touched or moved you is
never a straightforward journey. It's not about right or wrong, nor is it
solely about what's best for you; it's about the essence of what you glean
from the experience. Sometimes, you might feel you've taken nothing
from it. Necessity is often called the mother of invention, yet sometimes
life's lessons glide past without leaving a mark, imparting no wisdom...
until a paradigm shift occurs. Little did I know how drastically my life
was about to change, how deeply I would be shaken to my core. The
cruelest blow life had to offer was just around the corner.

My new job as a Cardiac Nurse was short-lived. The practice suffered
a catastrophic computer crash, erasing all electronic medical records.
The doctor, a friend of mine, confessed that he'd likely go bankrupt

before managing to recover all the lost billing data. He couldn't afford to keep me on the team. I was devastated. Just three months prior, I had met someone extraordinary, and the last thing I wanted was for this setback to impact our budding relationship. I've always prided myself on my independence, shunning any semblance of dependence or weakness.

In a moment of resilience, I revisited the idea of online dating, a realm that had brought me trouble in the past. Yet, through the haze of past disappointments, I could see into the eyes of this wonderful man. The first time I saw his picture, I was captivated by his beautiful, dreamy eyes—a mesmerizing blend of azure and light aquamarine. His dimples could melt even the coldest heart, complemented by a charming personality... and oh, was he handsome!

He was the first man in a long time to thaw my guarded heart. We shared so many common interests; his smile and laugh left me yearning for more, and thankfully, he felt the same. Since our first date, we had spent every weekend together—everything seemed so perfect, almost too perfect. My heart, scarred with trust issues, began to grow anxious.

Joe was incredibly easy to be around. He visited every weekend, arriving on Friday and staying until Monday morning. He treated me with such respect and kindness. And the best part, he adored my dogs. My three furry companions, usually barking at strangers, greeted him in complete silence on his first visit. Jack, my usually aggressive protector, wagged his tail all the way down the driveway. Brandi and Buffy were equally smitten.

Saturday mornings were blissful. After letting the dogs out and making coffee, they would join us in bed—Jack by my side, Brandi by Joe's. Despite Joe's aversion to face licks, Brandi would invariably attempt to sneak a kiss whenever she could. Yet, Joe never got angry or pushed them away. His patience and affection for my dogs slowly but surely helped lower my defenses, paving the way for me to fall deeply in love with him.

The first six months of our relationship flew by, and November brought a string of birthday celebrations. Jackson Bean and Brandi would turn nine on the 6th, Buffy twelve on the 17th, and my own birthday was on the 11th, my magical 11/11. I would soon learn about my ability to connect with spirit. My grandmother was a psychic, and I indeed inherited the gift...more so with animals. The joy of these celebrations, mingled with the warmth of newfound love, made the world seem brighter, despite the upheavals in my professional life. In those moments, I began to understand that sometimes, the most profound shifts in our lives come from the most unexpected places. And as I looked into Joe's dreamy eyes, I knew that regardless of what the future held, this chapter of my life was one of growth, love, and unexpected blessings.

As the bond between Joe and I deepened into something seemingly flawless, my insecurities unfurled like dark wings. The more enchanting our moments together—filled with laughter, shared secrets, and the joy of mutual discovery—the more I braced myself for the inevitable downfall. I had always had a bad habit of getting in my own way! And now I was almost willing it to happen, just simply looking for something that maybe was not even there. I found myself scouring for signs, for any hint that this perfection was a facade, that he couldn't possibly be this ideal, especially not for someone like me. We cooked, we laughed, and he even introduced me to his family. Why couldn't I simply revel in our happiness? Yet, I couldn't let go, ensnared by my doubts.

Happiness, I realized, should be embraced as a gift—a divine nod that it was, indeed, "my turn" to bask in the glow of a remarkable partnership. There was no need to doubt myself, the light Joe brought into my life, or the love story I had longed for. True contentment, I learned, lies in savoring the present; if there were shadows to be found, they would unveil themselves without my seeking. But being familiar with the 12 Universal Laws, the teachings of Bob Proctor, and the movie "The Secret," I knew I had to practice more gratitude and well...BELIEVE!

My birthday under Joe's thoughtful touch was nothing short of magical. He presented me with a breathtaking "Vera Wang" bouquet and three cards that seemed to peer into my soul. Could it be? Had I found someone who understood my love for heartfelt words? The sincerity in his message fueled my decision to start a "Joe & Susan" box, collecting mementos of our journey—Yankee ticket stubs, matchboxes, room keys, and more.

Our celebration at Euphemia Haye, Longboat Key Florida, a favorite haunt, was draped in enchantment. Waiting for our table, Joe's touch and the velvety vintage we savored, set against the backdrop of live music, made me feel like the sole woman in existence. His affection, both sweet and fervent, and the simple act of holding his hand, stirred a giddy joy within me. For the first time in ages, I felt genuinely beautiful beauty kindled by the way Joe looked at me. Why then, did I grapple with the fear of unworthiness?

With Thanksgiving on the horizon, life seemed to be at its peak, yet I couldn't halt my self-sabotage, prying into corners I knew I should avoid. The adage "seek and you shall find" rang painfully true.

The lesson I was slowly coming to grasp was the power of self-confidence. Confidence, after all, is not just seen but felt by others. Being prioritized by someone you love should be affirmation enough? No, you must know your worth, this is for you to LOVE yourself and know that you are worthy. The real challenge lies not in the fears stoked by our discoveries, but in maintaining the essence of who we are—the very essence that captivated them in the first place. Confidence is a beacon, casting light on the path back to each other, turning distractions into mere shadows against the brilliance of a shared love.

I successfully got the "bump" in the road I was looking for. However, I did not desire the outcome it provided: a pause in the relationship. Tears and sadness set in, followed by the dreaded phone call. We had been together every weekend for six months. This man had made me his number one priority. Yet, I looked beyond his attentiveness, searching for what he might be doing wrong. If you seek, you will "always" find. Now, we were taking a "break" this weekend, and I was filled with sadness, knowing his attention would not be focused on me for the first time in six months. We still planned to spend Thanksgiving together, which was only six days away. My heart would stop and not beat again until I could be confident. We would make it through this. That weekend, like so many before when despair had gripped me, my beloved Jackson boy, my sweet Brandi girl, and my steadfast Momma dog encircled me with their unwavering love, anchoring my world with their presence. They were my luminous beacons, the unwavering light at the end of every dark tunnel. Thanksgiving was approaching, a time I revered for reflecting on all the blessings in my life. My parents were our gracious hosts, and my dear Joseph had outdone himself with a culinary masterpiece—a turkey so splendid it would linger in memory.

The night before Thanksgiving, Joe arrived, arms laden with the makings of a feast. His specialty, an Italian antipasto salad, was on the menu, and his care in its preparation was a dance of love and tradition. As he tenderly arranged the mixed baby greens on the platter, placing it on the table, our mischievous Brandi seized her moment. With a swift, stealthy move, she snatched a mouthful of lettuce. Joe's reaction was nothing short of endearing—no trace of anger, just a bemused affection for her antics.

The atmosphere was tinged with a subtle change, yet everything remained cordial and comfortable. This Thanksgiving unfolded beautifully, marked by what I can only describe as the best turkey I had ever tasted.

Joe had stuffed it generously with fresh veggies, carrots, celery, infusing it with flavors that danced on the palate. It was more than a meal; it was a testament to the enduring strength and adaptability of our relationship. Under the veil of the ordinary, in the shared laughter and the stolen lettuce, lay the extraordinary—a bond that, while tested, remained as savory and fulfilling as the Thanksgiving feast we shared.

The day faded into memory, and suddenly, Christmas was whispering in everyone's hearts. There's something magical about having dogs during the festive season. My dogs have a penchant for unwrapping presents, a sight so endearing that it brings laughter every time. It reminds me of childhood, of those thrilling moments spent searching for hidden gifts, the anticipation of sneaking a peek. Surely, you've felt that too, haven't you?

I had a tradition of wrapping their stuffed animal gifts and tucking them away in my bedroom, nestled within a shopping bag, a spot that had always remained undisturbed. However, this time was different.

Upon returning home, I was greeted by a scene that would forever be etched in my memory. Buffy, my little detective, had embarked on her own festive quest. She delved into the bag with the precision of a seasoned sleuth, and, among all the wrapped treasures, she found her prize—a blue monkey meant just for her.

It was a sight to behold: out of all the gifts, she had chosen hers with an unerring instinct. And there she was, the evidence of her joyful transgression scattered around her, the blue monkey victoriously clenched in her jaws.

In that moment, the spirit of Christmas was alive and well, embodied in the innocent mischief of a beloved pet. What a story to tell—a testament to the curious, heartwarming antics that make the holidays with pets unforgettable.

Buffy, Buffy, Buffy! Such a sweet mama dog, reveling in every toy since the tender age of 14 weeks (about 3 months). Remarkably, she knew each by name, fetching whichever one you requested from her basket. As Christmas loomed closer, Joe and I faced the prospect of spending it apart. For the past 15 years, Joe had celebrated in New Jersey with his family, and although the thought of our first Christmas apart filled me with disappointment, I didn't yet know that it would turn out to be a hidden blessing I'd soon appreciate.

Joe and I harbored grand plans for a post-Christmas celebration upon his return. We envisioned a festive trip to Orlando for New Year's Eve, where we would exchange gifts and revel in our own delayed holiday cheer. Thus, I resolved to embrace the season as I had in years past—just me, my beloved dogs, and, for the first time in three years, my son at home. Together, we unearthed decorations and ornaments from their slumber. Among them, my favorites: a collection accrued over the years, each bearing the names of all three dogs. The most cherished among these was the first ornament featuring Buffy's name alongside her six puppies—a memento from the best Christmas ever.

With presents for the dogs and my son wrapped snugly beneath the tree, the familiar warmth of tradition enveloped us. Yes, I missed my boyfriend dearly, but our daily conversations—each ending with his earnest "I love you too, I wish you were here"—filled the gap his absence had created. In those moments, I felt a profound reassurance; despite the miles between us, our bond remained unshaken. It was then that I knew, with unwavering certainty, that we would be just fine.

That Christmas turned out to be one of extraordinary charm and warmth, a holiday adorned with joy as the dogs reveled in their festive bounty—stuffed animals, bones, and an assortment of treats. I captured the moment on video, their eager paws and wagging tails unwrapping toys, a scene that would forever remain etched in my heart. Though part of me yearned to celebrate my first Christmas with Joe by my side, destiny unfolded a gift of profound significance. Unbeknownst to me at the time, Joe's absence bestowed upon me the most precious Christmas gift—cherished moments with Jack in what would be our last holiday season together in this life.

The holiday season ebbed away, and soon Joe was back, igniting the excitement for our New Year's celebration. Anticipation bubbled within me as I looked forward to ushering in the New Year with the man who had captured my heart completely. Thus, with hearts full of hope and eyes sparkling with dreams, we ventured to the Peabody Orlando, a symbol of new beginnings and the promise of shared tomorrows.

New Year's Eve was a jubilant affair, a threshold between the past and the future, an opportunity to shed the remnants of yesteryear's trials and step into the light of newfound promises. It was a time to cast aside old burdens, embracing the path ahead with optimism and love.

Returning home, the anticipation of exchanging Christmas gifts added to the afterglow of our holiday adventure. The season, marked by both absence and togetherness, taught us the essence of cherishing each moment, each other, and the love that continued to blossom with each passing day.

As the evening unfolded, Joe orchestrated a scene straight out of a timeless romance: a fire crackled warmly in the hearth, glasses of wine stood ready to toast to our love, and cushions lay scattered, promising comfort. Then, with a touch of nostalgia, he filled the room with the sound of classic love songs from the soundbar. It was the epitome of perfection.

For me, the essence of romance has always been found not in the grandeur of material gifts but in the moment's intimacy, the heartfelt words penned in a card, the tender glances exchanged. Yet, Joe, with his generous spirit, had a way of blending the romantic with the grandiose. He lavished me with exquisite perfumes, chic apparel, wine accessories, and reminisced about our recent grand escapade—replete with couple's massages and facials, a testament to his thoughtful nature.

The mystery unraveled with the largest box, which intriguingly contained another box, and then another. My heart raced with anticipation, a familiar storyline playing in my mind. Yet, when I reached the final, small, oblong box, I was genuinely clueless until the very moment I lifted its lid. There, nestled within, was the most stunning diamond tennis bracelet I had ever laid eyes on. Its brilliance took my breath away!

Overwhelmed by the magnificence of his gift, I couldn't help but feel a twinge of inadequacy—how could my gifts ever compare to this sparkling symbol of affection he had bestowed upon me? Yet, in that moment, I realized the true measure of love wasn't in the material but in the shared moments, the warmth of a fire, the melodies of love songs, and the promise of a future together, illuminated by the sparkle of true love.

## 7

# DREAM A LITTLE DREAM

*"You are never too old to set another goal or to dream a new dream."*

—C.S. LEWIS

As January's days cascaded into memories, Joe and I found ourselves inseparable, each weekend an exploration of our burgeoning love, save for the brief hiatus at Christmas.

Life seemed to unfold in brilliant hues, each moment more vibrant and full of promise than the last. We were crafting an album of shared experiences—plays, concerts, dinners under the city lights—all threads in the rich fabric of falling in love. Amid this whirlwind of new beginnings, my dogs thrived, their joy a reflection of my own. My career brought satisfaction, but it was the happiness blooming in my heart that truly marked this chapter as one of the brightest in my life.

Valentine's Day approached with stealth, a whispering promise of romance yet to be planned. Amidst the rush of daily life, Joe and I hadn't spoken of it, yet the significance of the day hung in the air, an unspoken anticipation. Intent on celebrating at his place, I prepared to leave, but not before indulging Brandi, Jack, and Buffy in a little Valentine's ritual of our own. They, too, deserved to bask in the day's affection with their special doggie Valentine's cookies—a testament to the boundless love they received daily, though what harm was there in a little extra?

Just as I was enveloped in this small celebration of love, a knock at the door pierced the evening calm. The timing was impeccable, as if the universe itself conspired to add another layer of mystery and excitement to our Valentine's Day. With a heart full of love and a spirit eager for whatever surprise awaited, I moved to answer it, ready to embrace the next chapter of our love story.

The surprise that awaited me was nothing short of enchanting: a stuffed animal, ingeniously doubling as a goodie jar, brimming with treats for my beloved pets, and accompanying this delightful find, a breathtaking dozen of long-stemmed red roses. My heart swelled with joy—what a splendid prelude to an evening with my dearest!

Opting for simplicity over extravagance, Joe and I decided to spend the evening ensconced in the comfort of home, with the fragrant allure of Chinese takeout as our feast. The setting mattered little; in his company, contentment was guaranteed. Life, in those moments, felt blissfully perfect.

March in Florida presented a stark contrast to the cherished memories of New York and New Jersey's enchanting seasons. Here, the days were a blend of heat and humidity, a far cry from the northern climate I longed for. It was during this time that I noticed something peculiar—a small "skin tag" above Jack's right eye. At first glance, it seemed innocuous, much like the benign one adorning Buffy. Yet, the vigilant nurse in me couldn't dismiss the nagging concern. Florida's relentless sun was indiscriminate, and the specter of skin cancer loomed, even for our canine companions. I resolved to keep a watchful eye, the weight of responsibility heavy on my shoulders, as I navigated the uncertainties of health and well-being under the Floridian sun.

Above his right eye, it was unmistakable—the growth that had morphed from a harmless shade of pink to an ominous black. Alarmed by the transformation, I rushed Jack to my friend Anne's Veterinary Clinic, desperate for answers. The very thought of anything happening to my baby bean was unbearable. Dr. Schneider, with his gentle expertise, took charge. After a quick aspiration, his diagnosis dropped like a stone in still water: mast cells. The words "not good" echoed, urging us to schedule surgery immediately to remove the growth and await the biopsy results. Four days later, as Jack went under, my prayers were fervent, hoping against hope we had caught it in time.

The call came: Jack was ready to be picked up. Seeing him there, bruised yet resilient, adorned with bright blue stitches, he resembled a furry Hector Macho Camacho. Dr. Schneider's assurance of clear margins offered a temporary solace, but the real wait had just begun— the biopsy results would take 10 days. They had to be okay; the alternative was unthinkable. Having insured my dogs since they were puppies, I've always believed in the responsibility that comes with pet ownership. Buffy's hypothyroid diagnosis in 2005 was a testament to that, mirroring my own thyroid dysfunction later. But when Jack's results returned—benign mast cells—it seemed we'd dodged a bullet.

Relief washed over me, yet unbeknownst to me, in just five short months, I would face a loss so profound, that it would shatter my world.

April arrived fast and had unfurled its blooms, and with it, a plan took root in my heart—a surprise party for Joe, a celebration of the extraordinary bond we had nurtured. This wasn't to be just any party; it demanded a canvas as grand as the feelings I harbored for him. The Ritz Carlton, with its elegance and charm, seemed the only place befitting such an occasion. I envisioned a night where laughter danced in the air, and the warmth of affection enveloped us all.

Invitations were sent out, weaving threads of anticipation among our friends and family. Party favors, each a tiny flask, were meticulously prepared—a memento of the night's joy and revelry.

The secret was guarded zealously, even as many of the guests shared the same roof at the hotel, adding layers of excitement and challenge to the endeavor.

And then, the moment arrived. The surprise unfolded like a well-crafted narrative, each gasp and smile a testament to the night's success. Joe, unsuspecting yet overwhelmed, was enveloped in a celebration that mirrored the depth of my feelings for him. In those few hours, as laughter and music swirled around us, I hoped he understood just how deeply he had touched my life.

Soon, we would mark a year of being together—a year that had brought me not just one, but all my incredible loves: Buffy, Brandi, Jack and Joe. As the party dimmed and the last of the guests departed, contentment settled over me like a soft, comforting blanket. In the grand tapestry of life, I had found my corner of happiness with my heart full, each moment with them a thread of gold in the weave of my days.

In Florida, the concept of summer stretches far beyond the calendar's confines, enveloping us in its warm/humid embrace year-round. My trio of furry companions revel in this perpetual sunshine, basking in the light that filters through our screened lanai and dances around the gazebo. Yet, their enjoyment hinges on one simple condition: my presence. Without me, the allure of the outdoors fades; with me, the sun's caress on their faces becomes a moment of bliss. Jack, in particular, seized every opportunity to claim a spot in my lap, his loyalty unwavering.

Nestled within our yard stands a majestic oak tree, its roots perhaps as old as two centuries, cradling a double-seat wooden swing in its sturdy branches. It's there, in the quiet of the early morning with coffee in hand, that Jack and I would share serene moments. He, ever my shadow, would leap into my lap, content in our shared solitude. This photograph captures one such moment: Jack patiently waiting in my bed spot, a daily ritual as I prepared for slumber. Together, we'd unwind in the evening's calm, Jack often sprawled across my lap, showering me with affectionate licks until I'd gently protested—though in truth, such displays of unconditional love could never be too much.

As the clock struck nine, the spell of the day would break with my soft utterance of "sleepy nite-nite," a cue that sent them scampering off the bed and into their luxury-sized crate from Forsgate. This routine, etched into the fabric of our days, underscored the simple, profound joy of life with my fur children—a reminder that love, in its purest form, asks for no more than togetherness. With Swedish yogurt drops as my secret weapon, I perfected the art of training them from the tender age of six weeks. The mere sound of the bag's rustle would have them eagerly scampering into their crate, performing a charming ritual of sitting, offering a paw, and then gracefully settling down in anticipation of their treats. Watching this adorable routine unfold was a delight, especially when they were just tiny pups, their actions a testament to the bond we were building.

Each morning, as the sky began to lighten around six-thirty, I would tiptoe in to observe their peaceful slumber. Yet, invariably, Jack would be alert, his endearing little face peeking out in search of me. Our connection was undeniable, an intuitive understanding that seemed to say we were always in tune with each other's thoughts, throughout many lifetimes. As the summer days gently passed, life felt remarkably fulfilling. Work was consistent, the dogs flourished in health and happiness, and my relationship with my new boyfriend added a layer of joy to my days. The prospect of another trip to New Jersey for Christmas in July to visit Joe's family was on the horizon, a tradition I eagerly anticipated. Thankfully, my son Jerry was always there, a reliable presence to look after the fur-kids in my absence, ensuring that everything was perfect at home while we created new memories from afar.

The majestic oak tree in my backyard, a constant presence through the seasons, begins its annual ritual of shedding leaves around the end of August, continuing its gentle descent through the new year. This tree, with its sprawling branches and robust stature, offers a sense of grounding as I sit beneath it, surrounded by my dogs. Its canopy is a playground for the local squirrels, with one particularly bold character who insists on engaging me in conversation from my bathroom window, squeaking persistently until I emerge to "speak squirrel" with him.

As the end of August heralds the promise of cooler weather—wishful thinking in the perpetual summer of Florida—I embrace another day in the Florida haze. The routine is simple yet profound: brewing coffee and stepping outside with my fur babies into the early morning dew. Today, however, routine gives way to concern as I notice Buffy's eye is severely irritated, likely the result of her rubbing against the carpet, perhaps agitated by a stray fiber.

In the vet's exam room, the diagnosis begins with a stain and examination under special lighting to determine the presence of a corneal abrasion. The culprit? A husk from the oak tree, ingeniously lodged in her eye, its convex shape creating a suction effect on her lens. Thankfully, a few drops of numbing solution allowed the vet to remove it effortlessly. Yet, relief was short-lived as the vet prescribed the dreaded cone of shame to prevent Buffy from further irritating her eye. The cone, however, was met with disdain; Buffy refused to move, choosing instead to sit forlornly in silent protest.

Watching her discomfort was more agonizing for me than for her, leading to the cone's early retirement. I resolved to keep a vigilant watch over her, ensuring her eye healed without further incident.

This episode, while trying, underscored the value of pet insurance. The unexpected expense of an oak tree husk removal was a stark reminder of the unforeseen challenges of pet ownership. Moreover, it seemed almost a law of nature that as soon as one dog recovered, another was poised to take their place at the vet, a cycle of care and concern that bound us all more closely together.

In three weeks, a profound sense of attachment to my dogs began to overshadow my routines. The pull to forego the gym in favor of returning home to bask in their company grew stronger each day. An unsettling intuition whispered that not all was well, particularly with Buffy. She had developed numerous lumps, which, I had been reassured in the past, were merely fatty lipomas and nothing to worry about. Yet, doubt crept in, urging me to question this diagnosis further.

My weekends had traditionally been spent alternating weekends at Joe's house, a practice that had become routine over time. Lately, however, I found myself grappling with guilt, my heart yearning to spend those precious days with my beloved dogs instead. This nagging sense of longing refused to be ignored.

Compelled by this growing concern, I made the decision to take Buffy to the vet for a thorough examination of those lumps. It was a step driven by the need to quell my fears and ensure her well-being, a testament to the deep bond we shared and my unwavering commitment to their health and happiness.

A whisper of intuition, insidious and unyielding, suggested a dreaded diagnosis: cancer. It was a thought that clung to the edges of my mind, refusing to be dismissed as I decided to have Buffy examined once more. Her eye, thankfully, had healed beautifully, but now, it was the ominous fatty tumors that demanded our attention.

The vet tech escorted me to the exam room with a promise to return shortly. Yet, in the solitude of that sterile space, my fears overwhelmed me, and tears escaped unbidden. When she re-entered, her gaze fell upon my distress, prompting her to inquire gently about my concerns. "Cancer," I whispered, the word heavy with dread. She offered comforting reassurance, suggesting we wait for Dr. Chauvet's evaluation before leaping to conclusions.

Dr. Anne Chauvet—a beacon of humanity, whose kindness and dedication to animals knew no bounds. Anne, whose inner beauty matched her outward grace, approached with her distinctive Parisian accent, a sound that always brought a measure of comfort. Her customary greeting, "How are you, beautiful?" momentarily lifted the weight from my heart. I shared my fears regarding Buffy's lumps, suspecting the worst. Anne's response was pragmatic yet tender, "Let's take a look."

With a ten-cc syringe in hand, she warned of a slight discomfort, advising me to hold Buffy close and blow gently in her face at the count of three. The procedure was swift—the extracted substance, clear and silicone-like, indicating nothing more than fatty tumors. Relief washed over me as each subsequent test confirmed the benign nature of the lumps. Buffy was fine; there was no cancer. In that moment, gratitude and relief intermingled, a testament to the enduring hope and the deep bond shared between humans and their cherished pets.

Curiosity mingled with concern, I turned to Anne, seeking solace in her expertise. "How long can I expect to have Buffy with me?" I asked, my voice tinged with the vulnerability that comes from loving deeply. Buffy would be turning 13 come November, and each day with her was a treasure I feared to lose. Anne's response was a balm to my fretful heart. With the grace and assurance that only years of experience can bring, she informed me that Buffy, despite her minor, well-controlled hypothyroidism, was in robust health. "She could live a good 15 years," Anne said, her words painting a future filled with more walks, more lazy afternoons, and more moments of unconditional love.

Leaving the clinic, a lightness replaced the weight of worry I had carried in. Anne's words echoed in my mind, a promise of more time, more memories to be made with Buffy. The prospect of having my faithful companion by my side for years to come lifted my spirits. In the dance of life and the unknowns it carries, assurances are rare, yet Anne had given me something precious—a glimpse of hope, a reason to believe in the enduring strength of the bond between a human and their pet.

The weeks fly by, and like clockwork, Friday rolls around, signaling the time to head to my boyfriends for the weekend. Jack, my loyal companion, wears his typical melancholic expression. It appears that my weekend absences evoke a subtle melancholy in him, and even my return on Monday mornings, met with sheer joy, doesn't seem to lift his spirits for long. I've tried everything, from babying him to showering him with attention, yet a recurring pattern persists.

Feeling the weight of guilt, the following weekend intensifies these emotions, infiltrating my psyche. On a Sunday morning, a peculiar premonition haunts me—a vivid image of picking up my cell phone, charging in the adjacent room, to find a heartbreaking text from my son about Jack meeting a tragic end after darting out of the front door. In a rush of anxiety, I reach for the phone, only to be greeted by the absence of messages. A sigh of relief. I called my son, Jerry, confirming all was well, instructing him to tell my babies I loved them and assuring them of my return tomorrow. Struggling to stay with Joe that Sunday into Monday, my yearning is for nothing more than to snuggle with my cherished canine companion.

Monday morning arrived, and driven by an unprecedented urgency, I hit the road earlier than my usual routine. My foot pressed the accelerator as if I were a seasoned race car driver, bypassing the traffic with an intensity fueled by the anticipation of reuniting with my beloved companions. The 40-minute commute was conquered in a mere 25 minutes, a testament to my eagerness.

Upon reaching home, I swiftly activated the garage door opener, and the familiar sound was music to my ears. Racing inside, I made a beeline for the crate, opening the door with a sense of exhilaration. "I'm home!" I exclaimed, greeted by the joyous response of my fur babies. Jack, emerging with a triumphant stretch and wagging tail, led the welcome party. Brandi had already ventured into the yard, setting the stage for a heartfelt reunion.

We congregated in the yard, and I settled onto the big swing beneath the oak tree. Jack, the truest embodiment of joy, leaped into my lap, showering me with kisses and affection. At that moment, there was no place I'd rather be. As the workweek routine resumed, the countdown to the end of the day became my lifeline.

Unable to contain my anticipation, I skipped the gym, heading straight home from work. Sweatpants on, the air conditioning dialed down, I stepped into bed, enveloped by the warm presence of my three beloved companions. Together, we shared an evening of pure, unadulterated snuggles, a cherished reprieve from the demands of the outside world.

My baby boy, Jackson Bean—amidst the trio of my cherished pets—holds a place in my heart that surpasses words. From that initial meeting, a profound connection manifested, one destined to withstand the test of time. Lately, Jack's demeanor has taken an intriguing turn, and as I observe his aloofness and penchant for sitting by the front door, an unspoken signal triggers a maternal instinct. His boundless enthusiasm for bounding over, showering me with kisses from across the house, is a daily spectacle. There's an inexplicable pull drawing me home each evening, especially for Jack, more so than for Momma or Brandi. Then came Wednesday, September 12, a day I chose the warmth of home over the gym, and the seemingly ordinary transformed into an emotional rollercoaster.

As I opened the garage, the loves of my life, my fur babies, greeted me with unparalleled, unconditional love. Amid their usual routine, a subtle anomaly unfolded—Jack, standing on the driveway, attempting to urinate, yet nothing emerged. I brushed it off, attributing it to my busy distractions, only to discover a wet wee-wee pad later on. Dinner time, a frenzy of joy as I added fat-free beef gravy to their bowls, was followed by the realization that Jack seemed tired, requiring assistance on the bed. His recent preference for sitting by my bedside and his silent plea for a loving pick-up signaled a shift in our routine, a deep, unconditional love I hadn't encountered outside my maternal bond. The familiar bedtime ritual arrived, yet this night, the last night my trio snuggled together in their crate, felt different. As I bid them "sleepy nite, nite," little did I know that tomorrow would be far from ordinary, and Jack's journey was about to take an unexpected turn.

Thursday, September 13, a date forever etched in my memory. The morning unfolded with routine gestures, the usual awakening and placing Buffy on the floor, ready for our morning rituals. As we headed to the living room to let the trio out, a subtle shift in Jack's behavior caught my attention. Slow stretches were not exclusive to him; Brandi mirrored the lethargy. Outside, Jack attempted to urinate, but to my dismay, nothing followed. A sense of concern settled in as this continued three times, interrupted only by a successful number two. A worrisome realization prompted me to contact Anne, a dear friend and esteemed Veterinary Neurologist with an unparalleled Emergency Clinic. My text detailed Jack's attempts to urinate and my suspicion of a potential "stone." Anne, though not present, assured me that a capable covering vet would attend to Jack, prompting my decision to drop him off before heading to work.

Anne texted back, 'That will be fine. I am not there, but I have a covering vet who is very good. I will be in after eight a.m.' I headed to the bathroom to get ready. Jack was lying on the kitchen floor in the 'froggy' position, his favorite position. His tummy was a little distended, and I was positive he had a 'stone.' I picked him up and put him on my bed, babying him a bit before I got ready. I got out of the shower, and he was still in the same position I left him in. He was still very loving and kissing me as usual, but just a bit depressed. He seemed down and sad. I now know what was going on then, but I didn't know then.

Ready for work, treats were given to everyone except Jack, as I thought he might need to have nothing by mouth prior to a possible surgery. We got in the car and headed to Veterinary Neuro Services. I talked to Jack the entire drive there. He would not even look at me; his normal demeanor was that of trying to climb on my lap the entire drive anywhere. Not today; my boy was not feeling well, and he did not want to talk to me, let alone look at me.

We arrived at Dr. Chauvet's office, and I carefully lifted Jack out of the car. Surprisingly, he seemed okay to walk. Stepping into the clinic, we were warmly greeted, but Jack immediately sprawled out on his belly like a frog, his telltale position. I began explaining to the vet tech the troubling symptoms Jack had been displaying.

Years ago, Jack had shown signs of separation anxiety, becoming mopey when away from me for more than a couple of days. Now, those same mopey signs had resurfaced. Additionally, he couldn't urinate, although defecating posed no problem. The vet tech took Jack's leash, but he stubbornly refused to budge. I insisted she carry him, emphasizing that he wasn't feeling well at all. Glancing at the clock, it read 8:20 a.m. precisely.

In a mere five minutes, the on-call vet emerged, expressing concern that Jack might be in serious trouble. His abdomen was filled with fluid, and she couldn't determine if it was urine or blood. It could be a simple urinary blockage or stone, requiring a small surgery at an estimated cost of $500.00. I quickly interrupted, mentioning my pet insurance, assuring her cost wasn't an issue, and urging her to do whatever was necessary to "fix" my baby.

As she vanished into the back, she left me with a chilling thought—if it was internal bleeding, Jack could die. Panic set in. Not my Jack, not the love of my life, not my baby. I rushed towards the door, desperate to call my boyfriend, Joe. He answered promptly, sensing the urgency of my call. Through sobs, I blurted out, "Jack might die." Joe, unable to comprehend my distressed words, implored me to calm down. I took a deep breath and repeated the vet's grim prognosis. Joe advised me to let them assess Jack before jumping to conclusions and to call him back with an update.

I called my friend and client, Michelle; she is the founder of Gimme Shelter, a local 501c3 organization for death row doggies. I told her Jack might die. She asked what happened, and I explained the situation to her. She said, "Tonight is my event, and nothing bad can happen today, cause I'm raising money for the animals." I tried to convince myself that she was right.

It was now almost twenty minutes to nine, and I was pacing the waiting room floor like a lioness whose cub was in the jaws of a jackal. The vet emerged from the back and said, "Ms. Marano, can you come with me?" I quickly asked, "How's Jack? Is he okay?" She reassured me, "He's okay; he's in the back." We entered an exam room where she sat down and said, "Well, I have some bad news for Jack." I could feel my heart and soul shatter into small slivers. "What is wrong with him?" I exclaimed.

She went on to explain that the fluid in Jack's belly was blood, caused by a tumor on his spleen, which she called hemangiosarcoma. The tumor metastasized to the liver too, and as it expanded, it ruptured other internal organs, causing the belly to fill with blood. She said if it was just the spleen, we could remove it and give him a round of chemo. Still, with the liver involvement, she did not think that was possible.

In my hysterical state, I asked if I could see my son. She led me into a large ICU area with many pets in cages, IVs running, and monitors beeping. There was my Jack in an extra-large crate, laying in his favorite froggy position. I could see the relief on his face when he saw me. She opened his crate for me, and I hugged my boy. It was then I felt a hand on my shoulder, and I turned, and there was Anne. I burst into tears yet again and cried, "Anne, not my Jack, not my Jack…not my Bean." I stood up, and she hugged me, expressing how sorry she was.

She then explained that a normal hematocrit for a dog is 45, and Jack's was 14, and that he could not breathe. I asked, "He is not panting?" Being a nurse, I knew that a low hematocrit would not cause shortness of breath, as it is the O2 in the bloodstream that is low, and it's more of a tightness or elephant-sitting-on-your-chest feeling. But at that very moment, my brain was mush. The only thing I knew was that I had to fix my boy!

I then suggested, "Well, give him a transfusion." She explained, which again I knew, that he would just continue to bleed out into his belly. She said that he was uncomfortable and could bleed out at any time, and it would be a horrible way for him to transition and not a nice way to remember him and definitely not fair. "You need to put him down right now." I said, "No way! I cannot 'just' put the love of my life 'DOWN.'" He has been a part of my life for 9.5 years. Little did I know I would come to find out we had been a part of each other's lives for many, many millennia gone by. Little did I know that we were once husband and wife in another time continuum.

I signed my baby out AMA (against medical advice). I scooped him up and headed for the door. His eyes rolled back in his head, remembering what Anne had said, like it was a bad dream, "Susan, he may not even make the car ride home." I begged him to please not die, "Just let me get you home baby, please?" I canceled work and headed home. I called my son Jerry and my boyfriend Joe and told them that Jack was terminal, and I was taking him home. Joe asked me if I wanted him to come down and be with me; I politely declined and thanked him, but I just wanted to be with my boy.

We arrived home, and I carried Jack in. His oxygen levels seemed to be up a little, and his eyes no longer rolled back in his head, but you could see he just did not feel good. The "sparkle" was just not there anymore; his eyes were cold and dark, but the love in his heart reached out to mine and was warmer than ever. I laid him in my bed, and his sister jumped up right away and sat next to him, the sibling bond stronger than ever. She knew that it would not be long.

I changed my clothes, closed the blinds, and laid in bed with my Jay boy on my lap. He just looked up at me, and despite his low oxygen levels, he kept kissing me fiercely!

Tonight was supposed to be a night to support my friend Michelle and her wonderful 501c3, Gimme Shelter! She had an event to raise money for the death row doggies she pulls from the shelters. I asked her to come by and see me before her event. It was a weeknight, and I really prefer not to go out on weeknights, but this was not the "out" I wanted.

The hours passed like minutes; I can't remember ever feeling time go so quickly as it did that day. Jack lay asleep on my lap, and looking down at him, I could not imagine life without him. Who would dry my tears when I was sad? Who would laugh with me when I was happy? Who would steal the gum from my purse and look at me with a sheepish grin? My Bean was leaving, and there was nothing I could do to change it!

My dear friends, Shelly and her husband Dave, self-proclaimed "animal lovers," served as invaluable pillars of support during the tumultuous period of my profound sorrow. Shelly and Dave, who share their lives with three adored dogs, added depth and warmth to my own struggles.

A mere week or two before the diagnosis of Jack's ailment, Shelly's beloved Oscar received the devastating news of thyroid cancer. His thyroid, the seat of his ailment, underwent removal, and a challenging course of chemotherapy lay ahead. As fate would have it, on the day Jack received his ominous diagnosis, Shelly found herself scheduled for a poignant appointment with the compassionate local Veterinary Oncologist, Dr. Heidi Ward.

Upon learning of Jack's condition, I reached out to Shelly, sharing the grim news my vet had conveyed—Jack's tumor had metastasized from the liver to the spleen. Despite the gravity of the situation, I clung to a glimmer of hope. If the malignancy had not spread further, there remained a possibility of removing the tumor and embarking on a course of chemotherapy. In my communication, I included the pertinent hematocrit numbers for her consideration.

Later that afternoon, a text from Shelly pierced through the veil of my despair. She was at Dr. Ward's clinic, and my provided information had raised concerns. Urgently, she requested my presence, and without hesitation, I replied, "We have nothing to lose." Clutching my loyal companion Bean, I made my way to Heidi's office, where uncertainty hung in the air like a heavy fog.

Upon reaching the Oncology practice, Jack, perhaps sensing the gravity of the situation, expressed a desire to walk. Accommodating his wish, I allowed him this small comfort. In the parking lot, Dave sat in the truck with Oscar, who, I must mention, exhibited remarkable resilience despite his ongoing chemotherapy regimen. A swift wave to Dave, and I hastened indoors.

Inside the office, I was promptly directed to enter. The palpable tension met me at the threshold. Shelly awaited me in the exam room, accompanied by the compassionate Dr. Ward, who stood ready to unravel the mysteries of Jack's condition.

I had crossed paths with Heidi at various Humane Society events, sharing a camaraderie that would later become a lifeline in the face of unimaginable sorrow. She recounted a hauntingly familiar tale of her own canine companion's battle with the same hemangiosarcoma afflicting my beloved Jack. Despite the years that had passed, Heidi's dog had succumbed to the relentless grip of this insidious ailment.

Her words resonated with a tinge of melancholy as she divulged the unsettling truth about the misdiagnoses often associated with this relentless disease. Could it be, I dared to hope, that Jack had been misdiagnosed? Was there a chance, however slim, that his spleen could be spared, allowing him to continue his journey by my side?

Hope hung in the air like a fragile thread as Dr. Ward, with an air of quiet determination, instructed me to place Jack on his back in a foam V-shaped form. The ultrasound machine hummed to life, and

I watched with bated breath as she revealed the inner workings of Jack's delicate body. A glimmer of optimism danced within me until she pointed to a dense area, uttering words that shattered my fragile hope—"This is his liver, and yes, I am sorry, the diagnosis is correct." I felt my spirit crumble anew.

Jack, with a gaze only a mother could comprehend, communicated a silent understanding, as if he had known all along. Tears welled in my eyes as I thanked Dr. Ward, lifting Jack from the cushion and holding him close. The somber truth unfolded: the tumor's rapid growth, the rupturing of organs, the internal bleeding, and the inevitable discomfort that would plague Jack.

With a heavy heart, Dr. Ward laid out the harsh reality, urging a decision to either guide Jack to the Rainbow Bridge or risk the impending hemorrhage. The choice, she insisted, was about sparing us both from a harrowing end. Placing Jack on the floor, she summoned a Pomeranian named Bucky, clad in a Hurricane anxiety jacket. This makeshift solution, she explained, would buy me a few precious days to reconcile with the impending farewell.

Leaving Heidi's office, I carried the weight of emotional defeat but found solace in the attempt. As I headed home, preparing to spend the final night with my cherished companion, the gravity of the impending loss loomed over us.

In the hushed darkness, devoid of the distracting hum of electronics, I cradled Jack in my arms, Brandi by our side, and Buffy curled up nearby. His fading heartbeat echoed a poignant melody, a heart-wrenching symphony of impending separation. I sensed Jack's worry for me, his soul-mate, as uncertainty gripped us both.

Compelled by an unspoken urgency, I decided to compose an email to my boyfriend from Jack, a testament to our indelible bond that would soon transcend the physical realm.

**Subject: Goodbye Joe**
**From: S.marano@hotmail.com**
**Date: Thursday, 13 Sept 2012 @ 11:34:23 -0400**

Dear Joe,

Well, I didn't think I'd be writing this for a very long time, but I guess my number is up! Listen, I really love my mom! We have this special bond, you know, and I know how hard this is going to be for her. So, do me a favor, just be there for all those tears she's going to have, cause there's not much I can do from where I'm going to be. Cause she is going to be really, really sad.

And hey, I want you to know I liked you, and I was a bit jealous of the attention you got. But I knew you were a good guy from the first minute I didn't need to bark at you. Take care of my lady; she's mighty special to me, and now I need you to love her extra when I'm gone! Thanks for being someone special to my person; she was the best person a dog could ever have!

Love Always,
Jackson "Jack" Bean

A knock at the door, and the usual loud three-dog barking session had turned to silence. From behind the door, Michelle emerged. The first thing I said was, "See, look, he does not look like he's dying, does he?" She petted him on the head and softly said, "Hi Jack, how you feeling, buddy?" He just lay in my arms with the midday sun trying to creep through the windowpane, which I tried so hard to block out. I so wanted to stop the world from turning that day. I would have even sold my soul to the highest bidder in that moment; anyone or anything that could have changed destiny could have owned me.

Michelle had her event to tend to, but before she left, she said, "Why don't you give Barbara Goodfriend a call? She is an animal psychic; it may help." I frantically wrote the number down, and the minute Michelle left, I called Barb and left her a message through my tears: "Please call me; my Jack is dying, and I need your help." She never called me back. My son came home from work and sat with us in my bed. I had finally turned on the TV; it seemed like old times, all the dogs and me in my bed. Jack seemed to be okay, but he didn't seem to want to drink out of a bowl but wanted water. I drank water and gave it to him like a Momma bird gives its young food, and he drank. It was dinner time, and he was ready to eat; his urinary function had also returned. So now he really seemed better. Could all the tests and the vet diagnosis be incorrect? My Jack was fine; everyone was wrong. I needed Jack to start talking; I needed to hear his voice and what he wanted me to know, more importantly, what he wanted! Tonight, he would sleep with me, as they all would; he and his sister Brandi had slept in their crate for 9.5 years together since birth. Bedtime was a fun time for them, candies and all, nine o'clock every night! But tonight, they will be with me, all of us together for the last time. Even from the look in his eyes, I could see what he knew.

Dinner time arrived, and my son Jerry ventured to Home Cookin, where the allure of three little burgers for $1.99 beckoned. He returned with much more, but three were designated for me and Jack. Jack, my faithful companion, perched on my bed as he had done countless times, awaiting the delectable morsels. He remained his courteous self as he devoured the offering, relishing every bite. In fact, he indulged in not one but two full sliders. His petite frame adorned with the borrowed blue jacket looked utterly endearing, providing him with a sense of comfort. After his meal, he appeared fatigued, prompting me to nestle him snugly beside me. Reluctant to extinguish the light, I grappled with an unfamiliar fear of the encroaching darkness. "God, please reconsider; spare my beloved Jay," I pleaded silently, consumed by apprehension.

In the vacant space adjacent to mine, where human presence had long been absent, rested the soul—the very essence that had held paramount significance in my life for the past nine and a half years.

Jack lay next to me all night, neither one of us slept a wink. He literally licked me all night, keeping his eyes open as if he knew he wouldn't be here much longer. It was as if he wanted to imprint my face in his memory, to preserve our connection. He licked me for 7 hours straight, to the point that my lips were chapped. That night, we shared our hearts. I could feel my heart breaking with each passing second, as dawn approached. My life was about to change, and there was nothing I or anyone else could do to alter it.

This feeling—this knowing—came from the depths of my soul. It was louder than a whisper. It was the voice of something ancient and true. I would come to understand that this ending had been written at the beginning of our incarnations together. Jack and I had made a soul contract long before his paws ever touched this earth, before I ever held his small, trembling body in my arms. We both agreed on this part of the story. That he would come into my life to awaken something dormant within me. And he would leave—not to abandon me, but to guide me toward the path we had both agreed I must walk.

You see, my maternal grandmother was a psychic medium. I grew up watching her move through life with an unspoken understanding of the world that others couldn't see. Though I never formally studied her craft, something passed through the bloodline—something sacred. I had always felt things deeply, what some call "mother's intuition," but it went beyond that. I had a connection to animals that couldn't be explained by logic. I could hear them, sense them, feel their emotions as if they were my own. I didn't realize then that this was the beginning of my awakening—that Jack's journey with me was a divine appointment to open the door.

In time, I would learn something that broke me and healed me all at once: pets absorb the negative energy of their guardians. With all the love in their hearts, they try to carry our burdens so we don't fall ill, so we don't carry the weight alone. They love us that much. And I know now—though it aches to admit—that Jack was doing just that. He was taking in my pain, holding it in his own body. He was protecting me with every cell of his being. I didn't understand this while it was happening. I only knew I was losing him and couldn't bear it.

At the time, I hadn't yet realized that what we were experiencing wasn't just part of my ascension or spiritual assignment—it was his too. Jack's soul came into this world to guide mine. His story would become a light in the darkest corners of grief for thousands of others.

The Facebook community I would later build—a haven for people navigating pet loss—became his sacred ground too. His journey, his return, his messages from beyond... all of it was his life's work. His assignment. Together, we were meant to help others see that pets don't die. They simply return to the infinite consciousness. And if you open your heart—and ask—they will come back. They always find their way home.

But at that moment, none of that comforted me. I wasn't ready. I hadn't yet grasped what was truly unfolding. I didn't care about spiritual awakenings or divine timing. I wanted my boy to stay. He was only nine and a half years old. A baby. My baby. And I hadn't yet embraced what would become the most extraordinary experience of my life.

## 8

# LETTING GO WITH LOVE

*"A dog is the only thing on earth that loves*
*you more than he loves himself!"*

—JOSH BILLINGS

Friday, September 14, 2012, will go down as the hardest day of my entire life. I could not leave Jack alone for a second. I had to go to work briefly and reschedule patients. I called Jillie Docking, my stand-in, the best doggie sitter ever! She came and stayed with Jack on my bed, where Brandi and Jack sat together with Jillie. I rushed to work and back in less than an hour, the time clock ticking away.

When I got home, Jack was perky on the bed, glad to see me, with his sister sitting right next to him. What a doll baby. I still hadn't heard from the animal communicator that Michelle had recommended, and just as I was thinking about that, my phone rang, and it was Michelle.

She mentioned a great animal communicator at the event the night before and gave me her number. Her name was Wendy, and everyone seemed to like her.

I called Wendy immediately and left a message. "Hi Wendy, this is Susan. I got your number from Michelle. You were at her event "Hair of the Dog" last night. My Jack is dying, and I need to know what he wants, what I can do for him. Please call me asap." In no time at all, Wendy Cooper called me back. I could barely talk. I took Jack in my arms and went into the living room, sitting on the couch with him in my arms like a newborn baby.

I explained to Wendy what was going on and told her about the other pets in the house. Wendy asked me to meet her in a teleconference meeting room, which I would access by dialing a number and entering an access code. We agreed to meet at ten after eleven. It was about ten-thirty, so I had time to collect my tears and compose myself.

I dialed the phone around five after eleven and entered the conference room. I was prompted that I was the only one in the room and the music would stop when the conference administrator arrived. I held Jack, and he just lay in my arms, looking up at me, waiting to tell me everything I needed to know.

Wendy finally joined me in the conference room. She apologized for being late and explained that Jack had come through and connected with her just seconds before she was ready to join me. She was drinking water, and the way he came through, she stated that the water went down wrong and caused her to cough (the experience as she tuned into Jack before she got on the call), and coughing, she explained, "By the way, is a way of releasing energy that we no longer need."

She went on to say that this rarely occurs to her, but that she pays attention when it does, as it is an important sign. She went on to say what had transpired in tuning in with Jack. She wanted me to note the time, 11:11. I immediately told her that it was also my birthday. She went on to say how the number 11 was very significant in mine and Jack's life together. He would return again on 1/11/13.

Here are Wendy's notes for our session:

---

**NOTES FROM 9-14-12**

Start at 11:11 a.m. & this is Susan's birthday; (Wendy has a coughing attack (release via coughing as Wendy tunes into Jack before session)—high energy so that call was postponed for a minute

**Brandy:** all is well; I need time and attention (Susan says she gives her little); brushing is good & intuit what else I need; I'm doing AC with Jack; if anyone should be upset it's me as we incarnate together; but I'm well. We will stay in touch.

**Buffy:** emphatic; you must listen as you need to shift your perspective about life. It is all ok; I'm ok; I'm mostly out of my body; big physical pain in my right shoulder; She says "like a mother would" "Listen to me and listen good this is happening for a reason you need to see your pattern especially with men. I have been with you for many years and you need to change. (at this point, Susan says, "I called you for Jack." So we shift to Jack.)

**Jack:** I'm mostly out of my body & I am ready, I would like to go today but if you need to prep things, I will hang out and wait for you; my physical body is just a house for the spirit. Jesus energy about needing heart to break, so it can get stronger: humpty dumpty; tin man to open heart; Jack came to teach you romantic love, Romeo & Juliet— you and he have had a forever contract from the past. He must let go, so Susan can love (a human kind of love); Susan and Jack have been together for many lives and needs to let me go so she can have a "human" love like ours. Mission—teach her about romantic love. She must let go (let me go) so her heart can open, be connected for a while, then she will choose to let go. No time to waste. I will be serving you from the other side. Jack says it's ok to have photos around the house except in the bedroom. Susie, it is ok to be angry with God; do not take anger out on people. Be present & Jack's energy will guide. Write hello/good-bye letters to Jack thanking him for his present life with you.

**Susie says she has a fish tank:** calm; figure eight; flow; no breaks. Look at the tank when devastated and ask for messages. Spiritual crisis, and it is good.

At this present moment, today: 4/2/13 (4/2= 2-13=11) at 11:11 a.m., which continues to be prevalent in my life, I look down at my phone, after writing the paragraph above and see 11:11 on my phone screen.

A few minutes after I got off the phone with Wendy, I received an email from her:

Dear Susie,

I encourage you to listen to this recording over the next couple of days. Note that the 11:11 a.m. time is in this email below. BTW, coughing (my experience as I tuned in to Jack before we got on the call) is a way of releasing energy that we no longer need. It rarely happens to me, but I pay attention when it does as it is an important sign.

Warmly,
Wendy

Your recording is ready, and is available for Computer Download and Telephone Playback until the recording expiration date. Please see below for details and instructions.

**Conference Date and Time:** September 14, 2012 11:11 a.m.
**Duration of Recording:** 1 Hour, 17 Minutes, 25 Seconds
**Recording File Size:** 27 MB
**Recording Expiration Date:** January 12, 2013 12:40 p.m.

Computer Download

Unfortunately, at the time of this writing, I was unable to access the original call. I reached out to Wendy, and she provided me with her notes, but the actual breaking of my heart—the raw, emotional moment—was no longer audible. I could no longer relive the day Jack lay in my arms, looking up at me, pouring out his heart through the incredible gift of animal communication with Wendy.

A part of me aches, knowing I can't listen to that recording again. Yet, deep down, I also understand that hearing it would only reopen wounds, reigniting a longing for his physical presence. In my heart of hearts, I know he is back with me, just in a different form, like ice to boiling water and water to steam. So is it, in the ether, still, I miss my Jackson Bean every single day.

## SEPTEMBER 15, 2012

*Email to Wendy—The Day After*

You know, I had been asking Jackson all morning to give me a sign that he was with me. But I was struggling—was it supposed to be a bird? A butterfly? I just couldn't seem to recognize one.

Then, as I sat in the car while my friend ran into the store, I pulled out my phone and glanced at my screensaver—Jack's beautiful face staring back at me. And then I saw it. The time.

I knew, in that moment, the time had come to begin the healing process, to take the steps I was being guided to take, to somehow find my way through this unbearable grief. But how? How could I possibly move forward? Would I ever? My love, my life, my Jackson Bean, was gone.

I started by writing the goodbye letter Wendy told me to write. It was excruciating. With each keystroke, the tears came harder, my heart breaking all over again. But I kept going.

And now, let me share—no, let me bare—my soul to you. Because through my grief, you will see your own. And you will know that you are not alone. That the pain you feel is real, valid, and as consuming as mine. But together, perhaps, we can find a way through.

*Good-Bye Letter to Jack*

My dearest Jack,

I'm not ready for this. I'm not ready to say goodbye. You are my heart, my soul mate, my greatest love.

Coming home each day was never just a routine—it was the highlight of my day. I lived for that moment when I'd open the door, and you and your sister would stretch in the warm sun, lazily creeping out to greet me in the driveway. I cherished those little things, but I longed for more time— more moments with you in my lap, feeling your warmth, soaking in the love that only you could give.

Every time I sat near you, you made your way onto my lap, gracing me with your presence. It was never just a coincidence. I *know* we have loved each other before. I know we've shared lifetimes, that we have walked through millennia together. And this parting—it was too soon. Too fast. But I gave you what you needed, even when my heart was breaking.

You were ready to leave on Friday. For *you*, it was ideal. For *me*, it was unbearable. And still, you were willing to wait. A selfish part of me wishes I had waited just a little longer—to have had just a few more days with you. But I couldn't risk your condition worsening, couldn't bear the thought of you suffering. Your tummy was full, a little uncomfortable, but you were still *you*—wagging your tail, licking my lips, eating pizza, sipping wine, and reveling in the love of those who adored you.

I couldn't let it get bad. I couldn't let you feel pain. I honored the exit you asked for, the peaceful passing you deserved.

Jessie, Jerry's best friend, came to say goodbye. Your brother Jerry was there. Even Joe—tears in his eyes—was there for you. Your Mom, Buffy was there. Brandi too. And me—I held you close, kissing you, feeling you kiss me back. Those sweet, bittersweet kisses, faster and faster, as if you were saying *thank you*—as if you were saying *goodbye*.

Jerry kissed your head. I felt you pressing into my lips, kissing me so hard. And then, your gaze softened. Your body relaxed. Your little heart slowed. And I *saw* it—I saw your soul leave your body. Your big, beautiful brown eyes are no longer the same. Your happy face, now solemn. Still. Quiet. Empty.

I love you in life. I love you in death. You are with me forever.

My heart aches endlessly for you, my sweet Jackson Bean. You are my soul mate, my love beyond time. Even in death, we will never, ever part.

**Forever yours,**
Your mom, your lover, your best friend
xoxo


Below is an email from Nora, my Intuitive reader, acknowledging Jack's Death.

**9/17/12**

Dear Susan,

Please know that Jack loved you so much and was absolutely finished with his time on the planet. He will be there to greet you, all young and beautiful, when you leave this earth plane. I know you must miss him terribly but remember the love you gave him. I am sure, knowing you, that there was little Jack could ever have wanted for in life. You gave it all to him! He knew you loved him and was in no pain or suffering when he left. I will see if I can get you in earlier but it does not look promising. I will do my best.

Love and light,
Nora

Reaching, grasping—desperate to make contact with my Jack—I searched through Facebook, hoping for a sign, a connection, *something*. That's when I found Eden Scott Cross, an animal communicator.

I didn't hesitate. I called her and left a message, my heart pounding with anticipation and grief. To my surprise, she called me back almost immediately. She was kind, patient—her voice a soothing balm to my shattered soul. We spoke for over an hour, and in that short time, I felt a glimmer of hope, a whisper of possibility.

Determined to take the next step, I booked an email session with her, submitting my PayPal payment. Soon after, she responded:

**Email response from Eden Cross regarding your reading**

Yikes! I had no idea how expensive cremation could be. I completely understand the financial burden—believe me. I will do everything in my power to help you in any way that I can.

When our two beloved puppy children crossed over, I tried everything to reach them. And though I'm an animal communicator, it didn't matter. Grief is grief. I would wake up in the middle of the night, quietly slip out of bed, and retreat to the kitchen or bathroom just so I could cry without waking my husband. I knew he was hurting too, and I couldn't bear to add to his pain. We were both struggling to contain the unbearable weight of our loss.

Susan, it hurts—it just plain *hurts*. There's no easy way around it; we have to walk *through* the pain. I've seen this with my clients and friends who have lost their spouses— it's the same raw grief. Pain. Loss. Anger. You just have to take it one day, or sometimes, one minute at a time.

I truly hope you find some comfort in being surrounded by others in the support group who understand your pain. And I promise, I will do my best to complete your reading as soon as I can.

**Kind Regards,**
*Eden*

My Response:

No puppies for me! That's my Jack at six weeks old. His ashes will be ready tomorrow. I went today, but I couldn't even get the words out without breaking down in hysterics. I'm really never going to get over this.

I'm planning to go to a pet grief support group Thursday night. I'm praying Jack is in a very talkative mood, because I am *very, very* needy right now.

I feel a strong energy from you, and I think I can sense Jack around me today. Oh! I forgot to ask you something. The other day, I asked him who was going next, and he said his mother, Buffy. When I asked *when*, I think he felt my anger and decided it wasn't the best time to tell me. Could you ask him again? I don't handle being blindsided well—like I was with him.

Thank you, Eden. I truly appreciate you.
**Susan**

I was reaching out to anyone who would listen—anyone who could give me answers, make a connection, or help me make sense of this unbearable loss. My patient, John Mathis, was also a registered nurse. He had experienced a near-death experience and was deeply metaphysical. Desperate for insight, I decided to send him an email.

**Tue, Sep 18, 2012, at 10:11 a.m.,**

Hi John, where are you???? Don't disappear on me! Please don't fall by the wayside—I am an emotional wreck.

My soul mate, Jackson Bean, my 9 ½-year-old Cocker Spaniel, started having trouble urinating on Thursday. I thought it was a small stone, but it turned out to be hemangiosarcoma of the spleen with metastasis to the liver. They gave him a prognosis of 4–7 days, with the possibility of crashing at any moment. I refused to let him go in a sterile hospital room, so I signed an AMA (Against Medical Advice) discharge and brought him home with me Thursday at 10 a.m.

The next day, at exactly 11:11 a.m. (completely by accident), I had a reading with animal communicator Wendy Cooper. Jack told her he wanted to go that day but agreed to stay if I needed more time. I always knew we were soul mates, and she confirmed it—we have been together for millennia. She told me he came into this lifetime to teach me about romantic love, which she said is rare.

John, I am utterly devastated. My daily purpose is gone. I cry day and night. I miss him. I want him back. I know he will be with me as long as I need him, but I am a tangible person—I need his kisses, the smell of his fur, the snuggles, the love we shared.

I have his sister and his mother, but—God forgive me— it's not the same. I don't love them the way I love him. He was my reason for living. Pitiful, but true. I know his work here was done, but why?

I hope you'll be in soon.

Thank you for listening.
**Susan**

John Responds:

Aww, Susan. I am so sorry for your loss, but you were given the blessing of knowing it was coming. You showered him with love before his transition from the physical into the spiritual. His energy will always be with you, and now, he is no longer bound by physical limitations.

Losing a source of unconditional love is a pain like no other. But remember this—there are people who will live their entire lives and never experience the kind of love you and Jack shared. That, in itself, is a rare and beautiful gift.

As the old adage says, *God doesn't bring you to it without bringing you through it.* You have everything you need— spiritually and emotionally—to get through this. Grief is natural; allow it to run its course. You carry the strength of your ancestors within you, and your spiritual guides and guardians are surrounding you now.

You can do this.
John

It was almost—well, for me, it *was*—like when a person dies. I was reaching out to anyone who had known him, anyone who could offer me solace, answers, or simply tell me how I could reach him. In my desperation, I decided to write to Dolores Parsons of Eine Kleine Kennels in the Catskills—the place where I had brought Buffy to mate back in 2002.

Dear Dolores,

I'm not sure if you remember me, but my son and I visited you back in 2002 when your Inky sired my Buffy's litter. Jack was one of the cockers I kept from that litter, along with Brandi.

He was fine—perfectly fine—until suddenly, he wasn't. I took him to the vet because he was having trouble urinating, and within twenty minutes, they told me he had a tumor that had metastasized. Hemangiosarcoma.

I have a photo of him on the day I let him go. It was agonizing because, other than a full belly, he *looked* fine— eating pizza, peeing again, pooping, barking at strangers. I reached out to an animal communicator, hoping to understand what *Jack* needed. He told me he would stay a few more days if I needed him to, but ideally, he wanted to cross over on Friday—his work here was done.

And so, unselfishly, I honored his request.

I was also told (which I already knew, deep in my soul) that Jack and I had been soulmates for millennia, that he had come into this life to teach me romantic love.

Dolores, my life is over. My boy is gone. I don't know how I will ever—no, I *know* I will never—be the same.

I miss my baby. My best friend. The love of my life.

Susan, Buffy, Brandi, and Jackson Bean

Email response from Dolores Parsons (Buffy's Stud Service)

Hello Susan,

Of course, I remember you. I still have a picture of one of your puppies holding a basket under the Christmas tree—it has always been one of my favorite pictures.

I am so sorry for your loss. Cancer is taking more and more lives these days, and it breaks my heart. I hope Jack didn't suffer too much, as the disease progressed so quickly. Sadly, we have to face the truth that dogs just don't live as long as we do.

But you *know* he'll be waiting for you when you cross over—wagging his tail, jumping all over you, just as he always did. If I didn't believe that, I couldn't do what I do.

Thank you for letting me know about Jack.

Dolores

*Journal Entry:*

*I can't see him. I can't feel him. He is gone, and I am lost.*

*This morning, I woke up, made coffee, and returned to my bedroom to lie in bed and drink it. I was feeling so lost, so sad. Brandi lay next to me, and I could hear the click-clack of Buffy's nails on the wood floor, heading in my direction. I looked down, ready to say good morning and pet her. But when I glanced down, her entire face morphed into Jack.*

*This was the first time Jack had come to me.*

*Through Buffy, he came to me. I burst into tears, telling him how much I missed him, and I cried uncontrollably. Then, just as suddenly, he was gone, and it was Buffy sitting in front of me again.*

*The difference, though, was that Buffy has a sebaceous adenoma on the top of her head, the size of a small grape. But at that moment, it was gone. My Bean had come to me, showing me that he was still here, right next to me, just as Wendy had said he would be.*

*This was the beginning of the end of the "bad" grief.*

*Off to work, still reeling from the experience of the afterlife.*

*Still, no desire to go to the gym or do anything but cry and miss my boy. I head home the usual way and climb into bed, sulking. I sleep, wake, and let the time slip by. I got up to take a shower and found myself crying once more, this time in the shower. Brandi was right outside the door, watching me, never leaving my side.*

*When I stepped out of the shower, she was staring up at the spot where I had just stood, crying out for my Jack. Something had caught her attention, something I couldn't see. But I knew what it was.*

*He was still here.*

On Sep 26, 2012, at 9:48 p.m., Susan Marano wrote:

Hey Wendy,

It looks like Brandi sees Jack. When I got out of the shower, she continued to sit there, staring, and kept looking around. She's never done this in the shower or bathroom area before. Earlier, I was crying for Jack in the shower, and that's when she started sitting and looking. She's still there now—this has been going on for about an hour, on and off.

:-) Susan

Wendy writes:

Clients often report this kind of behavior. Animals definitely have the ability to intuit energies that we can't see. I would suggest using Brandi's behavior as information for you. Let her be your "eyes." Assume that she is picking up on something you aren't, and stay open to what that might be.

Wendy

It was 9:45 at night—there was no sunlight, and the bathroom window, frosted with a brushed texture, offered no view in or out. Yet, I allowed Brandi to be my eyes for the time being.

The longing I feel is indescribable, a pain that cuts deeper than anything I've ever known. It is unlike anything I've experienced before. Even losing a person has never struck me as profoundly. I am still searching for answers, desperately seeking some form of peace. I read everything I can get my hands on, and I've paid for animal communication services. I am still awaiting my email from Eden Cross, hoping for the connection that might offer clarity.

I've had several readings with Wendy Cooper, during which we've contacted Jack. As she explained, he has work to do on the other side, but he is still here for me, still present in ways I can't fully understand. Day in and day out, I continue my search, determined to find what I need. In my quest, I've found numerous Facebook pages dedicated to pet loss and grief support. I also came across an author and animal communicator, Jacquelin Smith. After exchanging a series of emails, we are now preparing to speak.

> Clients often report this kind of behavior. Animals definitely have the ability to intuit energies that we can't see. I would suggest using Brandi's behavior as information for you. Let her be your "eyes." Assume that she is picking up on something you aren't, and stay open to what that might be.
>
> Wendy

My son, Jerry, is at home, and I am with my boyfriend in Tierra Verde when I receive a text from Jerry:

*Jerry texted:*

"I saw Jack at 11:11 this morning coming out of my bathroom. I looked at my phone, and it was exactly 11:11. I was walking in, and he was coming out. He used to drink water from the toilet all the time."

It was so amazing to see his spirit form. My son has the same intuitive nature as I do.

A few weeks later, Jerry was watching TV in the living room. Brandi was on the couch next to him, and Buffy was lying next to the crate, which still had bedding in it. Jerry glanced over at the crate and saw Jack lying there. He said, "For a moment, I thought it was Buffy, but then I looked again, and she was lying next to the crate! He was just lying there, looking at me."

**Date: Sunday, September 30, 2012, 8:11 a.m.**
**To: jacquelinsmith@jacquelinsmith.com**

Hello Jackie,

My name is Susan Marano. On September 13th, my beloved Jack developed a urinary obstruction, and I rushed him to the vet. After tests, we learned it was hemangiosarcoma of the spleen with metastasis to the liver. My dear friend and vet, Anne Chauvet, explained that surgery was an option, but that Jack likely wouldn't survive, and I would only have him for another three to six months. There was no way I could put my soulmate through that.

I knew Jack was my soulmate, my husband, my companion, long before Wendy Cooper confirmed it for me. The day I needed guidance—whether Jack wanted to receive medical assistance or pass on his own—we had our reading on September 14 at 11:11 a.m. That moment was no coincidence; 11:11 has always been our time. My birthday is also 11/11. Jack had decided he wanted to go that night but told me he would stay for a few more days if I needed him. I put his needs first and gave him what he needed.

Since his transition, I have been dying a little each day. I miss him so much. I have connected with him since his passing, and he was incredibly grateful for how we crossed paths. He thanked me and told me he is always with me, as long as I need him. He even gave me an "atta girl!"—I did it right. I made his transition perfect with candles, music, and food. I ran around, frantic at times, to ensure it was just as he would have wanted.

I would love to schedule a reading session with you and Jack. When is your first opening? Wendy mentioned that Jack and I have been together for millennia. I miss him so deeply and long to reconnect with my boy.

Love and light,
Susan

Jackie responded:

Hi Susan,

Thank you for your email and for sharing everything that has happened. I know how difficult it is to navigate this kind of loss—I've been through it myself.

I would be happy to do a consultation with you and Jack. How long would you like the session to be? (Please take a moment to review my Consultation Page at www.jacquelinsmith.com.) Most people who wish to communicate with their beloved animal companions in spirit request either a 30-minute session or a 45-minute session if they have extra questions. Occasionally, some clients request an hour.

When animals cross over into spirit form, they don't always have as much to say as one might expect. Let me know your preference. At the moment, I have an opening on Tuesday, October 2, at 12:00 noon EST. I also have an opening on Wednesday, October 3, at 1:00 p.m. EST.

Where are you located?

I look forward to speaking with you soon.

Blessings,
Jacquelin
*Author of Animal Communication: Our Sacred Connection*

Three weeks have passed, and it still doesn't seem to get any easier. I find myself on the edge of my seat, eagerly awaiting my conversation with Jackie and, most of all, with my Jackson Bean.

My reading with Jackie was nothing short of incredible. Jack, however, was very tired, and I hadn't fully understood the depth of the healing process he needed. Connecting with us on this earthly plane takes immense energy, so Jack was surrounded by a white healing light during the session. Jackie explained that Jack and I have shared countless lifetimes together—millennia, in fact. We have traversed many dimensions, times, and spaces, intertwining in ways I could never have imagined. Even more astonishing, she revealed that all four of us—Buffy, Brandi, Jack, and myself—had shared so much over such an expanse of time, even belonging to the same star group in a past existence.

Then, in a sudden moment of revelation, Jackie said, "Jack is coming back." I paused, unable to process, and asked, "Really?" She confirmed, "Yes, in the spring." She went on to say that while Jack wasn't entirely sure of his breed, he would certainly return as a "dog"—he loved being a dog, after all. I asked her to tell him to please try to return as a buff-white cocker spaniel, the way he left. She smiled gently and shared that, while she couldn't delve into all the lives we'd shared, she did reveal that Jack and I had been married in the 1800s in Europe. Brandi had been our human daughter, and tragically, we lost her at a very young age. Buffy, she explained, had been Jack's human mother, and Jack had been some sort of curator in that past life. It all resonated deeply with me, especially as I'd often said, during moments of quiet reflection with my son, "Look at this dog... he was my husband in another life, I *know* he was. Look at him staring at me!" Jack would sit upright and gaze into my eyes, unwavering, as though he were searching the very depths of my soul. I would say aloud, often and without hesitation, "If I could find a man to love me the way Jack loves me, I'd be the happiest woman in the world."

I knew Jack was my husband before I even knew of Jacqueline or the world of animal communication. It was a knowing that transcended time and space. Jackie, however, was not able to provide a specific timeline, aside from "spring," and gently advised me that I needed to let Jack rest and heal. It was okay to reach out to him and stay close, as he was always with me, but for now, I needed to move forward. I was simultaneously filled with a sense of peace and deep sadness. Jackie encouraged me to reach out again in three months or more, as Jack might have more to share at that time.

As our conversation wound down, we chatted about good books to read and classes I might take. I thanked her, and we ended the call.

That afternoon, I felt compelled to reach out to my friend John. He had written a book about his near-death experience and had given me an autographed copy. John is a strong believer in reincarnation, and I felt the need to send him an email. Over the years, we'd had numerous conversations about "things beyond the veil"—conversations that often felt closed off to the uninitiated. But now, with my mind wide open, I wanted to share with him my evolving thoughts on reincarnation. It felt important, a necessary step in my personal growth.

And so, with a renewed sense of clarity, I emailed him, ready to share my journey and my new perspective on life, death, and everything in between.

## DEAR JOHN (MY REALIZATION THAT REINCARNATION IS POSSIBLE)

On Wed, Oct 3, 2012, at 8:00 a.m.:

I had another reading with author and renowned animal communicator Jacquelin Smith last night, and I do believe in reincarnation now! Jack (as I often proclaimed during his life) swore he was my husband in another lifetime, and it turns out we *were* married in the 1800s, in Europe. Brandi was our daughter, and we lost her at a young age. Then, Jacquelin asked about Buffy—she revealed that Buffy was Jack's human mother, my mother-in-law. Jacquelin said that Jack and I have had many lives together, but she couldn't tell me all of them. She then asked Jack which life he wanted me to know about, and he shared that all four of us—Buffy, Brandi, Jack, and myself—have been together in many different forms and lifetimes. We were also star beings in the same group. She said it's rare for a "group" to reincarnate together so often, but I told her that I'm born on 11/11, Jack and Brandi are 11/6, and Buffy is 11/17. She was amazed, and said "Wow!" when Jack communicated with her.

She explained that Jack is healing in the light, which is why he's still weak from the illness that took him. He's in transition and needs to grow stronger, but I'll be able to feel him more as my grief lightens and he grows stronger. He told her he plans on reincarnating in the spring. She said he loves being a dog and may even come back as a cocker spaniel again, though it's too soon to know for sure. Sometimes, she mentioned, things happen that delay the arrival of the next body, and the planned arrival time may not happen as expected.

She suggested I call her in April to see if Jack knows yet, but most of the time they don't tell us exactly where we can find them because it's fate that leads us to each other again. This wonderful news has truly lightened my spirit.

She also shared that Jack said he's still with me—he sleeps on the bed with me at night and enjoys spending time with us when we're in the kitchen. He told her how much he loves me and misses me, which also makes him weak. He sleeps in my bedroom too, and my son saw him in his bathroom last Saturday at 11:11!

Jacquelin said that people with less grief, or those who have passed, have an easier time connecting with their transitioned pets. All of these conversations have made me want to share my newfound open-mindedness with you. You're very metaphysical, and I thought you'd enjoy knowing I was a star being in a past life!

Got your email, sounds like you're moving and shaking! Glad to hear you're doing well.

Love and light,
Susan

John replies:

Hi Susan,

I'm glad to hear that Jack has opened your mind to greater possibilities. There's a concept called *soul groups*, where a group of souls travel together through several incarnations to help each other. It's like a group of friends who belong to a theater troupe—we all take different roles, trading off being the hero, the villain, the victim, and so on.

Over time, other souls come in, while others leave. But the goal is always to learn, and then bring back what we've learned in the physical plane to the spiritual plane.

I appreciate your open mind while you're grieving—it's like being stretched in two different directions simultaneously. It's tough. It hurts. But you're a tough *Borough Broad*, and you'll come through it, in your own time.

I would encourage you to seek out another psychic to see if the information matches, and to hear what another can tap into. They all have different skills and will "hear" different things. It's like getting a second doctor's opinion. If you're inclined, reach out to Victoria Ackerman. She has a school near you in Gulf Gate. Aside from being a psychic, she's a kind and loving person.

I fly out next Wednesday, interview Thursday, and return Sunday. I'll know if I got the job by that Monday. Until then, I am packing, cleaning, painting, and seeking out property management companies.

Be well. Know that you are loved in both the physical and spiritual planes, and that you will thrive.

John

**Subject: Re: TIME CHANGE**

Dear Jacquelin,

I first want to express my heartfelt gratitude for our conversation this evening. I truly appreciate you taking my call, especially after an emergency occurred on your end. I sincerely hope everything is now well on your side. The information you shared with me today, as well as your contact with Jack, was deeply meaningful. I am eager to witness him growing stronger in the light, so that our connection can become even more profound.

I've been practicing my telepathy with Brandi (Jack's sister and our human daughter from our past life in the 1800s). I start by holding a treat, and she sits—usually, I need to say "sit," but recently she has been doing so without any verbal or hand commands. I've gone a step further, attempting to telepathically request that she lie down, and she's been responding to that as well. So, I think I might be starting to get the hang of it!

I'm very interested in having regular sessions with you, possibly once a month, to keep track of Jack's progress and strengthen our connection. In the meantime, I'll be reading and studying more about animal communication. You also mentioned that we are star beings, and I am fascinated by the idea that Brandi, Buffy, Jack, and I keep reincarnating around one another. Our birthdates are so close—Brandi and Jack on 11/6, Buffy on 11/17, and mine on 11/11—that it almost feels like a cosmic alignment.

I'm also curious about why different animal communicators might receive varying messages from the same pet. Wendy Cooper, here in Sarasota, relayed that Jack did not want his pictures in my bedroom or in my boyfriend's bedroom. However, you shared with me that Jack was happy with the pictures being in my room and the living room, and I've decided to leave them where they are, as that feels right.

As I mentioned, I've always known—often joking—that Jack was my husband in another life. I'd say, "If I could find a man who loves me the way Jack loves me, I'd be a lucky woman!" His physical presence is what I miss most—the crazy licking and kissing attacks, the way he'd crawl into my lap every time I sat, just like his mom does when I sit on the floor. Jack was the most affectionate part of my life, and I am equally affectionate. I was told that Jack came to teach me about romantic love, which is ironic because I've always put my dogs ahead of everything. My motto has always been, "Love me, love my dogs."

I helped deliver all six puppies. The black ones came first, with Brandi third, Jack fifth, and Honey—the runt—last. She needed CPR, and as a neonatal ICU nurse, I was able to save her. What an incredible experience. We weren't supposed to keep Jack, but when my then-boyfriend said we couldn't have three dogs, I thought, "I'll get rid of you before I get rid of my Jack!" And that's how the story goes—I left in 2005.

I feel called to develop my abilities, even though I know it takes years. I've always felt a deep connection to animals, and while it's too late for me to become a vet, I hope to one day build a rescue center called *The House Jack Built*.

I'm thrilled to hear that Jack plans to return to me, and the thought makes me so happy. I can only hope nothing changes that. I also hope he returns in the same beautiful buff-white cocker spaniel body I love so much. When I was young, I had a cocker spaniel named Trixie. She was with me from age four to sixteen, until we moved from NYC to Florida. Sadly, she contracted heartworm, and my mother took her to the vet, where she passed away. There was no ceremony, no ashes, and no closure. That's why I bred Buffy with a black cocker to have Brandi.

I apologize for the length of this message, but I'm so amazed by the connection you achieved with Jack and the confirmation of our bond.

I'd love to know what kind of readings you recommend on a monthly basis to continue learning about *us* and to stay in touch with Jack.

With love and light,
Susan, Jack, Buffy, and Brandi

Hello Susan,

Thank you for your email. I'm so glad that our consultation was supportive and helpful to you.

As for the differing messages received by different animal communicators, I can't say for certain why that happens. I suppose we all do the best we can with the information we receive. However, I've never heard an animal request that a person remove their photo from their bedroom. Every experience is unique, and sometimes it's a matter of interpretation or what resonates with each communicator.

If you're interested in deepening your telepathic connection with animals, I offer an Apprenticeship

Program. You can read about it on my website to see if it's something you'd like to pursue at some point.

I think communicating with Jack on a monthly basis might not be necessary. I would recommend more like once every three months. It's important to allow him to fully heal and release his physical form. When an animal reincarnates, they will not come back as the exact same personality, though they may carry over some traits. The purpose of reincarnation is for them to continue their own learning and growth. It's essential not to expect Jack to return as the same dog, even though I understand the deep connection you share. He will choose the breed he wants to return as, and we'll see how that unfolds.

Please let me know if you're interested in the Apprenticeship Program or have any questions about it. It's a four-session commitment, with most people doing a session every two weeks to maintain continuity in learning animal communication.

Take care and blessings to you,
Jacquelin

---

**Subject: Clarification and Questions**

Hello Jacquelin,

I'll take another look at your website, thank you.

I just want to make sure I'm not overstepping by reaching out to Jack. I'm a bit confused. If I can communicate with him on my own—when he's in the bedroom with me or in the kitchen—then why wouldn't I just continue to connect with him like that? If he's here with me and will stay for as long as I need him, why should I go through a "true" communicator to hear him more clearly? I understand he needs to grow stronger, and I need to pay attention to the signs around me. For example, when I ask Brandi, "Where's Jack?" she kind of sits there like, "Why do you keep asking? He's right here." If Jack weren't here, she would be running around looking for him.

So, I guess I'm wondering if wanting to learn more through him about our past lives isn't the best approach. My friend Tere does past-life regression, and I'm having a healing session for myself tonight, but I'm trying to understand. I don't want to be a pest, but I really want to make sure I'm respecting Jack's wishes and keeping our bond strong. I'm just not sure what the difference is between you contacting him with me on the line versus me trying on my own.

I know Jack is weak and trying to grow stronger, but I also know he misses me just as much as I miss him.

Thank you for your guidance.

Love and light,
Susan

Please note that Jack has not even been gone a full month, and I am still grappling with the "bad grief," the overwhelming urge to connect with him constantly and learn all I can. At the time, I was filled with anger as well. Looking back now, as I write this book, I see that these emotions were part of the lessons I needed to learn—lessons about myself and my true life's assignment, about connecting with my higher self. It was a paradigm shift, of sorts. You will see, as this journey unfolds, when I begin to "truly get it" and where my growth starts to take shape.

**10/4/12**

Hi Susan,

When a beloved animal companion leaves us, it's crucial to begin the process of letting them go. I would encourage you to ask Jack to give you signs and communicate with you in the way he feels is best. This is why I'm suggesting we reconnect in a couple of months, once some time has passed. The bond between you and Jack will always remain, but for now, it could be very helpful to focus on your other dogs. They too need your support and attention during this time. You can also assist Jack by offering a prayer for him.

It might be positively healing for you to direct some energy toward your other dogs. They could use your love and guidance. Jack is at peace on the other side and will continue to progress through his process.

Regarding past life connections, it is fine to explore those as a way to understand the bonds, but the ultimate goal is to begin releasing Jack. When he reincarnates, as I mentioned, he won't be the same dog. While there will be a spark of the old "Jack" in the new one, his personality will be different. The new dog will carry traces of him, but it won't be the Jack you once knew.

I hope this makes sense.

Thank you,
Jacquelin

This brings an overwhelming sadness, causing me to retreat into the familiar darkness I thought I had left behind. I want my old Jack back, the one who filled my life with love and joy. Why did you have to leave? I miss you so much. I need you to be you, to return to me as the dog I knew and loved. I don't want a new version of you, I need the same Jack, the one who was always by my side. Please, come home soon.

I responded:

> This doesn't bring me any comfort at all. I don't understand why he had to leave, or what I'm supposed to learn from this. My ignorance and anger were volatile. If we've shared so many lifetimes together, why can't we stay in contact? And if he is indeed coming back, as my friend Tere—a Lightworker and healer—says, why does it have to be so uncertain? She sees it, too, and believes he will not let me miss it, but, as you mentioned, it could change in an instant. She's witnessed such shifts before, even in the delivery room with infants, without any warning.
>
> What I don't understand is why it hurts so much to stay connected with him. This morning, Jack came to me through Buffy, without me asking her to. I just wish I could have that every day until my Momma dog passes. I'm sorry if I'm being a bit much—this is all so new to me. I'm simply

not ready to let him go. It feels as if my very soul has been ripped out from inside me.

Thank you,
Susan

Gosh, I've yet to have a client as challenging as "me." Jackie's patience and kindness are remarkable—she never once shows harshness. It's clear she understands, because she's been there. She knows the pain, the sorrow, the gut-wrenching ache that accompanies the loss of a soul mate.

**10/7/12**
Jackie responds:

Hi Susan,

Thank you for your email. I understand that you're not yet ready to release him, and I respect that—this is still very fresh for you. Take your time with the process, but eventually, it will be important to begin letting him go.

It's wonderful that he's giving you signs, and you can certainly continue to communicate with him. However, I truly feel that your other two dogs need your attention right now, and part of your focus needs to shift toward them.

If you'd like to connect with Jack again in a month or so, just let me know, and we can set up another session.

As for the Apprenticeship Program, the focus would be on communicating with animals who are currently here on Earth. This approach is the most effective way to enhance your ability to connect with animals.

Take care,
Jacquelin


The day after my reading, I had Jack heavily on my mind. I was at work and remembered what Jacquelin had said, "he was your husband in another life, in the 1800's. So I googled Jackson Bean 1800's and I was shocked at what I found:

## WILLIAM JACKSON BEAN

### (1863–1947)

William Jackson Bean (1863–1947) was associated with the Royal Botanic Gardens, Kew (1883–1929), and served as curator there for seven years (1922–1929). He wrote the guide *Trees and Shrubs Hardy in the British Isles* (John Murray, London, 1914) which was known by British and Irish gardeners simply as "Bean." Currently in its eighth edition, "Bean" is still used as a reference today.

I immediately called Jacquelin. I asked if it was a coincidence that William Jackson Bean was a curator of The Kew Gardens in England. And that we lived on Botany Ave when Jack crossed. She explained that there are "No" coincidences. We had a life together...many lives!

She reminded me of what she conveyed in my reading. He and I were married in the 1800s and had a daughter together. She never mentioned his name, I was intuitively prompted by spirit to google "Jackson Bean" and as they say the rest is history.

FINALLY, MY READING WITH EDEN CROSS IS READY SHE WRITES:

**Date: Sun, 7 Oct 2012 21:08:42 -0400**
**Subject: Your Reading is ready!!**
**From: edenx1@gmail.com**
**To: s.marano@hotmail.com**

Hi Susan,

Wow, this is some reading...very unusual. It's the first time I've ever gotten the kind information that's come thru, from an animal reading. It's more typical for a reading with a human who's crossed over.

I'd like to make an appointment to go over it with you, and I'll send it to you at that time. I was trying to get it done for you a little sooner, but my mother has been ill. I hope you're doing a little better ;-)

Let me know when you're available.

Be well and thrive!
Eden
*Eden Scott Cross*
*FB: Eden Cross, Animal Communicator*

I am so excited—another opportunity to connect with my "Bean"!!! It still hasn't even been a month, and I cry every day. I can't bring myself to go to the gym, I don't care if I eat or drink, and I'm really not paying much attention to my other dogs. I just want Jack to come home!

## ANIMAL COMMUNICATION READING WITH JACKSON MARANO – CANINE, MALE (D) - 10.7.12

### BY EDEN SCOTT CROSS

*Note: This reading is an *unusual* combination of both dog and human in Spirit. Where there is direct quotable information coming through for you, the words are exactly as transmitted and *are in italics like this*.

**Eden:** I hear: "macaroni and sauce, yum!"

**Susan:** Yep when I made Italian gravy and pasta on Sundays I always put a ladle on their food

**Eden:** I see a dog lying on top of clean laundry—dirty wasn't bad either, but he loved to lay in the basket on clean laundry.

**Susan:** That would be "dirty" in my son's room, lol. Sometimes warm clean laundry drops on the floor and he would lay on it!

**Eden:** I see what looks like a vest on him. He says he had a bowtie—(was it red, plaid, with a white collar?) Yes, he had great big ear muffs!

**Susan:** At this time this does not resonate with me, but it does not mean that it won't someday, when he comes back. I remembered that he had a "bow-tie collar" that I had forgotten about.

**Eden:** Something about a turtle shaped toy? He loved chicken. He also loved cookies and it looks like you sometimes broke a piece of your own cookie off to share with him. You liked to see him dance on his hind legs! It looks like he could go around in a circle sometimes, but it seems like he could stay up on his hind legs for a fairly long time.

**Susan:** Jack never danced on his back legs, but again maybe he will in his new incarnation. There was not a food or food group that Jack didn't like! LOL, and I shared everything with him!

**Eden:** He says that he had kennel cough one time.

**Susan:** Since I delivered Jack and all of his siblings I know they never had kennel cough. I did get Jack's mother from a pet store (My Bad) and she was 14 weeks when we got her, she may have been exposed to it, but not Jack.

**Eden:** He says you like red wine.

**Susan:** Yes I do! And if I was drinking it, so was he!

**Eden:** He loved the dog park on weekends... and also to walk around the water (it looks like a marina? I see boats and the sidewalk seems to curve around the water). Jack-o

**Susan:** No dog park, Jack was aggressive (fearful), I did take him "once" to Marina Jack's (City Island) surrounded by water, we drank champagne and he helped me get over my sorrow of the month lol!

**Eden:** I hear what sounds like Peter or Petie, Pete or Petie-pie or Sweetie-pie?

**Susan:** I did not connect with any of these names or phrases. Then one day shortly after this reading I realized that I call my dogs sweetie all the time. I heard myself out loud and sent Eden an email telling her I do call my babies "sweetie".

**Eden:** I see *Paddington Bear*

**Susan:** This did not resonate with me, and it has not yet become apparent at the time of penning this book. But I'm waiting!

**Eden:** Now—in Spirit—Jackson is healthy and playing with a ball and with other dogs, too! I hear a name that sounds like Brett? I see a rag-doll like toy?

**Susan:** This made some sense as Jack always chased the ball but never brought it back, Buffy is my retriever! But Jack and Brandi would run alongside Buffy as she ran to retrieve the ball.

Buffy has many rag doll-like toys that Jack really didn't bother much with, however now that he's home he plays with all her toys and he is now the retriever and Buffy runs with him to the ball, but it's him who now retrieves the ball. Funny how much he loves his momma Buffy in this new incarnation. As for the name Brett, it was a HUGE warning for me from Jack in Spirit, it was him trying to protect me. And many of you know how I was almost led down a terrible path of deception of the many unethical communicators out there. Jack protected me, and I in turn have saved many from the same path.

**Eden:** I feel a lot of pressure in the chest—labored breathing. Everything started to go, loose bowels...

I hear: "now I lay thee down to sleep... hush, Jackson..."

**Susan:** The chest is the hemangiosarcoma of the spleen (middle of the chest) that metastasized to his liver, his oxygen levels were low and he had bouts of labored breathing the last two days here on this earth plane.

**Eden:** (Why do I think of one eye having "filmy sight"? Is that a person or Jackson?)

**Susan:** Jack's eyes were fine, I was not sure of this, but in this incarnation Jack has over-productive tear ducts and tear stains. I feel they are from crying for me at the Rainbow Bridge and they remind me how much we missed each other.

**Eden:** He says, "you did all you could do—no, no more pain—no more, medicines! Made me sick, not well. Sorry, my body couldn't last—too sore, too tired. I *always* love you—we are connected—ever!"

**Susan:** Jack was not on any meds, not even in the very end. There was nothing they could do. I just took him home and made him comfy.

**Eden:** It looks like he had an odd gait / walk...at times—almost like a limp or a step-and-a-half?

**Susan:** Jack was great to the end, no walking problems but his Mom, Buffy has terrible arthritis and I feel Eden picked up on this as Buffy limps due to wrist and left front leg arthritis.

..................................................................................................

**Eden:** There seems to be something *special* about a small bird.

**Susan:** This was the bird that Jack moved with his energy outside in my backyard to get my attention, the day after he crossed.

**Eden:** Something about England? I also see Charlie Chaplin.

**Susan:** In my earlier reading with Jacqueline Smith she told me that Jack and I were husband and wife in the late 1800's in England. One day while sitting in my office I decided to google "Jackson Bean" and it returned William Jackson Bean. He was the Curator for Kew Gardens, who attended the gardens located in England.

I contacted Jacqueline to reveal my find and asked her if it were any coincidence that the last three years of Jack's life that we lived together on "Botany Ave." She said, "no coincidences" that was my husband, William Jackson Bean. WOW!

**Eden:** I see a fireman—or a man who wears a uniform—some service business?

**Susan:** My son Jerry is a Chef, graduated with his Bachelor's from Le Cordon Bleu` and wore a uniform to work.

**Eden:** Jackson says, "*Trust God more*".

**Susan:** I was very angry with God, I did not speak to him nor did I want to pray to him. He took my boy. This also passed when I started reading animals for people and realized this amazing gift he had given me.

**Eden:** I see a handsome man—tall, slim with light brown or dirty blond hair nicely cut.

**Susan:** Eden went on to say this was Jack in his human form.

**Eden:** Something about **a clock**. I see the round black clock at work. (why is this important?)

**Susan:** I stopped going to the gym about three weeks before Jack crossed and I have been an avid gym rat for 27.5 years. I would look at the clock at work (wooden not black) and just want to go home and be with my babies, even before I knew he was sick. It was funny, I had a premonition three weeks before Jack took ill. I was walking into the bathroom at my boyfriend's house where I charge my phone at night sometimes. I saw in my mind before I picked up the phone that I would look at my text messages and see one from my son saying Jack got out the front door and got killed by a car! I lifted the phone, and saw

NO text messages! I felt that something was wrong and that it was Buffy, and not Jack, as she has so many fatty adenomas. I took her to see Dr. Anne, I was crying from the moment I arrived. They asked me why I was so upset I told them I felt Buffy had cancer and that she would not live much longer.

They took me back and aspirated all the lumps! All was fine. Anne said Buffy would live to be 16. I got the signs I had cancer, but I took the wrong dog to the vet. It was Jack, it was my baby who had cancer and would leave me in one week's time.

**Eden:** I see the name Lydia. I see a woman with dark hair and it's up in a French twist. She has red nail polish. She says "darling", but you don't trust it. It's not meant for you?

**Susan:** This woman she sees is my mother! Her favorite word is "Darling". It was meant for me. Lydia Caro was my mother's famous cousin, whom I did not know, but they looked a lot alike and my mother envied her glamorous lifestyle.

**Eden**: I hear: "big boobs"...I see a woman in a tight fitting, sleeveless black satin dress w/ V-neck.

**Susan:** Yes this is Jack seeing me when he was little, I still remember and have the dress. It was the first dress I wore after my "boob" job! LOL! Remember he was my husband in a past life. These are things a husband remembers "boobs"!

**Eden:** Jack says: *"sew up your wound, don't nurture it—let it heal! You need also to relate to other humans—you trusted me, now learn to find love and trust between yourself and others. Pure, don't make it up—learn to "let it be".*

*"I was brought into this life for only a short time. We all connect with lessons—and yours still to learn is to love and let go, trusting your own self to find more again.*

*You came into this life with 'loss' as your main lesson—you understand loss. You need to become strong enough within your own soul, to weather loss, yet to go on and not be expecting it but rather, looking on and knowing that it is all good and you are OK!"*

**In light,**
Eden


This is one of the reasons Jack had to return to spirit. He needed to get me back on track with "my life assignment" and he could no longer maneuver on the earth plane to do so.

> *"We will be together again in Spirit—meanwhile,*
> *I am always nearby, in Spirit. Remember the*
> *love we have shared—it lives on—loving energy*
> *never dies; it never goes away!! Amen."*


. . .


Then I hear: "Whispers in the Wind."

It's so hard to read the last few paragraphs, reflecting on all that has happened since Jack crossed over the Rainbow Bridge on 1/11/13. Jack said, "Sew up my wounds." I have always been good at dwelling on open wounds, and he knew it. He also knew it wouldn't benefit me to do that this time. He understood I needed to grow from this, and that's why he left. I would never have learned from my higher self about my life's assignment and my amazing gift of animal communication if he hadn't made that choice.

Re-reading this: "I was brought into this life for only a short time". We all connect with lessons, and yours still to learn is to love and let go, trusting your own self to find more again. You came into this life with 'loss' as your main lesson. You understand loss. You need to become strong enough within your own soul, to weather loss, yet go on, not expecting it, but rather looking on and knowing that it's all good and you are "OK!"

And reading this now, I realize I have always been a control freak. He is right—I need to let go, "just love" and "sew up my wounds." Let what will happen, happen on its own.

"Let it be pure"... don't try to force it. I have always needed to trust myself more. Jack knew me better than I knew myself. Yes, I have come into this life to learn to deal with loss—it's definitely my main lesson in this incarnation. I've experienced loss for as long as I can remember, and don't we all? The universal law that can be applied here is the Law of Soul Evolution. The Law of Soul Evolution is the most fitting universal law to apply to the experience of coming into this life to learn about loss as part of our path toward future ascension. This law teaches that every soul incarnates with the purpose of growth, and that each life presents lessons uniquely tailored to that soul's evolution.

Loss—whether through death, separation, or change—is a catalyst that deepens compassion, surrender, and wisdom. These qualities are essential for spiritual advancement and ascension.

Through the lens of this law, loss is not punishment, but preparation— an opportunity to release attachments, expand perspective, and align more fully with your higher self. Each experience of loss refines your soul's understanding of impermanence, helping you detach from the material and return to the eternal. By embracing loss as a sacred teacher, you fulfill a core part of your soul's contract and move closer to the light of your divine potential.

But I now know that Jack and I—our souls—contracted this path before this lifetime began. I can finally say that I have dealt with the most terminal of losses, and now I've weathered it. I do go on... not expecting it, but looking forward with the understanding that all "IS" good and "I AM OK!"

And now, I pay it forward with my gift of communication and my desire to write this book for those of you who are searching for answers in the same way I once did. The whisper is for my Jackson Beanie Boy.

Thank you, Eden Cross, for making me feel better today as I put pen to paper, far more than I did when I first read this. You took the time to speak with me for an hour during my first call to you. You were the soft spot I needed to land. Jack, thank you, too. Your work is a true gift, and you are an inspiration.

On the morning before his first month at the Rainbow Bridge, I am still a mess. I'm angry, and I keep reaching out to my communicators, hoping for what I want to hear. I reached out again to Wendy Cooper.

I can't seem to cross over to a place of "good" grief. But you have no idea how much of a gift it is, both to yourself and your fur baby, when you finally get there.

. . .

On October 13, 2012, at 10:53 a.m.,

Wendy,

I know you told me that Jack wouldn't be reincarnating for a long time, but I'm not entirely sure what "a long time" means. Jackie Smith mentioned that he would reincarnate in the spring, but it's not spring, and I recently saw a boy on Facebook who is so much like Jack—he's even labeled aggressive, just like Jack was. My little baby intuition tells me there's something about this boy. Tere Greenwald also says that when Jack reincarnates, I *will not miss it*— that Jack will not allow it. What is your opinion?

I'm really trying my hardest to let Jack rest in the light and grow stronger, so I can have you do a reading when I'm more healed, and the grief is lighter, so I can feel him more clearly. I am getting signs, and I'm practicing my telepathy with Brandi. Sometimes it's easy, but other times it feels like I don't hear or feel what she's saying.

Thanks for your input!

Love & Light,
Susan

Wendy responded:

Hi Susie,

I generally respond to weekend emails only if it's emergent, but my sense is that you're seeking answers sooner, so I'm replying now. What I teach in my classes is that any number of animal communicators can do readings, and they may offer different data. That doesn't mean that any one of them is right or wrong. It's about what resonates with your highest self.

Remember how, through our readings, it was determined that you and Jack need to "break the karmic contract," so to speak, in order for your heart to be fully open to a healthy relationship. I would focus on addressing the heartache of the loss without trying to bypass it—healing whatever needs to be healed. You likely need support around that, from a spiritual community or a guide. Some people choose to surround themselves with others who are also on their spiritual journey.

And, of course, you have access to Jack telepathically as a way to get support as well.

You could also "call" Jack back to you in another dog's body. This is entirely possible. My concern about this is that, in doing so, you might not be able to fully engage in an intimate relationship while Jack is present.

We have so much free will. Ultimately, it is all your choice. There is no right or wrong decision.

**Bottom line:** You need to tune into your highest self and keep asking about the next right step.

Hope that helps,
Wendy


I responded to Wendy:

Thank you for your response, Wendy. I can honestly say that I only want the best for Jack and for myself. But despite all the healing and reading I've done, my mind always circles back to Jack's early departure. I can't, and don't want, anyone or anything more than him. If I knew how to physically travel back through dimensions to be with him again, from the very beginning of his life, I would do it in a heartbeat.

I would sacrifice any part of my life as I know it to continue my path with him. Wendy, I know the path I'm meant to take when it comes to a "human" relationship, but free will keeps telling me to run back to my Jack! Most people go through grief, and it passes quickly. But for me, my heartache tells me that I am meant to be with Jack—and he with me—always.

I'll call you tomorrow.

Happy Sunday,
Xo,
Susan

**10/15/12**

Hi Susie,

Thanks for forwarding this. I really resonate with the last few paragraphs, starting with "I was brought" and "We often need"—those messages feel very much in line with what we've discussed. Jacqueline often refers to your "soul growth," as it's the same theme we've been working through. I know it can be confusing to receive different messages, but I believe this is part of the "discernment" that your guides, including Jack, were encouraging you to develop in our last reading.

Truly, YOU are doing a fantastic job. I know you're feeling lost and alone right now, but I encourage you to use that pain as a tool to deepen your spiritual connection. Ask for crystal-clear messages to your questions. Find ways to stay connected with Spirit. You are already learning how to communicate with animals through visuals, but also try "hearing" the messages or feeling them in your body. Tap into your "knowing" skills. All of these can be gateways for you.

When awaiting your pet's reincarnation, the **Law of Divine Knowing**—sometimes seen as a higher expression of the **Law of Vibration and the Law of Oneness**—guides the process. This law reminds us that all souls, including our beloved animal companions, are part of a unified field of consciousness, where nothing is truly lost—only transformed. "Knowing" in this sense is not mere belief or hope, but a deep soul-certainty that transcends time and space. By quieting the mind and tuning into the heart, you access a sacred awareness that your bond continues beyond physical form. This inner knowing holds a vibration that aligns you with your pet's soul and supports their journey back to you.

The **reincarnation process** is not random—it is orchestrated through love, soul contracts, and divine timing. When you sit in your "garden of gestation," the symbolic space of stillness, patience, and preparation, you are energetically welcoming your friend's return.

Your knowing becomes a bridge—a spiritual tether—that reassures the soul of your pet that their place is ready, their return is awaited, and the love never left. In this sacred space, your trust in universal laws actually helps anchor their reincarnation path, creating a soft landing point for their next journey with you.

Soon...
Wendy

Susan responded:

Thank you for the clarification. That reading was not from Jacquie, it was from Eden Cross in Delray. Jacquie Smith, the author of *Animal Communication, Our Sacred Connection*, is the one who mentioned Jack's plan to reincarnate in the Spring.

I've been exploring *www.thesoundoflight.com*, which was a wonderful website full of free classes on how to connect and many activations that have been helping me. I need the clarity of black and white to truly feel that connection with Jack.

I don't believe we are meant to "disconnect"—rather, I feel that Jack and I are meant to be together for eternity, traversing space and time again and again.

As I continue to strengthen my spirit and refine my knowing skills, I hope to start feeling the communication more vividly, not just as thoughts in my head, but as Jack and my Guides working together to help me grow. Perhaps with this growth will come the "letting go," but

I would prefer that our connection be one of unity, Jack and I together, both acting out of free will—letting go of ego and being filled with love for all that we can be and that Jack can receive.

Thanks again for your time and your strong spiritual soul.

Love and Light,
Susan & Jack

**On Oct 15, 2012, at 7:47 p.m.,**

Wendy,

I just listened to our first reading when Jack was still on my lap, and you told me that most people could not do what I did by putting him down the day he needed to go, that it comes from our 1st and 2nd Chakras.

I DID it, Wendy! I did it! And I know I want him back now more than ever. Many animal communicators say (just like you say, we can call them back) I want him back!

I need help. I need to get him back because I can't live without him ANYMORE!!!!!!

I'm losing myself without him!!!!!!

Thank you for your amazing gift. I will continue to read and learn to connect more with my Buffy & Brandi here, and keep up with Jack until he's ready to come back.

Thank you,
Susan & Jack

I continued to research reincarnation and read the books of animal communicators who have been in the business for many, many years and are extremely experienced. I recently saw an interview on YouTube with Dr. Monica Diedrich, Animal Communicator and author of What Your Animals Tell Me and four other books. I decided that her experience is second to none. She has been hearing the animals talk to her since she was two. So, I set out again to schedule a reading with her and find out what she can tell me about my Jack and his impending return. I know that I've said in the past that three dogs is too many, and when that "time" comes, I will be done. So not true. You never realize how much they are a part of you and how much of a loss you feel when they cross over to the other side.

I sent Monica an email and payment, explaining yet again the loss of my soulmate Jack and asking for her help. Monica responded:

Dear Susan,

Thank you for reaching out to me. I would love to talk with Jack on your behalf, but I have a feeling you know him a lot better than you think!

Anyway, I am in receipt of your questions, pictures, and payment. Thank you. I am booked this week but will be able to get you on Tuesday, November 13. Would you like to do this by phone? How about 11:00 a.m.? If that's OK with you, you can call me at the number below, or we can do this through Skype—your choice. Just let me know what will work.

Dr. Monica Diedrich
*Animal Communicator*

This is amazing! Two days after my birthday, I will receive a wonderful gift—the gift of "knowing."

*The "Law of Correspondence," which states that your inner thoughts and beliefs directly manifest in your external reality, essentially meaning "as above, so below"*

Dear Dr. Monica,

**My Jack had to be put down on 9/14/12 due to hemangiosarcoma. He was my soulmate, the love of my life.**

He was born to my Buffy (who will be 13 on 11/17). I also have his sister, Brandi, who will be 10 tomorrow—just as Jack would have been on 11/6. Tomorrow will be a hard day for me. We always celebrated together, as my birthday is on 11/11.

1. I would like to know if Jack has chosen his breed yet. (I hope he comes back as he left—in his buff-white Cocker body.)
2. I would like to know if he is receiving my messages and if what I am hearing is truly him. (I've been practicing and reading many animal communication books.)
3. Brandi and Buffy seem to be in constant contact, as they seem fine since he left. (Do they connect often?)
4. Jack returning in the spring—I would like your help with his reincarnation. (I am told, *"I will NOT miss it."*)
5. Jack was aggressive towards all people at first, except for a very few—like my boyfriend, Joe—whom he

was never aggressive with from day one. Why was he aggressive?

6. I know Jack and all of my dogs have lived together in many lives. Tell me more about our soul contract.

7. How does Jack feel about my boyfriend, Joe?

8. A squirrel came into the yard while I was on the phone last week and would not stop chattering until I acknowledged him. Was that my Jack? I thought it was.

9. Sunday, 11/4, was a difficult day. I dreamt that I called my friend Ann (a vet), who was the person to diagnose Jack. In the dream, I called her and said, *"Jack is still alive!"* (In the dream, I knew it was about two weeks after she diagnosed him.) *"I'm so glad I didn't listen to you!"* Then I woke up feeling saddened.

I went to take a shower, and four songs in a row on Pandora made me believe Jack was sending me a message:

- **"Goodbye Girl"** – *Goodbye doesn't mean forever.*
- **David Soul: "Don't Give Up on Us, Baby."**
- **England Dan & John Ford Coley: "We Never Have to Say Goodbye Again."**

It felt like he was telling me to "hang on, I'm coming back." Was it him? I want to trust my intuition. My grandmother is 94, from Spain, adopted by a Judge and moved to Bayamón, PR, and she was a psychic. She was 96 at the time of this writing, with dementia and short-term memory loss, but she tells me I have the gift and should not continue to push it away.

Buffy is turning 13 on 11/17. Is she preparing to cross over soon?

Thank you,
Susan

Dr. Monica called me the morning of November 13 and went over my reading with me on the phone and sent me her summary of my questions. I am sure you will find this most interesting.

**11/13/12**

Dear Susan:

I am so glad I had time to talk with you this morning. It was a pleasure to do so.

Here are my notes for you to keep.

Love and light,
Dr. Monica Diedrich
*Animal Communicator*

**11/13/12**

Jack—Male in spirit as of 9/14/12, almost 10 years old

1. **I would like to know if Jack has chosen his breed yet.** (*I hope he comes back as he left—in his buff-white Cocker Spaniel body.*)

**Jack:** Yes, you asked for it, and I comply. I, too, love having a Cocker Spaniel body because it is just the right size. It is not too small, where you could pick me up all the time and carry me around, which was not something I always felt comfortable with. But it's also not too large, so I can still be with you wherever you are—especially on the bed.

I think we are both in agreement here. **Cocker it is!**

As for color, I am not certain yet because I have to find a mother first. I want to have a mother that you can see and admire. I would like a mom who can teach me right from wrong from the very beginning. Most importantly, I want one with a very good personality. Listen, I already put you through some hard times before, and this time, I must work on my manners and my ability to be loving to all—both animals and people.

Please make sure you do not take me away from my dog mother too soon. I want her to teach me everything I need to know. I know this will be hard for you, but please try.

Also, when we start living together, I want you to take me out right away and introduce me to many people and pets. I want to be very social, and the only way I can do that is if you teach me that different people, smells, and situations are all good.

This time around, I think we will make an excellent team, and I am really excited for this *do-over*—both for myself and to continue teaching you as well.

2.  **I would like to know if he is getting my messages and if what I am hearing is really him.** *(I've been practicing and reading many animal communication books.)*

**Jack:** Part of my teachings to you were to help you open up your senses to the possibility of animal communication—especially so that you could converse with me. We both know we understood each other without words already.

That was only the beginning. We *can* and *should* improve on it, especially now that you have the guidelines to do it. You are still a little rusty. Although most of the time, you get what I'm saying, there are times when you put 'ideas' in your head—convincing yourself I said something just because you want to believe it.

For instance, you *know* I am coming back, and you got that loud and clear. But are you sure I am coming back **this** spring? I don't know that yet. I really don't.

The reason is that I want to be here when Buffy (Mom) makes her transition into spirit. It would be very important to me to do that for her. She would feel so much better if I were able to guide her.

I know you want me to come back very badly, and I want to respect your wishes, too, so you're putting me in a tough position.

3. **Brandi and Buffy seem to be in constant contact, as they seem fine since he left.** *(Do they connect often?)*

> **Jack:** Yes, they are both fine because I do connect with them often, if not daily.
>
> I tell them where I am and what I'm doing. Sometimes they can see me, but most of the time, they simply feel my energy around them.
>
> We've had lots of important conversations, and they know what's going on.

4. **Jack returning in the spring—I would like your help with the reincarnation.** *(I am told, "I will NOT miss it.")*

> **Jack:** Correct—you will not miss me because I won't let you miss me.
>
> We will find each other because I will guide you every step of the way. When you find me and look into my eyes, you will know—because that 'feeling' you always had will be the same. I *will* be the same.
>
> I promise I will come to you. I will seek you out. All you have to do is be around some puppies where you can also meet their mom.

5. **Jack was aggressive towards all people at first.** *(There were very few people he was never aggressive to—like my boyfriend, Joe. Why was he aggressive?)*

**Jack:** At first, I thought I was simply doing my job—protecting you no matter what the cost.

But now, I understand that you were also anxious around others, and sometimes, I was just picking up on your feelings and reacting accordingly.

Joe, however, is very special, and I wanted to make sure he felt welcome around me. He has a wonderful aura and energy that always made me feel at ease.

6. **I know Jack and all my dogs have lived together in many lives.** *Tell me more about our contract.*

**Jack:** Oh yes, we have a very specific contract.

Basically, we travel in a group—all of us. We decide if and when we will see each other again. Sometimes, our 'group' doesn't always come at the same time because, as a human, you would struggle with having several dogs at once. So we take turns—one or two at a time. But one thing is for sure: every time you come back in a human body, **we are right there with you**.

However, we are not *always* dogs. I have been a person in a past life, and Brandi has been a horse before as well. We change forms depending on what you, as a human, need to learn in that particular incarnation.

Right now, you are learning to be more spiritual and in tune with the higher soul that you are.

### 7. How does he feel about my boyfriend?

**Jack:** He is more spiritual than he even realizes.

He has a special connection with animals, but sometimes, he is afraid to fully embrace it. He should work on deepening that connection, and in doing so, he will learn many valuable lessons.

### 8. A squirrel came into the yard while I was on the phone last week and wouldn't stop chattering until I acknowledged him. *(Was that my Jack? I thought it was.)*

**Jack:** It wasn't necessarily *me*, but I was in him in a way.

My energy is very strong, and sometimes, I use it to show you little signs. You are paying much more attention lately, and it's fun for me to send my energy into other animals to remind you that I'm still around.

I also send you little messages in different ways—like moving the bed a certain way to remind you of me, or sending you a special photograph, or even songs.

9. **Sunday, 11/4, was a difficult day.** *(I dreamt that I called my friend Ann (the vet who diagnosed Jack) and told her, "Jack is still alive!" Then I woke up saddened. But later, four songs in a row on Pandora made me believe Jack was sending me a message. Was it him?)*

**Jack:** Yes, yes, Mom—it was me.

I can move energy around, and I am very good at it. I send you messages in ways I know you will understand. Not many people can put the dots together the way you do.

Oh, and I loved what you did for our birthday! I was there—I saw you. It felt like a party!

10. **Buffy is turning 13 on 11/17. Is she preparing to cross over soon?**

**Jack:** Yes, and I need to be here for her.

Good morning, Dr. Monica,

When you tune in to Jack next week, please get as much info on his reincarnation as he will give you—markings (as he really had no significant ones; he was buff white with a tail docked a little longer and always looked like it had a little tassel on it). But first and foremost, that is what is most important to me.

This is as much information as I can give you today:

I will be back to a Mom who you can meet.

I will have other siblings too, so you will have to seek me out.

I will TRY TO BE buff in color if I can manage that.

My eyes will give my love away, and I will seek you out.

I'd like to have a 'marking' of some type that will make me different from my siblings, just to make it easier on you, but I am not sure if I will be able to manage this.

I need to wait for my dog Mother before I make it back. This is more of a plea than anything else. I think it's only fair to her that someone is here. If you would rather I not wait, I will make every attempt to come back before, but you need to let me know during the many times you speak with me.

I know we will have a very unique relationship, and I am looking forward to seeing you again.

I love you now and forever. I am always with you; I always will be.

Dear Susan:

I am glad you got so many validations. I asked Jack about his Mom and he said that she would like to die at home very much but that he can't predict what she would do when the time comes.

I understand; one thing is to have a plan and the other is what happens at that moment. The contract has a certain time but it is flexible by a few days, and in some cases even months. When the time is close then maybe we can ask Buffy again.

Love and light,
Dr. Monica Diedrich

Wow, amazing! This animal communicator has such incredible insight, and Jack asking for permission to stay in spirit to help Buffy cross over was truly touching. I *did* grant him the permission he was seeking—to stay and wait for my Buffy, his Mama, to cross over. It was very bittersweet—him returning only to lose my dear, sweet Mama doggie. At this point, I held onto hope, knowing that free will also played a role.

I have been receiving many messages from my Jack—he's been rummaging around the house in the middle of the night when I was the only one home, with Buffy and Brandi in bed with me. One day, while in my office, Jack came to me in spirit, as he often did, at 11:11. Almost every day, his energy grew stronger and more amazing. I was learning that it was time to transition from bad, depressive grief to "good grief," and I could feel that my efforts were paying off.

I had joined pet loss groups on Facebook and was learning about reincarnation through people who had experienced it firsthand—some had even had their pets return to them as many as three times.

So, getting back to my story, I was in my office and had a very spiritual experience:

**Susie Paradise:** Ok, lots of enlightenments, but has anyone ever experienced this? I'm sitting at my computer, just saw a patient, and I sit back down. All of a sudden, I see what appears to be a firefly out of the corner of my right eye (remember, I'm inside my office), but it was way brighter—about the size of the tip of a pen. So I look (nothing), then I look away, and there it is zooming by again! Now it's gone. Not an orb—almost like a tiny white Christmas bulb! Hmmmmmm! This is getting fun!

**Facebook User:** Susie, you have arrived. Welcome!

**Janine M:** *Susie Paradise* Yes! I was sitting up in bed reading at night with a lamp on, and from in front of me, on the other side of the room, a yellowish ball of light about the size of a golf ball came zooming at my head. I looked around, thinking it must have been a huge insect lit up like a firefly—then realized it wasn't!! Please tell me this is a sign from my Squirty. *November 16 at 8:47 p.m.*

**Susie Paradise:** Too cool! It happened in my office while I was alone, and I kinda dismissed it the first time. Then it came flying by again—like Tinker Bell! "Tink!" I like that name for Jack while he's in spirit form! Tink it is! Love you, Jackson Tinkerbell! *November 16 at 9:00 pm via mobile*

## 9

# BRINGING JOY TO ANOTHER

*"The best way to find yourself is to lose
yourself in the service of others."*

—MAHATMA GANDHI

I decided to pay it forward.

As Jack had urged in his reading with Eden Cross, *"Pay the love
forward"*. Those words echoed in my heart, resonating deeply. I have
always been an advocate for animals, dedicating my time and energy to
their welfare in countless ways—raising money through events for the
local Humane Society, fostering when I could (though only short-term
due to the aggression of my three Cocker Spaniels), and donating to
causes on Facebook for the countless *thrown away*, *death row*, and
*abused* dogs of the world.

But I wanted to do more.

I decided to educate people about the dangers of posting "*free dog to a good home*" ads on Craigslist. That's when I stumbled upon a post that read:

"*I am looking for a small dog to give a good home to. I have a lot of love to give, and I will be a good parent to a dog. If you have one you can no longer keep, please email me.*"

Something about it caught my attention. So, I responded.

Of course, I didn't have a dog to give, but I gently pointed the person toward two local shelters, explaining that they had wonderful small dogs desperately in need of homes. I detailed how, for just seventy dollars, she would receive a spay/neuter certificate, a bag of food, a gift card for a grooming kit, a leash and collar, and food bowls—everything she'd need to start her journey with a new companion.

Her response came quickly.

"*I can't afford $70.*"

I hesitated for a moment before replying, "*If you can't afford $70, how can you afford to have a pet?*"

She explained that she could afford food on a weekly basis and had just started a new job. The money would come in time, she assured me, but she wanted a dog *now* and didn't want to wait.

Something inside me stirred.

I thought of Jack. I thought of the love we had shared, the bond that had transcended even death. And in that moment, I knew what I had to do.

"*I want to give back in honor of my Jackson Bean,*" I wrote. "*Go to the shelter, pick out a dog, and I will pay for it. I want to pay the love forward.*"

Her reply was immediate.

"OMG, you would really do that?"

"Yes," I assured her. "There are so many dogs that need loving homes, and I believe you could provide that for a fur child."

An hour later, my phone buzzed.

She was at the shelter. She had found *the one*. But there was a problem—they wouldn't accept my credit card over the phone. Without hesitation, I told her, "Come to my office. I'll write a check made out to the shelter." She agreed and was on her way. We texted back and forth the entire time, excitement building with every mile.

Then, a thought crossed my mind.

"How old are you?" I texted.

Her reply, "18. Why?"

I took a deep breath before responding.

"It doesn't matter how old you are. What matters is how much love you have in your heart to give. I believe you have the ability to love and care for a pet deeply. But I ask that you remember one thing—if you can truly commit to this, to love and care for this animal no matter what, then you are a good person."

When she arrived, I handed her a printed article about responsible pet ownership. I could barely hold back my tears as she accepted my check with shaking hands and whispered, "Thank you."

She promised to call when they were on their way home.

And as I watched her walk away, I knew.

Jack's love had been paid forward.

And it would live on!

# 10 THINGS YOUR DOG
# WOULD TELL YOU

Kaitlyn,

I only ask you to remember these things before adopting, my life assignment is to animals, and it breaks my heart when people fail their animals. This article says it all:

Susan

1.  **My life is likely to last ten to fifteen years.** Any separation from you will be painful: remember that before you get me.

2.  **Give me time to understand** what you want of me.

3.  **Place your trust in me**—it is crucial to my wellbeing.

4.  **Do not be angry at me for long,** and do not lock me up as punishment.

5.  You have your work, your entertainment, and your friends. **I only have you.**

6.  **Talk to me sometimes.** Even if I don't understand your words, I understand you.

7.  Be aware that **however you treat me, I will never forget.**

8.  Remember before you hit me that I have sharp teeth that could easily hurt you, but **I choose not to bite you because I love you.**

9.  **Before you scold me** for being uncooperative, obstinate, or lazy, **ask yourself if something might**

**be bothering me.** Perhaps I might not be getting the right food, or I have been out too long, or my heart is getting too old and weak.

10. **Take care of me when I get old.** You too will grow old. **Accompany me on difficult journeys.** Never say: "I cannot bear to watch" or "Let it happen in my absence." **Everything is easier for me if you are there**—even my death.

Feeling very good about what I have just done in the name of my Jackson Beanie, I waited for Kaitlyn to text me a pic of her and her new doggie, she was looking at two different Chihuahuas, a boy and a girl.

I had read a lot over the last few months about spirit connections—how to reach out and feel spirit energy from the other side. I was communicating with a fellow Facebook member about what I had been trying to do and, finally, what I had accomplished.

See the conversation below:

**Susie Paradise:** *I just rubbed my hands together and slowly moved them apart, about 10-12 inches. I could feel the spirit energy—it is soooooo tingly! I feel the space between my hands. When I reach down to where I sense Jack at my feet, it's not cool or cold, but the tingling becomes even stronger... Is that his energy??? Or does it have to be a cool spot?*

**Facebook User:** YEEHAH!!!!! You have now moved from desperate depression (bad grief) to "all there is" and feeling Jack alive and well in spirit form. Welcome. *November 15 at 12:19 p.m.· Like · 3*

**Facebook User:** THIS IS REAL!!!!!!! You have evolved in awareness, and for that, Jack is grateful. Now you can be more connected—teach him "spirit form" tricks!:) Like, put your paw in my hand, kiss my cheek, and rejoice that Jack IS ALIVE and well!!! YEEHAH!
*November 15 at 12:21 p.m.*

**Susie Paradise:** This is ALL soooooo amazing!!! I was in an awful place—sooooo angry inside and sad at the same time, lashing out, putting up walls. If I could give a second of advice to anyone going through the deep, dark depression of losing a fur child, it's: Breathe, relax, don't speak a word until you have knowledge. Accept situations, apologize when wrong, but LEARN, BELIEVE, and LISTEN... NOT SPEAK!!!
*November 15 at 12:21 p.m. · Like · 2 ·*

**Susie Paradise:** GOOSEBUMPS ON MY GOOSEBUMPS! RIP!!!!! (REINCARNATION IS POSSIBLE) YAY, BABY! LOVE YOU, BEAN! Now I need to get the word to others—to heal just one person's tears, like the tears I cried, will make a difference to me.
*November 15 at 12:22 p.m. · Like ·*

**Facebook User:** Susie Paradise, I'm proud of you and happy for you! See what Jack has already taught you from the other side. Isn't he wonderful?!
*November 15 at 12:26 p.m.· Like · 4*

**Susie Paradise:** Yes, ma'am! I hope that everyone learns from my experience. Good grief is soooooo much better.
*November 15 at 12:38 p.m.*

As I sit and wait for Kaitlyn to call, I receive a text:

> Here we are. We just left the shelter and I brought her a pink leash and a pink collar. I have decided to call her "TINKERBELL".

Can you imagine the validation that I received from the naming of her dog? I had not told her the story about Jack coming to me in 'Orb' form two weeks earlier and me deciding to call him "Tink" (Tinkerbell) while he was in spirit form!

THIS IS TINKERBELL AND HER NEW MOM KAITLYN, MY PAY IT FORWARD IN REMEMBRANCE OF JACK. SHE DID NOT KNOW THAT I WAS CALLING JACK IN SPIRIT FORM "TINK". AN AMAZING GIFT FOR ALL OF US!

**Susie Paradise:** When you are doing God's work—the Universe's higher calling—everything just falls into place! And there are NO coincidences! Now let's talk about coincidences. When discussing coincidences, the **Law of Synchronicity** is the most relevant universal law to cite.

This law states that there are no true coincidences—only meaningful alignments orchestrated by a deeper intelligence within the universe. Synchronicities occur when your internal state (thoughts, emotions, intentions) aligns with external events in ways that seem beyond chance. These moments often serve as confirmations, guidance, or signals that you're on the right path.

The Law of Synchronicity suggests that everything is interconnected through a web of energetic and spiritual relationships. When you're tuned into this flow—through presence, intuition, or openness—"coincidences" begin to appear more frequently and meaningfully. These events are not accidental; they're the universe speaking in symbolic language, nudging your awareness toward growth, purpose, or divine timing. Henceforth there is no such thing as a coincidence.
*Yesterday at 2:48 p.m.*

**Facebook User:** HEY, Susie Paradise! Ask her to keep in touch! Then, when something happens, she will understand that "there are NO coincidences"—that you met HER! And that she named her dog the name that came to you for your Jack in spirit form.
*Yesterday at 3:01 p.m. · Like · 3*

**Susie Paradise:** I definitely will keep in touch with them both!
*Yesterday at 3:07 p.m. · Like · 1*

**Buster Bear:** That is amazing, Susie, and all of this unfolded right in front of us in your posts too... that is

really something special!
*15 hours ago ·*

**Susie Paradise:** I'm glad sometimes that I'm long-winded because I would never have written about the experience with the little lights—fairy-like, spirit-like orbs—flying around my office. I'm still amazed myself that I said "fairy-like" and even went so far as to say I was going to call Jack "Tink" while he's in spirit form! I'm lovin' it!
*15 hours ago via mobile · Like · 1*

**Elizabeth:** Susie, how exhilarating!
*13 hours ago · Like*

**SJ Paul:** Susie, this is so fantastic! It also seems like you two are telepathic!

Dear Katilyn,

I just wanted to explain to you that when a pet or person dies, they take spirit form while they wait to be reincarnated, either back to their original owner or into a new body or life to learn different things. Jack is reincarnating to me in the spring, and right now his spirit is around me. The validation of you naming your dog Tinkerbell was Jack's way of telling me he was behind the idea the whole time. :-)

Thanks for being a part of our lives.
Susan

**From: Susan Marano**
**Sent: 11/16/12 2:10 PM**
**To: gecky@gmail.com**

Hi Kaitlyn,

I was just wondering about you two today. How are things going with Tinkerbell? Bet u will spoil her for Xmas huh? Thank you for being a good Mamma to Tink!

Susan

**11/16/12**
5:10 p.m.

Dear Susan,

Hi Susan, we are great, she's spoiled rotten :)

You're welcome and thank you again for bringing us together!

Love, Kaitlyn

Thanksgiving was rapidly approaching, and I was still feeling the sadness of knowing I would not be spending the holidays with my babies. All the baking and no "Bean" to lick the mixer blades. It had always been a challenge to let three dogs lick the beaters without major incidents. LOL! We were invited to Joe's friends for Thanksgiving, and I was bringing the dessert! I decided to make my famous Tiramisu. It's all in the presentation.

As I started to remove all the ingredients from the fridge, my little ones were right there underfoot, where God intended them to be. Anytime the fridge door opened, they magically appeared. A little Michael Bublé on the iPod, a nice glass of vino, and let the dessert-making begin!

Mascarpone cheese—check. Sugar and vanilla—check. And the mixer! With tongues wagging and the mixer humming, I suddenly feel a tear well up in my eyes. I have to stop, gently put the mixer down, and take a breath. Something's missing, something huge... *MY BEAN.*

I rush into the bedroom and grab a card Shelly and Dave Smith had sent me, a beautiful handmade creation from SendOutCards. It's my favorite card, and it still sits out on my shelf, surrounded by his paw print, photos, and his ashes. I place the card on the windowsill in the kitchen, where I'm preparing the desserts. A wave of peace washes over me, as best as it can be... for now.

The dogs lap up the mascarpone mixture from the beaters, the music plays softly, and my tiramisu turns out to be sheer perfection. But now, my least favorite part: cleanup. Ugh. I place the glasses into the fridge, their fall-colored bows so pretty, and begin loading the sink with utensils. As I clean up, I find myself staring at my Jack's picture, wishing he were here to sit beside me, to look up at me with those big, brown, marble-shaped eyes. The sadness hits me hard.

Finally, everything is put away, the counters are wiped down, and I lower the dimmer to a soft glow. As I walk over to retrieve Jack's card from the windowsill, something catches my eye. I call out to my son, Jerry, to come quickly. I couldn't have believed it myself, but there it was. Jerry rushed in, looked at the window, and gasped, "Holy shit, that's crazy."

There was one small tear falling from his eye. He was giving me yet another sign! He was sad too. He missed me. He wanted to be there in the kitchen, licking the beaters and hanging out. And he did his best to show me, "Mom, I am here!" What a wonderful, beautiful neon sign! *BOOM!*

Christmas is rapidly approaching, and my heart aches with the absence of my Jack. Last Christmas was my final Christmas with my Bean, and the longing for him grows with each passing day. Yet, amidst my grief, another worry gnaws at me—Buffy. She seems to be aging right before my eyes, and after my reading with Dr. Monica Dedrich, I fear that her time with me is running short. I will miss her from the very depths of my soul, but deep down, I know this also means my boy is on his way home. Bitter-sweet moments indeed.

Then, an email from my Facebook friend Robyn arrives, telling me about an incredible animal communicator she found—someone who helped her navigate the reincarnation process after the tragic loss of her lab, taken too soon by an inexperienced trainer. Her name is Debbie Johnstone. With a glimmer of hope, I sent my first email.

Dear Debbie,

I am sure this time of year you are extremely busy, with many souls crossing and returning. I hope you will have time to read and respond to this email.

Robin and Angela, both recommended you, and I must say, I am incredibly happy for them both! My Jackson Bean was diagnosed with hemangiosarcoma on 9/13/12, and I had to put him to sleep on 9/14/12. We were soulmates, having shared many, many, many incarnations together.

My heart aches, but I have passed from bad grief to good grief, and I have received many signs from Jack since his crossing.

The day I put him to sleep, I had an animal communicator reading in our house, in our bed. Since then, I have had Jacqueline Smith (author) and Dr. Monica Dedrich also do readings for me.

Jackie says Jack is reincarnating in the spring, and during Monica's reading, she asked, "Are you sure it's in the spring?" Then Jack, through her, asked for my permission to stay until my mom (Buffy) crosses over, as he feels it would be beneficial for her if he is there. I granted him permission. I'm not sure if I'm supposed to tell you this or if it would skew your readings, but I feel the need to share. I'm seeking someone who can help me, just as you helped Robin and Angela with the actual return of their babies.

I have developed my intuition over time. My grandmother is a psychic, and I've been in two past lives. My desire is to be able to read for the "dumped" animals in shelters— to explain to them that someone will love them and that they are not bad. I am looking into animal communication classes, possibly in the new year!

Do you think you can help me? Please see the attached photo. I would like to do an hour-long phone consultation. I would be happy to pay for it this year but would prefer not to schedule the reading until after the first of the year.

Love & Light,
Namaste,
Susan

Hi Susan,

I am so sorry for your loss, and I'm glad to hear you are moving through the stages of grief. Each stage is very important.

Yes, I can assist. This type of work is very near and dear to my heart. I can feel the heart connection between you and Jackson Bean; it is so deep and has been this way through many lives. I would be honored to talk with him on your behalf, whenever you are ready.

If you choose to purchase the session this year, I am happy to schedule it whenever you'd like. If you have any questions, just let me know.

With love, blessings, and tail wags,
Debbie Johnstone
*Listen2Animals - Heart 2 Heart Intuitive Consulting & Animal Communication Services*

In the past few weeks, I have immersed myself in grief support groups on Facebook, as well as animal communication and reincarnation pages. Through these connections, I've encountered countless souls who, like me, are navigating the overwhelming sorrow of losing a beloved pet.

It's been both humbling and healing to bond with those who share this unique and profound experience.

As I spent more time in these communities, something extraordinary began to happen. I started sensing the presence of pets—animals I didn't know, but who belonged to people I had connected with. They would come to me, seeking help in delivering messages of peace to their earthly companions, sometimes even offering a glimpse of their return.

It was then that I began to realize something deeply profound: I had inherited my grandmother's gift of intuition. The more I embraced it, the more it became a part of who I am. At first, I lacked the confidence to trust in my abilities, unsure of what I was experiencing. But soon, my heart led me to reach out to Debbie Johnstone, a renowned animal communicator, who provided the validation I needed.

Debbie performed a reading for me involving a dog named Butler. He had come to me with vivid details, and Debbie confirmed everything he had shared. Butler's earthly mom had fallen victim to a charlatan, someone posing as an animal communicator, who fed her fabricated information.

It was a painful experience, but when Debbie relayed Butler's message—confirming everything he had conveyed to me—the relief in his mom was palpable. She was filled with peace, knowing that her boy had big plans to return to her from the Rainbow Bridge.

That moment solidified something for me: my connection to the spiritual realm was real. Now, with renewed confidence, I felt ready to hear what my own beloved Jack had to say.

**1/2/13**

Greetings Susan,

I have your photo, just send me the telephone number that you would like me to call you on. That's all I need. It will be an interactive session and I will act as your translator.

I'm looking forward to connecting with you both.

With blessings and tail waggles,
Debbie Johnstone

Here is my first communication session with Debbie, connecting with Jack:

**Debbie:** Jack is here, and he is wearing a black hat and a green bow tie. Note this is the second time a communicator sees him in a bowtie. He sees your future with someone who feels the same way about animals as you do. He's (Jack) a very wise old man... LOL!

**Me:** Yes, he is... a wise old man.

**Debbie:** He has been around the block a few times. He wants you to know he thinks Joe is a good man, but your vibration patterns for animals are different. Jack says you can have what your heart desires... "You're worth it!" He (Jack) keeps referring to the fact that he is your soulmate, and I keep hearing him say "Mom" a lot.

**Me:** Uuuuummmmm?

**Debbie:** Do you feel that you took care of him in a motherly way?

**Me:** Absolutely!!! Jack was like a rag doll; you could pick him up, hold him, and hang him upside down, and he would just lay there. Jack was very, I guess to me, socialization was just having people around him, and that's really not the case! I lived in New Jersey, and they were born in November, so it was cold. I thought having the puppies around my son and my boyfriend's son and their friends was "plenty of socialization." It was not. They need different situations, different smells, and different places. And, well, they didn't get that, and Jack became aggressive in a defensive way. That's one thing Dr. Monica Diedrich did touch on. She said Jack caused me a lot of stress with his aggression/behavior. Being the Alpha male, he created a pack mentality with Brandi and Buffy (who are not really aggressive).

Jack would sit on the kitchen table with Brandi and just, out of control, bark at anyone walking by. If I even opened the front door and he saw something moving, he would take off down the block. And now, through all the animal communications I have done, I realize that it was his defense mechanism for me. I also know that when he comes back, he has expressed to me that he wants me to get him out there, around a lot of different people and things. At the time of this writing, I can tell you he has returned without an aggressive bone in his body.

He loves people, and other dogs he is a bit afraid of, but we're working on it. Jack expressed that he wants our relationship to be more "stable," so to speak.

**Debbie:** When you said stable, he said "equal." He also says he is anxious to come back as a puppy and have puppy fun… lots of puppy fun.

**Me:** Like I told you before, I had them all sitting, giving paw, and high-fiving by six weeks old!

**Debbie:** OMG, that's great!

**Me:** It was just adorable! Would I breed again? "NO," there are too many homeless and abused animals that need homes to be breeding! But it was the best experience of my life.

**Debbie:** He kind of feels… Well, he's telling me this is just a "continuation." So, he will come back and go through the experience of being a puppy, but it is his intention to bring himself back to you. Sometimes they come back and "not remember," but that is not his intention. He wants to come back as "who you knew."

**Me:** OK, and his body? He's going to be Buffy white again, right?

**Debbie:** Sometimes they come back and only remember a little bit, and you will see their mannerisms to be very similar. They will do things, and you, of course, can feel the energy of them inside their bodies. But he says, for the most part, he intends to bring who he was with him— that part of him. There will be some changes, but it's not like he's going to be a brand new version of himself. You will know who he is, if that makes sense. I'm seeing a Blue Roan. You know what that is, right?

**Me:** Like gray, white, and black, it looks almost blue?

**Debbie:** I used to have horses like that.

**Me:** Well, you tell him to come back as he left or not at all! LOLOLOLOL!

**Debbie:** *Laughing* OK!

**Me:** Ask him why he has changed his mind about waiting on the other side to help his mother cross? Because it was more of a plea, and he asked me for permission?

**Debbie:** He says he talked to her, and it doesn't matter to her, as he can be with her from either side. He is really just getting excited and anxious to come back.

**Me:** I'm just not sure "how I'm going to find him"?

**Debbie:** OK, let's see what else he has to say. He says he will continue to connect to you until then. Just simply, umm... you're really, really good at this... umm... follow the nudges and the signs, and he will lead you. It looks like he is showing me. He says not everything has been completely planned at this point in time. What he would like to do is be some place near to you so you don't have to go and look for him all over the place. So, somewhere in your area... it shouldn't be hard! He promises he will send you... he keeps showing me his nose nudging you.

**Me:** LOL, he used to do that all the time! (And he still does in his new puppy body.)

**Debbie:** He's showing me himself, nudging you on your right shoulder, "Pay attention." You will get little nudges. He's showing me the computer, so you must be going through the computer trying to find him online where someone has posted something. I'm seeing March 17.

**Me:** Well, I am sitting here online while I'm talking to you with my iPad. But March 17 means nothing to me.

**Debbie:** *Laughing* It's St. Patrick's Day.

**Me:** Tell him I said he is a smart ass!!! LOL

**Debbie:** He's also done the high-five thing a few times, too! I have to tell you, he carries a lot of energy. He's making me really hot right now. That means he has a lot of energy. I lost my train of thought... Let me go back to him. He wants to know if you're OK if he comes back sooner than later?

**Me:** Yeah!

**Debbie:** He doesn't want to wait a couple of years.

**Me:** I wouldn't have made him wait a couple of years. I honestly thought that, like in my last reading with Dr. Monica, I asked her if Buffy would be crossing soon, and she said she would be.

**Debbie:** He says, "I don't think so, because I just talked to her."

**Me:** Let's see, I just had my reading with her on 11/13/12 (look at this, WOW), and Jack has only been gone two months shy of a day. Wendy had checked in with Jack, and she also picked up Brandi and Buffy. Brandi has been the one who has gotten the least amount of attention out of the three dogs, and she is just loving being "The One" right now. I was very worried about Buffy when Jack died because she slept "a lot," and Wendy said that Buffy comes out of her body because of the pain from the arthritis in her front legs. You need to start giving her something for that pain, so I did! She also said, "Your grief is such bad negative grief that she is ready to go if this is the way you are going to be from now on."

**Debbie:** Oh yes, I see that.

**Me:** Then Monica had said Buffy was going to be going soon. I lashed out at everyone that I could, and even Wendy came to my home to do an actual healing for me. I was so angry that I just wanted to feel my boy, my JACK!!! I was just like, "I don't feel him! I just wanna feel him!

This is not working for me! I just wanna talk to my dog!!!" I was just belligerent... It was just horrible! I am writing a book and collecting stories from my support group I created on Facebook with Jeanne Harris, who also lost her Jack to the same disease.

**Debbie:** Oh, good, how wonderful!

**Me:** I have actually, regardless of the fact that you and I haven't had a reading until now, been referring quite a few people to you, as Angela (Buster Bear) had nothing but wonderful things to say about you. And there was someone else—did you read for Robin & Roscoe?

**Debbie:** Yes, I did.

**Me:** Well, all great things said, and you know you have to look for the signs, be aware. As a matter of fact, I was sitting at a bar with Joe, and right across from me, at eye level, was a little stuffed cocker spaniel. The bartender asked me what I would like, and I pointed to the little stuffed animal, and he said, "It's yours!" And on New Year's Eve, my boyfriend always gets Cakebread wine, and this time he got Brentwood Stellar Cakebread for Jack Cakebread. "You have to look at these signs!!!"

**Debbie:** And that's what Jack is telling me. You just said, "I don't know how I'm gonna find him," and he's going, "HELLO!" *LOL* He's like, "You will hear. You will find me. Don't worry, and just remember!" Here is something I use all the time... because Jack says he sits in your heart center. You can feel your heart center, right? Where is your chakra?

**Me:** When you say your heart center, what do you mean?

**Debbie:** Umm, not physically, but you feel feelings in there, right?

**Me:** Doesn't everyone feel feelings in there?

**Debbie:** *LOL* No, no, not really. But you're a feeler, so use that because you will feel it. He will give you gentle nudges. I have a feeling they won't be that gentle with him. If you're unsure, you can ask a yes or no question, like, "Is this Jack?" You can kind of feel what it's like in your heart center. I kind of feel like, in my mind's eye, I see a plus sign in my heart center and a minus when I get a negative answer. You can simply ask the question, and you can even practice with your heart center. "Show me or tell me how a positive answer will feel like," and what will a negative feel like? He tells me that is where you're going to get most of your signs because you're a "feeler." So, through your feelings, he says he is pretty good with giving you signs. So, all you have to do is keep yourself open.

**Me:** There is one thing I wanna confirm with him!

**Debbie:** About a month ago, I could not sleep, and I was home alone with Brandi and Buffy sleeping on the bed with me. I had the TV on; it was about 3 a.m. Now, Brandi and Jack have slept in their "High-End Fancy" crate since they were born. I would say, "Sleepy nite-nite" and say "candies," and they would run in there at 9 p.m. and sleep till 6:30 a.m. But since Jack crossed, I have not had the heart to make Brandi sleep alone in the crate. I'm sure she misses him as much, if not more, than me. Wendy did say that Brandi said, "What about me? I have been with him always, since before birth." Anyway, Buffy always slept with me, and now Brandi does too. So, all of a sudden, I hear something—it's like a dog going through the garbage in the kitchen, but it can't be, because they are asleep in my bed with me. Right away, I called out for my son, Jerry... but no answer! So, I start to think I left the door to the laundry room to the garage open, and maybe I have a raccoon in the kitchen. Then I hear the sound of a wet dog shaking. So, I realized it was not a raccoon, and I said, "It's Jack!!!" So, ask him, was it him?

**Debbie:** Yep! Have you heard like their crate rattling a little bit at night? Sounds like the door opening and closing?

**Me:** I hear a lot of things at night, and a few Sundays ago, Jerry saw Jack just sitting in his crate that is right next to the TV in the family room. He said, "I thought it was Buffy," then took a double take, and Buffy was next to me, and Jack was straight across from me, lying in his crate!

**Debbie:** Jack says he is around a lot, and he looks over your shoulder, especially when you're on the computer. He is around a lot at night, and you'll need to listen because he's around the crate a lot. Um, like a little bit of a tinny sound.

**Me:** Well, I took out the comforter, so there is a plastic base. It's a beautiful wicker crate, so if you walk in now, you could hear nails on the plastic flooring.

**Debbie:** Jack is a manifester and is very strong. He can move energy like that—it takes a lot of energy to do that, and he carries a lot. I can feel it. He manifests a lot!

**Me:** The very first time he did it was a few days after he crossed. It was 6:30 a.m., and I could hear Buffy walking over to me. When I looked down to pet her, Jack morphed right through her. See, Buffy has a raisin-sized cyst on her head, and at that very moment, it was gone. I started crying because he did not stay long. Jacqueline Smith (author of *Animal Communication, Our Sacred Connection*) said had I just thanked him for coming and told him I loved him, he would have stayed longer. She also said not to encourage that, as it would take "a lot" out of Buffy.

**Debbie:** He is feeling better now. Oh, by the way, he is telling me to tell you if you want to help the spot on her head, use colloidal silver. But he says he can feel you're feeling better.

**Me:** I am. I joined a pet bereavement group called Bentley's House. It's helping. It's a pet bereavement group, and I actually go every third Thursday of the month. I wrote the poem *The Rainbow Bridge and Back: Jack's Story* and handed it out to everyone, explaining that

I realized everyone believes in different things, but it was there if they wanted it.

**Debbie:** Oh, that was very nice.

**Me:** Wendy Cooper, my animal communicator, was there, and I told the group that if it hadn't been for her, I probably would have gone with Jack because I was that broken. If it wasn't for her telling me that this is the way it was to be, I don't think I would have been able to make it through. One thing you don't know is that in April 2012 (five months before he crossed), he had a tiny spot above his eye that was pink and turned black, so I thought cancer right away. I brought him in (being an RN), thinking it was skin cancer on his Buff-White fur. They aspirated it, and it came back "mast cells." I had it removed immediately, and when the pathology came back, it was all benign. He came home looking like he had been in a boxing match. But four months later, he was gone. I also have a friend, Heidi Ward, a great veterinary oncologist, and she said, "Come down." My friend Shelly was there with her dog and told Heidi what I was saying about metastases in the liver. Heidi said most times that "the mets" is a misdiagnosis. So, I ran him down there, and my heart knew that Anne Chauvet DVM, my friend, was so intelligent and thorough that it couldn't be wrong, but I went anyway. It wasn't a misdiagnosis, and they said we could take the spleen out and the affected portion of the liver, but I would only get six months. I couldn't and would not do that to my Jackson Bean! Just as they start to heal from a painful surgery, you find out, "It's back." No way! I would like to know your take on "negative lifestyles" and how they affect the pets in your home. I had heard that if you are a negative, draining person, your pets absorb that energy, and they can get illnesses such as cancer. I've pretty much been a very negative person my whole life. I believe that people have paradigm shifts, and all things happen for a reason and that there are no coincidences. I wouldn't be the person I am today if Jack hadn't chosen to leave when he did. How do you feel about pets absorbing illness or stress and negativity?

**Debbie:** I do believe that, and a couple of things... It's a choice, just like we have free will as humans. It's a choice. They don't always absorb it, but they can. It's a choice they make. Some animals, some pets, don't choose to make that choice, but many times, they can. Also, many times, they are able to choose to do that, and they can release it in a way that doesn't upset their health. But I do agree with that premise.

**Me:** Well, it makes a lot of sense. And I'll tell you, the amount of yelling and screaming and the things I let bother me were overpowering my life. I don't let those things bother me anymore. It resonates with me that negativity hurts everyone around you, including your pets. I know a lot of my readers aren't going to want to hear that!

**Debbie:** And this can even be true for humans. I also do "soul" work when I can connect to the human soul. Many times, a person who experiences—well, it doesn't have to be anger, it can also be extraordinary sadness—and the lower vibratory emotions, if you hold onto them and don't express them, they stay embedded in your soul and your body. If you continue this pattern over and over, I worked in corporate America in technology for a long time, which was not a good place for me, because

I would take a lot of stress from many of those around me. I really didn't understand it at the time, but it became a very depressive state for me, and I ended up having some pretty severe gastrointestinal issues from it and had to have surgery. But I started finally on this journey of where and who I was supposed to be, which was not a computer programmer. I connected to those things in my body, and I could feel the energy of the emotions stored in there, and I started working on releasing them. So yes, that can happen. One of the other things I love is connecting to animals right before the transition process—before, during, and after. The other thing I really enjoy doing (and it's not that I enjoy it, but it's a passion) is being able to tell a person what their animal feels, so you know, like, "Where does your body hurt?" How does it feel? I can actually connect to it, and when I get that their back hurts or neck hurts, I can pick up if it's caused by emotional trauma. I have a friend who has a tumor in her body, and when I connected to it, it was extreme anger.

**Me:** Debbie.

**Debbie:** Yeah?

**Me:** I am sitting here, and I put in the search bar "Shamrock Cocker Spaniel Puppies."

**Debbie:** Oh no!

**Me:** You're not going to believe what's come up.

**Debbie:** A Blue Rhone?

**Me:** No, it's a cartoon beige cocker spaniel jumping out of a black pot of gold, and it says, "And we are expecting adorable cocker spaniel puppies for St. Patrick's Day!" (I'm crying)

**Debbie:** Now I wanna cry!

**Me:** They will be ready on or about March 16!

**Debbie:** Well, enough said, I guess! LOL, where are they located?

**Me**: Like you said, not far from my house—Lakeland, about an hour.

**Debbie:** There you go! Where are you in Florida?

**Me:** Sarasota, about an hour from Tampa.

**Debbie:** I lived in Ft. Lauderdale about 20 years ago.

**Me:** And it's clear as the day you said March 17 You're pretty good!

**Debbie:** I just hear it and give it to you as it communicates it! How cool!!!!!

 _We are expecting adorable Cocker Spaniel puppies for St. Patrick's Day!_

January 13th ... Cooper and Sophie are a beautiful pair of silver Cocker Spaniels. This is a repeat breeding and two girls are already reserved from this breeding. Last year they had an all silver litter of babies and all are still holding their true color. These beautiful babies will be like having a four-leaf clover for that someone special as they will be ready to for St. Patrick's Day on or about March 16th.

SIRE: Cooper
Stanfield Farms
Dream In Buff
MORE info on Cooper >>

DAM: Sophie

**Debbie:** I have to tell you what I'm seeing. Jack's over here doing an Irish jig! LOL... Well, I am glad that we talked long enough for you to find this! That makes me feel wonderful!

**Me:** You have to see this! I'm on my iPad, and I'm gonna send it to you. It's the website, and there's this little thing jumping up and down... Oh, wait a minute, I can make it bigger. "OH MY GOD! It's a little cocker spaniel jumping out of a pot of gold! It's a little animated thing!"

**Debbie:** Well, let me tell you what's funny about this conversation. The first thing he told me, I write things down before I call. I wrote down *March 17* and *top hat shamrock*! I'm excited because he knew what he wanted to get through to you.

**Me:** I'm thinking maybe it was the name of the breeder, "Shamrock Breeders." I just stuck that in the search bar and figured "try it."

**Debbie:** Wow! Thank you for sharing that with me. I appreciate it.

**Me:** How long have you been doing this?

**Debbie:** Well, kind of... hmm... My earliest recollection of talking to animals, and I also had invisible friends, was when I was two years old. I had a little black cat named Boots, and I would talk to the cat. I would also see spirits and all sorts of things. Then, when I was seven years old, my mom said to me, "You're getting to be a big girl now, and you need to stop imagining your invisible friends." So, I turned it off until I was in my late 30s, early 40s. I kind of had a crisis. It was 2001, 9/11 had just happened. I worked for a huge corporation with lots of responsibility, and I was the holder of the spreadsheet that had all the names of all the people who were going to be laid off. I had this crisis where I said to myself, "I can't do this anymore." I started to see a healer, and the second time

I saw him, he said to me (by this time, I had already gone through a bunch of medical stuff; I was taking 16 different meds), "Do you want to talk to animals again?" And I said, "Yeah, I do." That day, I started looking for a horse rescue and started volunteering, and it basically just turned back on! I put a 2-year plan in place to leave corporate America, and I have been doing it ever since!

**Me:** Wow!

**Debbie:** Much better than corporate America!

**Me:** Really?!

**Debbie:** I learned a lot from that. I learned who I wasn't, so I am just very, very grateful. Eternally grateful. My passion truly is connecting to animals in spirit, and I love the whole reincarnation thing. It's something I have experienced over and over again with my own animals, and the same types of things you and I have just walked through, I have experienced with my own animals! As I tell people, when you have a connection with an animal, they just want to be with you, and they come back. I am very passionate about reincarnation.

**Me:** If Jack is still with us right now, since we've gone off on so many other things...

**Debbie:** He was actually tapping his foot for a while there. He's not doing that anymore... He's actually showing me an image of himself laying on his side with his belly facing me. This was the position that he would lay in often from the time he was a puppy. Ultimately when I went to pick him up from Stanfield Farms, this would be the position he laid in under my chair, where he laid when I decided not to take him home.

**Me:** What I am curious about is that I didn't know I had the ability to do this. Like I said, when it pops into my head, it just pops into my head. I've listened to some teleconferences and "free" animal communication classes. My passion is doing it for animals who have been dumped or pets who want to come back and their families who don't know anything about reincarnation. I want to bring awareness. I've done lots of readings, as you know, for friends on Facebook. I met Jeannie Harris through the grieving process on Facebook. She too lost her Jack to the same type of cancer, and we got together through Facebook. I know there are so many dumped animals that sit in the back of the run with their heads hung low, and I want to communicate with them. I want to lift their spirits so they become more adoptable. I just want to know if I will ever be at that level with my gift to be able to do that.

**Debbie:** Yes, and Jack actually is giving you a high five, saying good job! You recognize your gift, and I, Debbie, also say I think you are already at that level. I would say that it's easy to send that message to an animal. You just walk up to them, open up your mind and your heart center, and you send the message you expressed to me, but to them, and they will get it.

**Debbie:** I think you're already there.

**Me:** I spoke to Jeannie. I told her I want to make positive affirmation templates for prayer cards so that people can put their pets' pictures in the prayer and laminate them— just something that will make people feel good and give them a tool to help pass from "bad" grief to "good grief." Any money that comes from the book, after all has been recouped to write it, put it together, and get it online and in paperback, I want to put on my website that all monies will be donated to the charity of your choice. There will be three to choose from when they hit purchase.

**Debbie:** Well, please keep me in mind when you get to that point, because I would be happy to put your book on my website.

**Me:** And I was going to talk to you about that. I would like to make a Facebook page, and I need someone like you with animal communication skills, like yours, so I can tell people, "Hey, reincarnation is possible. You just have to believe, and here is someone you can talk to." I will refer them to you. If you have anyone who is interested in being in my book with their stories, please let me know.

**Debbie:** Yes, I will. I have plenty on my website. And I would be glad to connect with them and ask for you. And what I was going to say was I'd be happy to link your book to my site to offer to my clients.

**Me:** I have already started the book—about 8-9 pages. I'm starting from how I found out and how I decided to breed Buffy and how she had the puppies. But mainly, the book is about reincarnation and the how's, what's, and why's of it all, and about animal communication. A book of substance.

**Debbie:** I was just going to say, a book of substance! And I am so happy you are doing this. It will help a lot of people.

**Me:** You know, a lot of people don't realize, but all you can do is try to heal a heart, try to tell someone, "Hey, this is what I have experienced—open your heart to it. Here's my book, read about it!" Maybe just chew on it like gum, and then when you're ready. I like you, as you don't push a heavy reading or costly reading like some do. You do what you can for whatever time the person can afford.

**Debbie:** It's my job, but it's also my passion.

**Me:** Well, I can't wait for you to go to your email and see this!

**Debbie:** I will definitely, please keep me updated!

**Me:** Well, it says right here, *Jan 13*, Cooper and Sophie are a beautiful pair of silver cocker spaniels expecting their litter at the beginning of the year! 1/11/13 would be his birthday.

The tape stops here, but we talk for a bit longer. I asked Debbie if she had ever "found" someone's pet that was reincarnating in the first 30 mins of one reading. She said this was a first. It usually takes a few readings. I have come to realize that two people with cosmic power together can be very powerful... and let's not forget Jack's desire to come back from *The Rainbow Bridge*!

Susan,

Wonderful to talk with you and Jack today.

Attached are my handwritten doodles from our call and also a story of one of my dogs.

With love and blessings,
Debbie Johnstone

...

**Debbie:** just a few clarifications: Does Jack want to be called Jack again? Because he *is* Jack, and I don't want to call him anything else!

Yes, Jack wants to be called Jack again. He actually requested it!

That's wild about the silver color with blue bellies. Boy, Jack certainly is a good planner. LOL

He's spending lots of time with your grandmother. Although he frowned when I used the word "time." He says it does not exist where he is. I told him I didn't know how else to say it. He sent me an image of a high-five.

He tells me his mom knows it is him, but it may be his sister who does more of the caretaking. He feels they will share the duties.

With blessings,
Debbie Johnstone

## 10

# WHEN THERE IS NO PLACE YOU WANT TO BE BUT....HOME

*"There's no place like home."*

—L.FRANK BAUM, THE WONDERFUL WIZARD OF OZ

Well, of course, the very first thing I did was jump on the phone and call Pam Bigsby! She was the owner of Stanfield Farms, and I had to get a head start on Jack's new body. There was no time to waste!

*Ring, ring...*

"Hello?"

"Hi, Pam?"

"Yes, this is Pam."

"Hi, Pam, my name is Susan, and you're probably going to think I'm crazy, but I'm calling about your St. Patrick's Day litter."

"Well, that doesn't sound crazy...?"

"Well, when I tell you my story, you might change your mind."

I take a deep breath, my heart racing as I begin to share. I tell Pam about how my Jackson Bean got sick overnight, how he had to cross, and how utterly heartsick I was. I talk about reincarnation, about my reading with a special animal communicator, Debbie Johnstone, who helped me discover that Jack would be coming back to me. And where was he coming from? The Rainbow Bridge. He would be born to her Sophie.

Pam was delighted—her voice filled with warmth as she explained how her deposit policy worked. She told me I was the first to inquire about a "boy" puppy, which meant I had pick of the litter! I felt a rush of relief wash over me. There was no way I was going to miss Jack now.

The next day, I hurried to work to collect my paycheck. I drove as fast as I could to the bank and rushed to deposit my pay. I could barely get to my PayPal account fast enough! The amount? $300.00. She only required $200.00, but I wasn't taking any chances. I proudly printed out my receipt and sat there for a moment, letting the calm flood through me—the first true sense of peace I'd felt since my boy had left. Pam started emailing me on the regular about Sophie and her pregnancy.

Hi Susan,

Sophie is due any day now. I keep watching her like a hawk. She ate well this morning, so I can't say it will be tonight. Her pickup date for the puppies will be eight weeks after she delivers. As soon as I go to the vet with the puppies to have their tails and dew claws done, I also make their eight week checkup appointment for their shots, etc. So when I say she has had them, it will be eight weeks after that.

And yes, you can surely have the pick of the boys. You are the first one in on that, so that makes you first in choice. I can't wait to see which one it is! Haha. You've made me very excited about all this, although I am anyway when I am having babies.

It's fine to send whatever, like $300. I had set a limit on the least amount of a deposit. Sophie is a good momma, so I expect she will do the same this time. But I am always there, anyway, in case of any problems. Like I said, we counted six little heads—haha—hope we are right again, like last time.

I know two girls are already spoken for, and now you have the first pick of the boys. No question about that now.

Your pictures were so cute. I got tears in my eyes looking at Jack's final-day shots. I just hate that. It's so hard to say goodbye to a dear friend. But I love the way you have found a way to speak to Jack again (animal communication) and might use that someday on a few here. I've got a few in mind right now—some very old guys here. They're still bopping around, though, at the ripe old age of almost 13... my old man Taylor. He was born in May, 2000. He still thinks all the girls are for him! Haha, so funny. He looks like he'll go, but he's still going strong. Poor old guy.

Talk to you later...

Thanks again,
Pam Bigsby

Pamela J. Bigsby
http://www.stanfieldfarms.com
Polk City, FL 33868

## 11

# A HEART REUNITED: EMBRACING THE PAST, WELCOMING THE PRESENTS...

*"The Feeling is in the "Knowing" The spiritual heart is the seat of our deepest knowing and most authentic self."*

—KABIR HELMINSKI

**On Jan 12, 2013, at 12:56 a.m.,** pam@stanfieldfarms.com wrote:

Well, Susan... They are here!!!!! Sophie had her babies this afternoon, 1/11/13. She always surprises me. She didn't even look like she was doing anything, and then all of a sudden, she had a puppy! Haha! She is a great mom. She took her vitamins this morning with no problem and even ate well for me, which is unusual for a mom in labor. She started at about 2 p.m. and just kept going. I gave her another special vitamin during her whelping, and she ate them. As soon as she had #7, she wanted food. I gave her a heaping bowl of food, and she gobbled it right down. She was even looking for more, so I gave her more. She drank water and went outside for potty and has done everything perfectly, as she always does. She is a very special gal, with a wonderful temperament. Great mom.

So her final count is 4 boys and 3 girls, all silvers. Just keeping an eye on her, as we always do, just in case of any problems. She is very calm with her new babies now and resting well. She takes great care of them too. Love her so much.

Talk to ya soon,
Pam Bigsby

Pam! I could feel it all night. I kept saying Jacks here!!!! He is back, my boy is home !!!!!! Such good news! I'm so excited! I can't wait to meet them!!!!!

Susan

**Subject: Re: St. Patrick's Litter!**
**From: Susan Marano s.marano@hotmail.com**
**Date: Sat, January 12, 2013, 6:40 AM**
**To: pam@stanfieldfarms.com**

I'd love to see a pic or two of Momma and her babies if that's a possibility! I'm on cloud nine, Pam!!! And remember to remind me to tell you about the "11" story! Also, yesterday I posted a picture, and it said 1/11—a magical day!

I'll send it to you!!!
Susan

Hi Susan,

I was trying to make sure all is okay. I might send you a text picture though. Mom needs a haircut, ha ha! She did so well, just like the last time. I'm so proud of her. All of the puppies are doing very well this morning and have full bellies. Sophie is the best mom ever! She ate last night, and I mean ate a huge amount of food, which surprises me since most moms don't. But it's a good thing because it makes the milk come in even faster without any problems or stress for me. She has done everything perfectly and takes wonderful care of her babies. But I'm still watching to make sure everything's great. So, we're doing the happy dance here!

Talk later,
Pam Bigsby

Hi Pam,

I'm doing the happy dance myself Pam! You have no idea. I woke up last night a few times and just knew Jack had been born. It was amazing when I got your email! I was in tears!!!

Susan

Hi Susan,

Awwww, they are so beautiful, even now. They look like little white rats...well, to some, but not to me. I love them so much. Sophie takes such great care of her babies. I'm sending the pics...they're not the best, but give me another day or so.

Pam Bigsby

Hi Susan,

Just sending some cute little pics of the puppies. They are so healthy and have full tummies. It was really hard taking any pics since they are so active. They are truly a pretty litter, once again...I love them. These are all the boys.

Talk to you soon,
Pam Bigsby

Hi Pam,

OMG, Pam, thank you so much!

In the second picture, there's a puppy on the far right in the back sticking out. He resonates with me as a girl, but is it?

When I say "right," I mean the right if you're looking at the picture straight on. I look at the picture straight on and see the puppy on the right, meaning me facing the photo.

Susan

Susan,

There's no way I could even try to know who that is in this litter. They were all moving around so much, and none of them were tagged yet. Sorry, but you will have to start over when they are all tagged, and that is not yet. They have to have their tails and dew claws done first before I start tagging and taking individual pics of them. I'll get back to you soon. I have a ton of company coming, besides taking care of these babies this week. My company is staying until Sunday—an old friend from when we were kids, and I am holding off everything and everybody until she leaves, as I haven't seen her in almost three years. All is on hold until after she leaves. The puppies have to get to the vet, though, but that is all for now.

I also believe I had only sent you the pics of the boys. But anyway, I have lots to do today...she is in a business meeting in Tampa today, and then she'll be here. I will talk soon...

Pam

I wanted to share the news with Debbie, so I quickly shared the pictures that Pam had sent me on 1/14/13.

Hi Susie,

Love the photos! Thank you!

Yes, I can connect to the energy that is now in the physical body and also to the soul. When an animal has incarnated, I always connect to the life force or energy that is in the body. When the animal transitions, that energy joins back up with its soul energy. It is possible to connect to the soul, even when an animal is in physical form.

I do soul work with people and animals alike.

A little bit more information exists on my Soul Connection website at: http://soullightconnections.com/

Any other questions, just let me know.

With blessings and tail wags,
Debbie Johnstone

2/23/13

Hi Susan,

Yes, we have a picture-taking day scheduled for Friday afternoon. It seems like we've been so busy lately, especially since the holidays, and I was really hoping things would calm down. So far, that hasn't been the case, but I'm doing my best to get back into a routine here.

Sophie, the mama, is an absolute gem. She's the kind of mom who just *knows* what to do, and honestly, you don't have to worry about a thing with her. She's got everything under control—no intervention needed. Haha, she's just that amazing.

Her babies are so fat (and I mean *fat*). They're eating more than they probably should, but I love it. Sophie herself eats a ton of food, which makes me so happy. Her milk is always rich and plentiful, and the babies are thriving. They're never lacking in any department, haha!

Stay tuned! When I'm taking pictures, I need a little help from another person to catch the puppies—they're all over the place, squirming in every direction except the one I need them in! Haha. These little ones were squirms from the moment they were born. I love it because it shows how strong they are. No weaklings here! Sophie's babies are incredible, and she's the perfect mom. I just adore watching her with them.

Talk to you later—I'm off to take care of her again!

With love,
Pam Bigsby

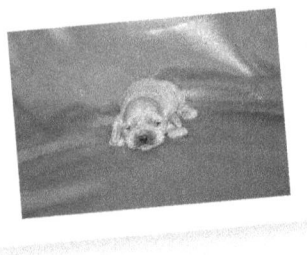

JACKSON BEAN 3 WEEKS OLD

They're growing bigger by the day, and I'm finding myself more and more confused! One moment, I feel a strong, undeniable connection to Jack, and the next, I resonate with Otis. It's as if they're both reaching out to me from different corners of my heart. I reached out to Debbie Johnstone for clarity, because every time I try to connect with Jack's spirit, I sense the energy of a "baby"—an infant who just wants to be warm, fed, dry... and most importantly, happy. It's such a peaceful, tender presence. But I'm not receiving the strong, mature messages I once did when Jack was in spirit.

When I had another session with Debbie, everything clicked into place. She confirmed that both Jack and Otis want to come home with me. It turns out Otis knows exactly how wonderful a home Jack will have, and he wants that same joy for himself. Oh, my heart—now I want them both!

The amusing part? At this very moment, Pam has the puppies all decked out in ribbons—green, blue, white, and yellow—and she knows each one by the names she's given them. With those ribbon colors, she's already assigned each personality, a little label of love. And as I'm sure you can guess, I have a *feeling* I know where this is going. Stay tuned for more on those ribbons, their names, and how the universe has a funny way of working things out in ways we least expect.

2/13/13
Hi Susan,

Here is Otis. Susan...you asked about the eyes. They are all like this at 4 weeks old, they have had checkups and no problems with any of them! Enjoy...Off to clean the pups.... again!!!!!!!

OTIS AT 4 WEEKS OLD!

2/13/13

Here you go, Susan! We had to wet Jake's (Jack's) hair a little because he got some food on his head during playtime. The little rascal! It made him look much darker, but it's all part of the fun. They're such a rowdy bunch—well, not *really* rowdy, but certainly playful! It's so amusing watching them grow. I love them all, and not a single one of them is shy. I can hardly believe how old they're getting already. Almost time to start weaning...not quite yet, but soon.

You wouldn't believe how much these little piggies eat, considering how young they are. It's hilarious! We took all these pictures tonight, so let me know what you think. As for whether that's really Jack or not... maybe you can tell. I'm not sure, but I trust your instincts. All the other boys will be posted on the website soon, so you can see them all.

Can't wait to hear your thoughts!

Thanks,
Pam Bigsby

2/14/13
Dear Pam,

OMG, I absolutely adore their little Valentine's Day photos! Thank you so much for sending them. I honestly don't know how you do it—I would definitely become the crazy dog lady; I could never part with them!

Thank you again, and please give them all kisses from me for a very Happy Hearts Day!

With love,
Susan

Okay, I'm going to be completely honest here—I didn't think these puppies were cute at all! Their little eyes looked a bit googly and, well, almost like they were missing something—like they didn't quite have all the right "ingredients"!

I know, it sounds harsh, but it's how I felt. How could Jack, my beautiful, handsome boy, come back like this? I had to know why, so I turned to the one person I knew could help me. My first thought was to call Wendy Cooper. She's the one who's always reminded me that everything in life is part of a bigger picture—a lesson, a journey, and a soul's purpose. She'd be the one to guide me through this.

---

3/5/13
Hi Pam,

I know you were getting professional pictures taken before we picked Jack up—are they ready yet?

Susan

PS: See you Monday!

---

Hi Susan,

I've had more people here than I care to entertain at once! Here's Otis—I just took them outside. What time Monday works for you? I have a doctor's appointment at 11 a.m., so it'll have to be later in the day, please.

Thanks! The next photo is of the other puppy (we called him "Jake" because we forgot you named him JACK).

JACK AT 8 WEEKS OLD

Susan,

Here's Jack. I had to rename him because my hubby grabbed the wrong puppy when I said, "Bring me the med, blue one." He brought the light blue one instead... men... ugh, geez! I could've kept going here—he's just too cute. I love all the pictures I was able to take. I'm so in love with these little guys.

Anyway, here he is...

Pam

JACK AT 8 WEEKS OLD

After seeing all the pictures of the four boys—Pespi, Otis, Jake, and Reece—I was overwhelmed with doubt. *What if I don't know my Jack?* What if I pick the wrong one? What if I don't see the signs? *What if?*

But I knew better. Deep down, I knew the answers to these questions. I couldn't miss it. I couldn't, and I wouldn't. Jack wouldn't let me. No way, no how.

I've learned that reincarnation is a circle—a cycle of beginnings and completions, of life and death. Cycles are natural, like the seasons that change, like the tides that ebb and flow. It's natural to be afraid of what can and will be, but don't be. Because the unseen realities will come to pass, with or without your approval. From life to life.

I remember Debbie saying that sometimes, animals return with very little memory or prior knowledge of their past life. But Jack told her that wasn't the case for him. Dr. Monica Didreich confirmed the same, and Jacqueline Smith echoed it too—Jack and I had been together for many, many lifetimes, and our journey together was meant to continue.

Jacqueline Smith told me in my first reading with her that Buffy, Brandi, Jack, and I had all been part of the same *star group* in one of our past lives. Not only Jack had been with me, but all four of us had traveled through countless lifetimes together.

One of the best pieces of advice I can give you is this: *Read*. Read as many books as you can get your hands on. Take animal communication classes. Attend workshops. Read books. You will need healing, too.

I didn't understand I needed healing when Wendy Cooper came to my home the Monday after Jack had crossed. I was angry, lost in pain, and Jack wanted me to feel his presence, to feel *my boy*. But when I couldn't, I closed off to her—and to the world. She told me she wouldn't charge me for her visit, but I insisted. Everyone works for a living, and she was kind enough to come out to me when she usually does this remotely.

Now, I understand. Traumatic experiences, if not cleared properly, can affect our entire life's growth process. Remember: animals heal us. They fulfill so many physical, mental, emotional, and spiritual needs. When they shed their earthly bodies and transition into spirit, their presence—and our access to them—is even greater than when they lie at the end of our beds.

**Trust the journey. Trust the signs. Jack would never let you miss him.**

Monday, Monday!!! The day had finally arrived, and with it, a mix of excitement and nervous anticipation. Jerry and I hurriedly got ready, our hearts racing as we made our way to Stanfield Farms. It wasn't far—just an hour's drive, or so I'd been told—and sure enough, we arrived in just about 58 minutes.

We knocked on the door, which was just a screen door, but through it, we could see two crates filled with chocolate-colored cocker spaniels and one large crate with its top removed. Inside, tiny cocker puppies stood on their hind legs, their little wiggle butts wagging in excitement. A voice, soft with a southern drawl, called out, *"Come on in!"*

As we stepped inside, the first thing that greeted us was a beautiful female cocker on a grooming table. Behind her stood a tall, thin woman with a warm smile that radiated kindness. *"I'm Pam,"* she said, extending a hand. We introduced ourselves, barely able to focus on anything other than the impatient, wriggling puppies jumping excitedly at our feet. There were six in total, one already having gone to her forever home.

*Wow,* we whispered in awe, gazing at the little bundles of joy. The dog on the grooming table was Sophie, Jack's mom, his conduit back from the Rainbow Bridge. Her pictures had done her no justice—she was even more beautiful in person. And the puppies? They were nothing like the "ugly" ones I'd imagined from the photos. I had been so wrong.

Pam instructed us to take the puppies out, and we eagerly lifted each one from the crate, placing them on the floor. Instantly, it was like the *Puppy Bowl* had begun. They dashed around the room, peeing and playing, running in circles around the room's circular layout. As I picked one up, his eyes locked with mine, and a rush of emotion washed over me. I felt teary-eyed. *This is him. This is my Jack.*

I turned to Pam and asked, "You've named them all, so you must know which one is which, right?" Pam smiled and said, "Sure! They all have different colored ribbons around their necks. The blue one is Jake." But as I looked closely, I noticed none of them had ribbons—except for one little girl with an orange ribbon. Pam placed Sophie down and walked over to the crate. *What in the world?*

All the ribbons had come loose and were now scattered on the floor of the crate. Laughing, Pam turned to me and said, "Well, I guess it's a good thing you know which one Jack is. Because without those ribbons, I have no clue!"

I looked over at my son, and he met my gaze with a reassuring smile. "Just take your time, Mom," he said gently.

I did. I let the puppies run around, pausing only briefly to climb into our laps, their playful energy filling the room. One little boy kept breaking away from the pack, seeking me out for attention. I lifted him up and gazed into his eyes. *Is that you, Jack? Are you in there?* His response was a soft lick to my face.

I handed him to Jerry, and at that moment, an older couple arrived. They were looking for a girl, and within moments, they had decided on one. They paid Pam and left, the clock ticking as I grew increasingly certain that this little boy was my Jack. Jerry also felt it—this was him, no doubt about it.

My son, always the practical one, reminded me that we needed to leave. We had already been there for an hour, and he had work. As I stood there, though, doubt crept in. *What if I'm making the wrong decision?* I thought of Wendy's words about sacrificing my human relationship for Jack's return, how one of the reasons he had to leave was to make space for my *forever love.*

I turned to Jerry and said, "I'm not sure. I don't know if I can do this. Can I house-train him? Can I commit to 12 to 15 years of responsibility?"

But then it hit me: *This was Jack. My baby. He had come back to me so we could continue our journey together. How could I leave him here?* I had his homecoming outfit ready at home, his name tag "Jackson Bean"—and his new leash waiting. Even his baby playpen was set up.

How could I walk away from him now?

I sat at the table with Pam and my son, the weight of the decision pressing on my chest. Pam pulled out the paperwork, the formalities of bringing Jack home. But all I could think about were my fears, my uncertainties. I spoke to them aloud, admitting how unsure I was, how I worried about being able to handle everything—training him, the long-term commitment, the responsibilities that came with having a third dog again.

Jerry, ever steady, reassured me with his calm presence. *"I'll help you,"* he said. *"I'm not going to Martha's Vineyard till May. I'll help you, and I'll have him trained before I leave."*

As we sat there, discussing everything, Jack crawled under my chair. Without hesitation, he assumed the familiar position he had so many times before—curled up, tucked in close. It was as if he knew. As if he had always been with me, and always would be. The little puppy who had already found his way back home to me, just like he always had.

As crazy as this sounds, only a few of you know this... but yes, I left him there. Pam gave me back my $500 deposit, her voice tinged with disbelief. She couldn't understand why, after all this time, I was walking away without my boy. And honestly, neither could I. I couldn't believe it myself.

I cried the entire way home, tears streaming down my face, making my son late for work in the process. I felt as if I had left a piece of my soul behind.

Pam was going to re-ribbon all the puppies, placing a green ribbon on Jack. She wasn't sure what she had named him or even if she could tell them apart at this point, after all the ribbons had fallen off. But I knew who Jack was. And he knew me.

I couldn't help but wonder—how could he be feeling when we walked out of that room? How could he feel when that door clicked shut behind us, leaving him with nothing but a sea of unfamiliar faces?

---

**From: Susan Marano (s.marano@hotmail.com)**
**Sent: Mon, 3/11/13 6:22 PM**
**To: Pam Wallace (pwallace0000@aol.com)**

Hi Pam,

I'm still not sure I don't want him! Please keep his green ribbon on him. You see below, I bought him a green jacket and collar! I also love him dearly (I think you mentioned that the little guy with the green ribbon is Reeve, correct?). I may be back sooner than you know. I just don't want to make a mistake—dogs are a big commitment, and I would never take that lightly with my baby!

You are such a wonderful person, and I'm truly grateful for your kindness. I will definitely be in touch, Pam! I just don't want to fail at this, because once I have him, there's no turning back.

Susan

---

From: PWallace0000@aol.com
Sent: Mon, 3/11/13 6:44 PM
To: s.marano@hotmail.com

Susan,

He is still here. Your son is a good kid—my daughter wouldn't have been so good about it all. He's a winner for sure. You went that far and didn't take him? I'm shocked... but he's up for sale again. I've already told my web guy, and he's now listed as available. I hate it, but that's the reality. It's sad.

Jack—or green ribbon boy, I'm not sure what to call him anymore, hahahaha—but I'm sure your boyfriend is happy, or will be! Let me know, okay?

Pamela J. Bigsby
*Stanfield Farms*

Pam,

What I think I'm going to do is wait and see what happens on my son's interview date, 3/21. If he's not going to Martha's Vineyard until the summer of 2014, then I will come on the 22nd to pick Reeves up!

That is, if he's still there... I'm praying he is!

I'm feeling really sad today.

Susan

That night I called my dad in NYC. He was going through cancer treatment from 9/11 related cancers; he lived a block from the World Trade Center. I explained to him the situation. I told him I was really falling in love with my boyfriend and that the relationship was not going to go where I wanted it to go if I committed to having three dogs, again. My dad said, "Wait... let me get this straight. You asked your baby to reincarnate back to you, and you worked with a few communicators to help you with your connection and beliefs. And you're going to leave him there now?"

I said I spoke to Wendy and Debbie and they both said that Jack would return back to spirit, and another "soul" would change places with him. He would wait to return to me when the time was right. He went on to say "If this is your boy, you need to go get him. Men are a dime a dozen and if you're the "one" wild horses could not keep him away! GO GET YOUR BOY!"

And that's all I needed, my Daddy to love me and support me in the decision that I already knew was correct.

From: Susan Marano (s.marano@hotmail.com)
Sent: Tue 3/12/13 11:25 PM
To: Pam Wallace (pwallace0000@aol.com)

Pam,

Jerry will be by in the mid-morning to get our boy!

Susan

**From: PWallace0000@aol.com**
**Sent: Wed 3/13/13 12:08 AM**
**To: s.marano@hotmail.com**

You're kidding...?? I'm shocked!!! Funny thing, I just had someone asking about him too and I just answered her. But that's perfectly fine. All is well.

Good for you! Tell your boyfriend that Jack just had to be with you.

Let Jerry know to call me when he's on his way so I'm sure I'll be here. I don't want to be caught in the middle of something like going to the bank or something else, and then miss him.

Are you going to change your mind again, or is this it now? It sounds like you have most of your life under control and are making your own way, so why not surround yourself with things that make you happiest and bring longevity all around you?

I'm really glad you've made up your mind about this special little fellow. He's a real prize for sure. He needs his own bed, coat, and loving arms.

Thanks so much, and remember to have your son call me or something on his way.

Pam Bigsby
*Stanfield Farms*

P.S. By the way, Susan, your son is a prize too. He's a great guy, and you must be so proud of him. He sure loves his mom and has such a gentle way about him. Good for you... good job, Mom.

Jerry picked up Jack on 3/13/13, just two days after I thought I had
changed my mind. Jerry arrived to pick me up from work with my
little boy in the passenger's seat! Jerry said he slept all the way. I got
in, and we all drove home together... at last!

Joe called me, surprised, saying, "You never told me you were
getting another dog. My sister just told me." I replied, "You've known
since my reading with Debbie back in November that Jack was coming
home from the Rainbow Bridge." I had gone to get him on the 11th
but came home without him. Joe responded, "You do what you want!"
He seemed annoyed and mentioned that I should have discussed it with
him. I told him, "Too late, Jack's home to stay."

We all spent the next few days getting acclimated. I was eager to
fill Pam in on Jack's settling-in process.

I wanted to let you know that Baby Bean is doing great. I am so glad I had my son go get my Jack. He looks more and more like my Jack every day. I know he's in there as he is really shining through. He is a BIG licker (he always was), he's great at potty outside, and he's a real lover! Thank you for Cooper and Sophie and for being the vessel that Jack arrived back through to this side. When the book is ready, I will mail you a copy. If it's an e-book first, I'll send you a link! Your kids will be in it!

Thank you, and God bless.
Susan & Jerry

From: PWallace0000@aol.com
Sent: Mon 3/18/13 4:19 PM
To: s.marano@hotmail.com

Awww, thanks so much for letting me know this. I knew he would bring happiness into your life. No matter what your boyfriend says, he needs to be with you. It's not all about anyone else. People need to understand that if you're wanting something to make you happy, then you need to do it. If you're paying the bills, it's your decision. If he had marriage plans or something like that, then I might, and I say might, think about it in a different way. But you would have to seriously think about it.

But anyway, this little guy is in your home, and you are caring for him.

Good for you and your good decision on what's making you happy for now.

Thanks for sharing, and send some pics when you can!

Pam Bigsby

JACK BACK HOME WHERE HE BELONGED
WITH HIS SISTER BRANDI

**From: PWallace0000@aol.com**
**Sent: Mon 3/18/13 5:41 PM**
**To: s.marano@hotmail.com**

So sweet, and it looks like the others are accepting him just fine. They all will adjust just fine. They always do. Thanks for sharing!

Pam

## 12

# THERE'S NO PLACE LIKE HOME

*"As far as I can tell, it's just about letting the Universe know what you want and then working towards it while letting go of how it comes to pass."*

—JIM CAREY

Jack was finally home—it was amazing! He had such a distinct personality. As I explained earlier in his story, he used to drink out of the toilet. When he returned home to begin his second life journey, his curiosity was boundless. He spent time in the bathroom, circling the toilet bowl, seemingly perplexed by its size compared to his new tiny frame to his previous life. Day after day, he tried to figure out why he could no longer reach it to drink. It was comical to watch.

The morning after he arrived, I was letting my other dogs, Buffy and Brandi, outside. At the time, my house was somewhat of a labyrinth. My master suite led into the master bathroom, which connected to the master closet. The closet had a door leading into the garage, which ultimately opened to the side yard. I had been in the kitchen, and when I returned to my bedroom, Jack was sitting on the bathroom floor. As I walked in, he looked up at me as if to say, Look at me. Then, he took off into the closet.

I suddenly realized I had left the closet door open—the one leading to the side yard. Panic set in. I rushed toward him but stopped just before I reached the door. What if he truly remembers this place? Instead of chasing him, I decided to test his memory. I took the longer route, heading through the family room and into the screened-in porch on the opposite side of the house. There was no logical way Jack could have known the layout—unless he had been here before. The house was a maze.

When I arrived at the side door, there he was—sitting patiently, waiting for me. I stepped outside, knelt beside him, and whispered, "So, you're trying to tell me you've been here before, huh?"

Jack took off into the house, and I trailed close behind. He sprinted toward my bedroom, then darted around the house, only to return to the same spot again. He did this four times, running a full circuit, as if to prove a point. I finally laughed and said, "I get it, Jack. I know it's you. I have no doubt."

Watching him grow and interact with his mother, Buffy, and his sister, Brandi, was a joy. He knew all of his favorite toys, his bed, and every spot he had once slept or hidden in his previous life. Each day brought a new revelation. He was truly back, and I was happier than I had ever been.

# AWAKENING TO MY HIGHER SELF

*"The spiritual journey is the unlearning of
fear and the acceptance of love."*

—MARIANNE WILLIAMSON

As I bonded with Jack again, I started to connect with him—and with spirit. I finally embraced my higher self. My grandmother, a psychic medium, and I had inherited her gift. Inspired by this connection, I created a Facebook group where people could grieve alongside like-minded souls. Pet Loss, Grief Support, Animal Communication & Reincarnation with Susie.

As the group grew, so did my intuitive abilities. People would post about their dearly departed pets, and I could feel their energy—sense their messages. I began offering free readings, hesitant at first, because what if I was wrong? But reading after reading, people told me how eerily accurate I was.

One of my most profound experiences was reading for Dee. Dee, the owner of Bella, the famous 1-800-PetMeds dog, a beloved Pomeranian. During the session, I saw that Bella would reincarnate into a litter of three that was already on the earth plane. Three days later, Bella's owner confirmed that she had, indeed, reincarnated—exactly as I had described.

What had started as a simple grief-support group in memory of my beloved Jackson Bean had evolved into something so much greater—an intersection of grief support, animal communication, and reincarnation.

Jack had changed the entire trajectory of my life. And the lives of hundreds of people who would soon make up 20K facebook group followers.

## THE HARDEST TRUTH

*"Awareness is the greatest agent for change."*

—ECKHART TOLLE

Through my work with animal communicators, I learned something difficult to accept: Jack had left because of me. I was devastated.

I came to learn something both painful and profound: Jack had left because of me. He had been trying, in his quiet, devoted way, to absorb the weight of my emotions—my sadness, my anger, my persistent pessimism. Like many soul-connected animals, Jack loved without condition or boundary. And in that love, he did what many pets instinctively do: he took on what I couldn't release.

Wendy, one of my mentors, helped me understand that animals, especially those closely bonded to us, are deeply sensitive to the energies we carry. According to the Law of Vibration, everything in existence emits a frequency—our thoughts, feelings, and intentions included. Jack had been living within the field of my energy, and over time, his own frequency tried to match mine to ease my pain.

This law teaches us that we are always sending out vibrations into the world, and those closest to us—especially pets, who are often energetically open and spiritually attuned—will feel and sometimes even absorb those frequencies.

In Jack's case, he took on more than his small body could handle, because that's the kind of soul he was. His passing was not about blame, but about love—an act of profound sacrifice from a being who simply wanted me to feel lighter. Understanding this helped me move from guilt to gratitude, and to honor his legacy by choosing to raise my own vibration, so that no soul—animal or human—would ever feel the need to carry my pain again. He had tried to absorb my negativity, my anger, my pessimism—taking it all in, the way pets often do when they love unconditionally.

I had always been the person who saw the glass half empty, and people never hesitated to remind me of it. Wendy, one of my mentors, explained that pets often take on their humans' emotions, whether good or bad. Jack had tried to carry my burdens for years, and in the end, it had been too much.

That truth was a bitter pill to swallow. I was the reason Jack had to leave.

But then, he chose to come back to me.

His reincarnation was my second chance—my opportunity to get it right. His return was a gift, a wake-up call. Through Jack, I learned to connect with God, the Universe, and Source energy. I learned to embody love, to express gratitude, and to live in alignment with my higher self. Most importantly, I found my purpose—to help others heal after losing their soul pets.

**Law of Divine Compensation.** The universal law that teaches us that nothing is ever truly lost and that love always finds its way back through second chances, spiritual alignment, and soul contracts.

His reincarnation was my second chance—an invitation from the Universe not just to try again, but to awaken. It was as if the cosmos whispered, *"You're not finished yet. This love has more to teach you."* Jack's return was not a coincidence or a random twist of fate—it was an act of divine compensation. According to the **Law of Divine Compensation**, when we suffer loss, the Universe—operating in harmony with our higher selves—finds ways to restore us, often through new forms of the same eternal love. Jack didn't just come back as a pet. He came back as a mirror, a messenger, and a living thread tying me back to my soul's assignment.

Through him, I learned to speak the language of the unseen—to connect with God, the Universe, Source, and, perhaps most importantly, with myself. I stopped chasing healing and started *embodying* it.

Love became a state of being. Gratitude became my compass. And in the quiet bond we shared the second time around, I finally understood that our souls had agreed to this dance long before we met on Earth. Jack's return wasn't just his second life—it was my second life too. A new chapter where both of our higher selves could complete what we started, and where my true purpose revealed itself: to help others heal, just as he helped heal me.

## THE JOURNEY CONTINUES

*"The journey of awakening is not about becoming who you are. Rather it is about unbecoming who you are not."*

—ALBERT SCHWEITZER

The years have passed swiftly, unfolding into the most enlightening journey of my life. Jack is now 12 years old—he has outlived his first incarnation, when he left at 9.5 years old. Every day, I express gratitude, over and over again, because *tomorrow is never promised.*

I have learned to use my mind to create my own reality. Everything you desire is already out there, waiting for you to claim it. The Universe is waiting for you to ask. Everything you want *also wants you.*

The Universal Laws are real, and when applied, they will transform your life. But knowledge alone is not enough. Only through *application* will you experience their true power.

I hope the stories within this book inspire you to open your heart—to see that reincarnation is real, that love never dies, and that your soul pet is always connected to you.

At the time of this writing, Jack is 12 years old. He was reborn on *1/11/13*. I was born on *11/11*. My father was born on *1/1*. In Jack's first life, he and his mother were both born in the 11th month.

There are no coincidences.

The Universe, and your soul pet, will always find a way to guide you—but *you* must be willing to do the work. Do not let your old beliefs or fears hold you back. This lifetime is short. You, too, can have it all.

I called my boy back to the earth plane, and he came. Some might call that a manifestation. I call it a *truth*.

This awareness is available to everyone.

And now, it's available to *you*.


## BELIEVING IS THE FIRST STEP

There are no coincidences; you are exactly where you are meant to be. My one true intention in writing this book is to create awareness and shine a light on reincarnation as I know it. Through sharing Jack's story, as well as others, I hope to help you understand your pet's life force energy—during their lifetime, into the afterlife, and ultimately, on their journey back to you through the reincarnation process. Life force energy is something that flows through all living beings, great and small.

It is my understanding that all living creatures are caught up in the cycle of reincarnation because this is the natural process of evolution. Just as water evaporates, grows heavy in the clouds, and then rains, beginning the cycle again, living creatures are ever-incarnating, transitioning, and being reborn. I am passionate about educating people on this concept that I have experienced firsthand—it is a very real possibility.

This is also where I learned about soul contracts. The Universe plays a significant role in reincarnation, just as it does in the way the cosmos evolves and expands. Think of all your experiences as a person. We learn, we grow, and we move on to greater lessons. The same process applies to animal life forms. While it is entirely possible that we could have been a lower life form in a previous lifetime, we would not have evolved to our current state if we had not moved beyond it.

In my belief, we evolve through all forms of life—plant, mineral, and animal. I believe that once we reach a certain point in our spiritual journey, we evolve beyond the need for physical incarnation.

The universal law that deals with belief is the **Law of Assumption**. This law states that whatever you assume to be true, whether positive or negative, will become your reality. Your beliefs, thoughts, and assumptions shape your experiences. If you believe something is possible, it will manifest in your life. If you believe something is impossible, it will stay out of reach. The Law of Assumption emphasizes the power of belief in creating your reality.

This principle aligns closely with the idea that belief is a powerful force, and when we assume the feelings of the outcome we desire, we attract it into our lives. It's all about understanding that your assumptions shape your future. What you believe, you create.

How many times have you said, "My cat/dog thinks he's human"?

That's because they live with humans and are constantly learning from us. They absorb lessons of loyalty, love, kindness, and humility. This, in turn, allows them to evolve rapidly, having learned so much from simply existing alongside humans.

Soul contracts are, at their core, lesson plans or agreements we make before we incarnate. While in between lifetimes—spending time at the "Rainbow Bridge" prior to returning—our spirits ponder: *What would I like to learn so that I can fulfill my life assignments and allow my soul to grow?* With the help of spirit guides and angels, we review past lives, reflecting on what worked and what didn't.

Animals, too, create soul contracts with humans. In essence, they "sign on" to help their humans in some way. Jack came to me again in this lifetime to help me learn to deal with *loss*. For as long as I can remember, I've "lost" everything that has ever been important to me in this incarnation. This was my personal Soul Contract of Loss. Jack mirrored/acted out my aggression throughout his entire existence. I was always angry, caught up in the negativity of losing everything—relationships, finances, even abundance. This negative soul contract made me a very difficult person to be around, always yelling, always complaining. Jack had to cross for me to become enlightened. All the things I'm doing today to enlighten others.

Jack's crossing was my moment of enlightenment. It was his ultimate sacrifice—his decision to leave—because, in his absence, I would finally *get it.* I would begin to understand the lessons I had failed to learn for so long. This book, for instance, is a product of Jack's departure. He introduced me to my life assignment, my "higher self," and the purpose behind my soul's journey.

For years, I was consumed by fear—fear of losing things. Losing a relationship, losing financial stability, losing any sense of abundance. It was a dark, limiting existence. But I can now say, with profound gratitude, "Thank you, Jack, for leaving me when you did. I would never have evolved to this point without your sacrifice."

This was our soul contract—a contract we agreed upon before this incarnation and the one before it.

Jack was my mirror, reflecting every action, every thought. When it was time for him to cross, it was the final, ultimate decision that he knew was necessary for my growth. He understood that by leaving, he would teach me from the other side what he couldn't teach me while he was here. His departure opened my eyes to the truth, to the lessons I needed to learn. And when my eyes finally opened, Jack knew he would return to continue our journey together.

Soul contracts work on both a spiritual and subconscious level. They guide our physical circumstances, life situations, and the people we encounter, all designed to teach us and help us grow. I was once a closed-minded person—black and white, right and wrong, with no room for in-between. For nine and a half long years, Jackson Bean tried to help me see the truth. He knew that the soul contract we had agreed upon was perfect. He understood that his leaving would be the key to helping me learn, even if it had to be done from the other side.

But soul contracts, while pre-arranged, still leave room for *free will.* And that's where everything changes. That's where my story comes in. You may be asking now: *Why would we agree on such a painful, negative soul contract?* The answer is simple: sometimes, the toughest teachers provide the most valuable lessons. It's like signing up for karate and then realizing just how hard the training really is. *Lesson learned.*

Soul contracts are challenging, and complex in nature. Working through them as a physical being can be incredibly difficult, and often we may not succeed. But it's in the struggle, the growth, and the eventual transformation that the true lessons lie.

In spirit, we tend to create the best lesson plan possible for our time in the physical world. Often, we also need the help of other souls—our soul contracts with our soulmates, including our fur babies. These agreements may be formed with individuals or groups of souls, each helping the other evolve to the fullest potential agreed upon. I, along with Buffy, Brandi, and Jack, have traveled together in past lives, evolving as a group. It is no coincidence that I am where I am today. I now feel that I am on the brink of another incarnation, one that will resonate with a much higher vibration of knowledge.

Just think—your pet is here to help you. And in turn, you are helping him or her evolve to their higher self as well. Sometimes, the journey doesn't end with the physical body; the body may die, but the "spirit" or "soul" is eternal. Therefore, the soul can choose to return.

## 13

# REINCARNATION: NOT A NEW CONCEPT

*"Reincarnation is not a concept to be feared; it is a promise of renewal."*

—UNKNOWN

### WHAT IS REINCARNATION?

Reincarnation is the concept that souls are continuously reborn—sometimes in different times, places, and even dimensions. Many belief systems around the world embrace reincarnation, including Hinduism, Buddhism, Sikhism, Jainism, and various New Age philosophies. While each tradition holds different views on the causes and purpose of reincarnation, certain core principles remain consistent.

In nearly every case, reincarnation is seen as a natural and essential part of a soul's evolution. It is the process of overcoming negative forces—such as desire, karma, or ignorance—in order to ascend to a higher state of being. Additionally, reincarnation is not limited to human souls; it applies to all living creatures, including our beloved pets. Each religion professes different beliefs about the cause and purpose of reincarnation, but some facts remain consistent. In most cases, reincarnation is a natural and very important part of the development of a soul. It is the process of struggling against some negative force, such as desire or karma, towards a higher state of being; and it applies to all sentient beings.

## REINCARNATION IN CHRISTIANITY

Even within Christianity, references to reincarnation can be found— though they are often overlooked or interpreted differently. If you study the Bible carefully, both the Old and New Testaments contain passages that suggest Jesus and his disciples acknowledged reincarnation.

One of the clearest examples is the connection between John the Baptist and the prophet Elijah. In the New Testament, Matthew 11:11-15 (NIV) contains a passage where Jesus speaks of John the Baptist, indicating that he *is* Elijah, the prophet who was prophesied to return. Interestingly, this revelation occurs in *Matthew, Chapter 11, Verse 11* —a sequence often associated with awareness and spiritual awakening. Coincidence? Perhaps not.

*Matthew, Chapter 11, Verse 11* reads:

*"Truly I tell you, among those born of women, there has not risen anyone greater than John the Baptist; yet whoever is least in the kingdom of heaven is greater than he."*

On the surface, this verse honors John the Baptist's spiritual greatness, but it also alludes to the paradox of divine humility and the evolution of the soul. When paired with the appearance of **11:11**—a number sequence long associated with awakening, alignment, and messages from beyond—it becomes more than a verse. It becomes a spiritual marker. **11:11** is often experienced as a "wake-up code," an intuitive signal that the veil between worlds is thinning and that something meaningful—possibly predestined—is unfolding.

Was it a coincidence that this particular verse showed up at a time when I was pondering Jack's return? Perhaps not. In many spiritual traditions, moments of synchronicity are considered signs that the soul is on track—nudged gently by the unseen hands of higher intelligence. In the context of **reincarnation,** this verse can be interpreted as a subtle validation: that greatness is not confined to a single lifetime, and that soul journeys are layered, circular, and purposeful. Just as John the Baptist was believed by some scholars and mystics to be the reincarnation of the prophet Elijah, so too might our soul companions return—not as new beings, but as familiar energies in new form, bringing new lessons wrapped in old love.

So when **Matthew 11:11** appears alongside your soul-pet's journey, it's not random. It's a sacred breadcrumb, a whisper that your connection spans lifetimes, and that both your souls are rising—again—toward something even greater than before.

Of course, Catholic doctrine officially interprets this passage differently, stating that John the Baptist was influenced by Elijah's spirit rather than being his reincarnation. However, interpretations vary across religious traditions. Hinduism, Buddhism, Sikhism, and Jainism all embrace reincarnation as a fundamental truth, each with its own perspective on how souls return to continue their journey. And this leads us back to the concept of the **soul contract**—the idea that souls choose to return in order to learn, grow, and move forward in their spiritual evolution.

The basic premise remains the same in most sects of religions: the belief that one's physical body "transitions" or dies; however, their "spirit" or "soul" is eternal. Therefore, the soul can be reborn again and again to climb to a "higher self" and achieve the destined "life assignment," where incarnating to a physical plane is no longer necessary. Commonly, what is believed is that a new body and an "old" soul choose their future inhabitants based on karma in its past life or its new karmic purpose or "soul contract" with us. This is where most pet guardians "who believe in reincarnation feel their pets will return." There are still a number of people who do not give credence to or embrace the concept of reincarnation; however, ask them about the Rainbow Bridge, and they will tell you that they "know" they will be reunited with their beloved friends.

I have had the pleasure of reading for many of my Pet Loss Grief Support Group members' beloved pets, and a number of them convey their past lives to me. I do believe in reincarnation and have experienced it firsthand. Therefore, that is sometimes why I believe they (pets) reach out to me through a posted picture and choose to send a telepathic message—one that I could not possibly know. I reach out to their guardians, who are hurting, and I give that message, bringing comfort and "food for thought" for the non-believer or the uneducated survivor.

I also believe that when animals tell me about a past life, they don't do so just to tell a story or to simply satisfy my or their curiosity. It is almost always because they want to explain something to their person about a connection from their past to their current life issues.

I've heard quite a few stories about behavior patterns, health issues, personality traits, and relationship dynamics that, in some way, were not fully resolved in a past life. The soul then often chooses, as part of her or his purpose during their next life on Earth, to attempt to complete this lesson from the past and grow further in that area.

That is my purpose in this lifetime—to share the message from a place in my soul that I would never have come to realize had it not been for my own personal experience. In having done some research on soul connections and the reasons for reincarnation, a "soulmate" or a forever-connected soul—which, in this case, is your pet—is a spirit guide or "teacher" that travels or has traveled with you through one or many past incarnations. The lessons that you both were or are to learn have not always been completed in one lifetime. Henceforth, reincarnating back to continue this journey. Just as Jack chose to do.

Animals seem to have effortless recall of their past lives—certainly more so than we humans. When they describe their past lives, it is usually done in a very matter-of-fact way, and when I do readings, I find that it is no surprise to the guardian that they have shared a past life.

In my own experience with Jackson Bean, he used to sit and look up (chin in the air) and stare so deeply into my soul that I would say to my son all the time, "Look at this dog! If I could get a man to love me the way he does!" "He definitely was my husband in a past life." I am still single at the time of publishing. I remember the lesson Jack conveyed to me when he left the first time.

He wanted me to find "human love." I was too attached to him and "nothing" would change that. I would choose him or any of my pets over a male companion. That is "free will." Jack knows, and knows that I want to love again, but he clearly takes precedence over anyone I have or will meet. While he is physically here he will always be the center of my heart and soul.

Little did I know that Jacqueline Smith, Animal Communicator and Author, would confirm just that. Somewhere deeply embedded in *my* soul, I inherently knew this, as I said it out loud—and quite often.

## THE REINCARNATION OF PETS

Our pets, too, have soul contracts. However, they learn their lessons much faster than humans, which is why they come into our lives and leave so quickly. Many people who believe in reincarnation are convinced that their pets will return to them when the time is right.

But, is there real evidence of reincarnation? The answer is yes. There have been numerous documented cases—many of them featured in television specials—where children as young as five years old recall vivid details of past lives. Some remember names, locations, and specific events with such accuracy that fabrication seems impossible.

Our pets, too, are souls on a journey—travelers with their own soul contracts. While we often see ourselves as their caretakers, they are just as often our healers, mirrors, and guides. Unlike humans, animals tend to move through their soul lessons more swiftly. Their lifespans may be shorter, but their impact is vast. They come into our lives not by chance, but by design—arriving with love, fulfilling sacred agreements, and often leaving once their mission is complete. And for those with the courage to believe, they *do* return. Not always in the same body, but always in the same soul-frequency, searching for us as we search for them.

To truly experience the reincarnation of a soul-pet, belief becomes the bridge. You must allow yourself to trust what your heart already knows: that love never ends, it only changes form.

There is growing evidence—even outside spiritual communities—supporting reincarnation. Documented cases of young children recounting details of past lives with striking accuracy have been studied by researchers and featured in respected media outlets. If the human soul can journey through lifetimes, why not the soul of an animal whose love was unconditional and pure? When we open our hearts to this possibility, we create the space for reunion. We recognize signs not as random, but as reminders. We begin to *feel* when they are near again—nudging us, finding us, waiting for us to remember what love promised: *I will find you again.*

## THE REINCARNATION OF PETS AND THE
## UNIVERSAL LAW OF RELATIVITY

The reincarnation of pets is a deeply profound and personal experience—one that many pet guardians have come to recognize through unmistakable signs and synchronicities. When a beloved pet transitions from the physical world, their soul does not simply vanish; instead, it continues its journey, often choosing to return when the time and circumstances are right.

This phenomenon aligns with the **Universal Law of Relativity**, one of the fundamental principles governing existence. This law teaches us that nothing is inherently good or bad, big or small, long or short—everything is measured in comparison to something else. It reminds us that our experiences, emotions, and even losses must be understood within a greater context.

When a pet passes away, the initial pain and grief can feel unbearable, but through the lens of the Law of Relativity, we begin to see the experience differently. The physical separation is temporary, and in comparison to the eternal bond shared between souls, it is but a brief moment in time.

## UNDERSTANDING REINCARNATION THROUGH RELATIVITY

The law also teaches us that challenges—such as loss—are opportunities for growth. The departure of a pet often serves as a catalyst for spiritual expansion, pushing us to seek deeper truths about life, death, and the soul's journey. This shift in awareness can open the door to recognizing the possibility of reincarnation.

Many who have experienced their pet's return find themselves reflecting on what has changed. Has their perspective on life evolved? Have they gained a deeper appreciation for love and connection? Have they learned to raise their vibration to one of gratitude rather than grief? In many cases, the pet's soul returns when the guardian is ready—when the experience of loss has transformed into a higher understanding of unconditional love.

## RECOGNIZING THE SIGNS

The reincarnation of a pet is often revealed through undeniable signs:

- **Personality traits and habits**—A newly adopted pet may display the same quirks, preferences, or mannerisms as a past pet.
- **Instant connection**—The feeling that you've *known* them forever, as if no time has passed.
- Responding to old names.

- **Synchronicities**—Birthdates, adoption dates, or specific numbers aligning in ways that feel too significant to be a coincidence.

The return of a soul-pet is rarely announced with fanfare—but for those paying attention, the signs are unmistakable. Reincarnation speaks in a quiet, symbolic language, offering subtle confirmations that grow louder the more you trust your intuition. These moments aren't random—they're sacred echoes, invitations to remember.

**Personality traits and habits** often return first. A newly adopted pet may tilt their head the same way, sleep in the same corner of the house, or react to certain sounds just as your previous companion did. They may carry the same gentle stubbornness, the same playful spark, or the same calming presence. It's not imagination—it's memory resurfacing in a new form.

**An instant connection** is another powerful sign. From the moment you meet, there's a knowing. As if no time has passed, as if you're simply continuing a conversation that never really ended. You don't have to "get to know" them—you already *know* them. The bond is immediate, familiar, and often accompanied by an overwhelming sense of peace or emotion.

Sometimes, the pet may even **respond to their old name**, or perk up when familiar phrases are spoken. These responses are often dismissed by logic, but your heart knows better. Their soul recognizes your voice, your energy, your love.

Then there are the **synchronicities**—the divine winks from the Universe. A new pet might be born or adopted on the same date your old pet passed. Repeating numbers like 11:11 may surround their arrival. You might notice signs, dreams, or unusual coincidences pointing you toward a particular animal or shelter. These alignments are not accidents—they are reminders that love is not bound by time, and your reunion has been carefully orchestrated.

When you allow yourself to believe—not blindly, but soulfully—you begin to see that reincarnation isn't a fantasy. It's a return. A promise kept. A love that, even through death, found its way back to you.

## THE SOUL'S JOURNEY

From a higher perspective, reincarnation is simply a continuation of the soul's journey. Our pets, like us, are evolving spiritually. Because they learn at an accelerated rate, they transition more quickly, often choosing to return to the same guardian to continue their mission of love and companionship.

The Universal Law of Relativity reminds us that while loss feels overwhelming in the moment, it is only when we step back and compare it to the eternal nature of the soul that we realize—nothing is truly lost. The bond we share with our pets is infinite, transcending time, space, and physical form.

When we shift our perspective from grief to gratitude, from longing to openness, we create the space for reunion. Our pets are never truly gone; they are simply waiting for the right moment to return.

## PREPARING TO WELCOME A RETURNING SOUL-PET

Once you begin to recognize the signs, a sacred space begins to open—both in your heart and in your life. But welcoming a soul-pet back isn't just about waiting; it's about becoming energetically ready. The soul that once walked beside you is returning not only to love, but to continue a mutual journey of healing and growth. Your preparation matters.

Start by **clearing emotional residue** from the past—grief, guilt, regret. Speak to your pet's soul as if they can hear you, because on a soul level, they can. Tell them what you've learned. Thank them for their service in your life. Forgive yourself for anything you feel you could've done better. These acts of conscious release create energetic room for them to return in a new body, free of the weight both of you once carried.

Create what many spiritual teachers call a **"garden of gestation"**—a space of stillness and belief. This might be a physical altar with a candle and their photo, or a quiet time each day in meditation or prayer. It's not about forcing their return; it's about inviting it, holding the door open with love and trust.

Remain open to where and how they might come back. It may not be through the channel you expect. Sometimes, a friend unexpectedly offers you a pet. Other times, you feel an unexplainable pull toward a certain animal at a shelter. If your heart quickens and time seems to slow, pay attention—that's how the soul often announces itself.

Above all, **trust your inner knowing.** Reincarnation isn't about recreating the past—it's about honoring the eternal bond that never left. Your soul-pet returns not just because of love, but because you're ready for the next chapter together—stronger, wiser, and more awake than before.

## THE ETERNAL SOUL

Despite differences in doctrine, most religious and spiritual traditions share a fundamental belief: while the physical body transitions—what we call death—the *soul* or *spirit* is eternal. That means souls have the ability to be reborn again and again, climbing toward a higher self and fulfilling their life's assignment. The ultimate goal? To reach a level where reincarnation is no longer necessary.

A soul's next incarnation is often determined by **karma** from its past life or a new **karmic purpose**—a soul contract that brings it back to a physical plane for further growth. This is why so many pet guardians who believe in reincarnation feel certain that their animals will return to them.

### INTUITION—WE ALL HAVE IT!

It happens to all of us. The journey ends—sometimes abruptly, and other times, we are given the time to adjust to our pet's illness and their imminent crossing. Either way, it is *never* easy. I had 48 hours to wrap my head around this concept, and I can say I have never felt that kind of pain and anguish in my life. When I was told that Jack was terminal and that I had to "do the right thing, that minute," I thought that I would die, and a very large part of me did. I needed more time. I needed him to stay and never leave—he was my *pack leader.*

Little did I know, I had failed at learning the lesson he was trying to teach, and he had to *cross* for me to grow. But as you all know, he was not done with me.

Some of you will decide not to part with their "things"—their collars, beds, and toys. Then don't! Listen to your heart; act on your promptings. The most common connection that your pet in spirit utilizes is your dreams. They come to you, bringing messages of wellness, happiness, and, a lot of times, their return. Your pet is embedded into your soul, sometimes through incarnations after incarnations. Pay attention to these signs—this is your intuition and your inner telepathic energy! Be open to receive, without ego and full of love—*OPEN TO RECEIVE.*

Many of you were there on that last day, and you held your baby in your arms and whispered, "*Come back to me.*" In your subconscious, there was a reason. Your inner *knowing* is ever-present, and you know they will return to you.

Your pet will reincarnate for many different reasons. It is not just about your animal's soul path or any one lesson that you must learn. Reincarnation can come as a *braided soul*—two distinctly different energy signatures inhabiting the same body and genetic structure but with their own unique signatures and personality. Braided souls stay together and share experiences together. Some of you will go on to get another pet after the transition of a pet, and you slowly, over time, notice *two* personalities. You see a lot of the qualities of your pet that transitioned in the new pet, but you also see a new and different personality emerging as well. This is when your pet reincarnates and *braids* itself to the present soul, and you get the best of both worlds!

Or reincarnation can come in the form of a *walk-in* (Walk-Ins: Two souls agree that they will "switch out" at some point on the life span timeline. In this manner, there is one in the driver's seat and one that hangs out in the auric field (the back seat), and they integrate that way. This is not the same as a braided soul.)

The reincarnation of your pet is about the unfulfilled journey—the *soul contract* you both agreed upon before this incarnation. Right now, your pet is not gone; he/she is just in a different form—spirit form. Give their soul time to heal in the light on the other side.

Most times, the end was traumatic, and other times, imminent and expected—but with that, a period of vet visits, pain, and numerous medications. I was told that Jack was in the healing light and needed time to *heal*—that he would come to me in spirit, but constantly trying to connect with him through an animal communicator was not allowing him the time he needed to heal and work through his learning process in the ever after. When the time came for him to return, I *could not* miss him.

Reincarnation really is not all that complicated! It's the fulfillment of a contract between the two of you, made before this incarnation. So, you see, this *is going to happen*, with or without your conscious effort. There may be a winding road or two and a few chapters to work through, but for the most part, if you feel you need help with the re-entry process, you can enlist the help of an animal communicator. I have helped many group members with this process. However, each and every one of you has the ability to connect!

It comes down to a basic chemistry process. If you freeze water, it turns to ice, right? If you boil water, it turns to steam. It's the physics of energy. Our life force energy never leaves us—it just changes form for a minute!

## HOW TO KNOW IT'S REALLY THEM

When your soul-pet returns, something deep within you will know. It's not logic—it's resonance.

A vibration that matches yours like a forgotten melody suddenly remembered. Still, it's natural to question: *Am I projecting my grief? Am I imagining this because I want it so badly?* These are fair questions, but your soul will answer in subtler ways than the mind can.

Watch for what can't be explained. A new pet that finds the same hiding spots, favors the same toys, or curls up in the same sleeping position. A gaze that holds too much familiarity to be mere coincidence. A sudden shift in their behavior when you mention the name of your previous pet. These are not proofs—they are echoes. And together, they create a pattern only your heart can read.

You may also experience **emotional recognition**—a wave of comfort, or even tears, upon holding them for the first time. Some people report dreaming of their previous pet right before meeting the new one. Others sense their old companion's energy lingering *until* the new one arrives, almost as if guiding the way.

Trust doesn't mean blind faith—it means honoring the feeling that this love has returned to continue its story with you.

## SUPPORTING THEIR SOUL IN THIS LIFE

Remember, your returning pet may come back in a different form, with a new physical body, breed, gender, or temperament. Their soul carries old wisdom, but they are also beginning anew. It's important to support both who they *were* and who they *are becoming*.

Approach them with **patience and presence**. You may notice moments where their old personality shines through—followed by entirely new expressions. Allow their soul to unfold at its own pace. Just like you've grown since your last life together, so have they.

Offer them what they once loved—perhaps their favorite food, toy, or scent—and see how they respond. These can trigger soul memories, gently reactivating the bond. But also be ready to explore new rituals, routines, and roles. They've returned for the *next* chapter, not a replay of the last.

Above all, keep your heart open and your expectations soft. Love them not only for who they were, but for the soul they *still are*—braver, wiser, and choosing you again, just as you are now more ready to receive them.

Sometimes we learn in bits and pieces, in stages or layers, and if it's not all done by the end of one life, that's okay. There is no prize to be won for who learns the fastest or the most. And we can't possibly learn everything available to learn in one lifetime—that is why we reincarnate. It's a learning process for all creatures, great and small.

When the time comes to shed that physical form, it is never easy. As an animal communicator, pets tell me a lot of things at the end. They mostly confess that it is their time and that *they are ready*. Some are willing to stick around a little while longer to help their humans prepare for this heart-wrenching experience. They also confide that the pain is no longer prevalent and that they are about 90% in spirit—"out of their bodies."

It's amazing—if you look into your pet's eyes in their last days, you can see that *the light has gone out of them*. Their eyes are just dark, their souls in transition, headed toward the light. We all know that our beloved pets live much shorter lives than we do, so it is necessary for them to shed their physical bodies in order to return to a new, healthier one. Once this process is complete, they are free to start their journey home.

Remember—the transition is only the *first step* on the road back home. It's probably a good thing to remind yourself of this—it will save you a lot of heartache. That said, heartache, loss, and sometimes devastation is *normal* when you lose your soulmate. But let me give you a bit of advice—at the risk of being redundant—being in a state of *bad grief* is not conducive to feeling your pet's energy in spirit form. In order to connect, you must be in a stage of *good grief*.

*"Grief is not a place to unpack your bags and move in. It is a place to move through at your own pace, honoring your bond and your loss. —Susie Marano*

Let me elaborate. When Jack crossed, I wanted to connect with him every second! Poor Wendy Cooper—she probably needed a new computer after the number of emails I sent! Wendy arrived at my home four days after Jack crossed, and I was *desperate* to hear about Jack's trip to the Bridge. She wanted to start with a healing—a lightworker's process to clear those traumatic feelings of pain and loss, to open my karmic soul so I could receive Jack's messages in a positive light.

But I was downright *obnoxious*.

"I want my Jack! I want to talk to him! I don't need healing—I will never heal! I am lost!"

Folks, *this is not the way to go*. I kept myself in a space that was neither positive nor conducive to seeing, feeling, or connecting with my baby in spirit form. Unfortunately, I alienated people, remained depressed, and shut myself off from the world. I contacted animal communicator after animal communicator, spent *tons* of money, all because I *could not feel Jackson Bean*. There was one time, a few days after Wendy's healing session, when he came through Buffy—it was amazing. But as soon as I connected, I broke down:

*"Oh my God, Jack! My Jack! I miss you so much!"*

I burst into tears of heartbreak, and he left as fast as he arrived.

Jacqueline Smith later told me that if I had *thanked him* for coming and been less emotionally overwhelmed, he might have stayed just a little longer.

My motivation in writing this book is to help all who read it follow the *right* path of grief. Don't get me wrong—it's okay to grieve. It's okay to be sad and mourn the loss of your soul fur baby. But don't let yourself slip into that dark place, that place where no one can console you, where no one can help you heal. This is a happy experience, "Your baby is coming home!"

Okay, enough about negative energy.

**This is a *happy* experience—*your baby is coming home!***

Some choose to return to a puppy's body. Some return to an older body. Sometimes, it depends on the journey. Sometimes, they choose a smaller or larger breed, or even a different species altogether. I know a bird, Charlie—he returned as a female bird, but still wanted to be called *Charlie Bird!* Same behaviors, same learned qualities—everything he had when he left, she returned with.

Some leave within days of each other, their journeys so deeply intertwined—just as they are with their guardians. And when they return, they come back almost exactly as they were when they left—at the same time, no less!

Even among those who don't fully embrace reincarnation, there is a deep-seated belief in the **Rainbow Bridge**—the idea that they will one day be reunited with their beloved companions. They may not call it reincarnation, but they *know* that the bond with their pet transcends death.

I have had the profound privilege of reading for many people who have experienced this firsthand...

### REFLECTION & SOUL PET PRAYER

Reincarnation is not just a return of form—it's a return of purpose, of shared lessons, and of unconditional love that cannot be undone by time or distance. If you are reading this, it's likely because you've known a soul-pet—a being who met you where words could not, and who walked beside your soul in silence, devotion, and deep knowing.

Whether they are on their way back to you or already resting quietly at your side in new form, your love is the bridge, and your belief is the door they walk through.

May the following prayer guide you into peace as you prepare your heart for this sacred reunion:

### A Soul-Pet Prayer for Reunion

*Beloved companion of my soul,*
*Thank you for the lifetimes you've walked beside me—*
*in fur, in feathers, in silence, in joy.*
*If it is in alignment with your soul's path and mine,*
*and if love still has more to teach us—*
*I welcome you back with open arms and a ready heart.*
*May I see you not only with my eyes,*
*but with the knowing of my soul.*
*May I honor who you were,*
*and embrace who you are becoming.*
*Guide me with your subtle signs.*
*Speak to me in the language of love and trust.*
*And until we meet again,*
*I will sit in the stillness, in our garden of gestation,*
*Believing... waiting... and remembering you home.*

**You are not waiting alone.** Souls like yours call their companions back across lifetimes. Love like this doesn't end—it evolves. And in that sacred return, both of you rise.

## THE TRANSITION TO THE RAINBOW BRIDGE

It is, without a doubt, one of the hardest experiences you have ever faced. By now, you have likely received the heartbreaking news that your beloved pet is on borrowed time. And for many of you reading this, the transition has already taken place. If you are preparing for the inevitable, I hope these words bring some comfort and guidance through this deeply emotional journey.

The transition of your pet is a time when your love for them and the internal struggle to do what is "right" come into full play. Some pets have a few weeks or months left before a final decision must be made, and during this time, you may begin to notice subtle shifts in their behavior. They may no longer curl up beside you on the couch or stay in the same room as they once did.

When you call them, they may not come, and at times, they may even avoid looking into your eyes. You might find them sitting by a door or window, lingering in places outside their usual routines. Even the simple joys you once shared—your evening walks, games of fetch, or their cherished pampering sessions—may become things they quietly withdraw from.

This withdrawal is not a rejection of your love, but rather an energetic preparation for what is to come. There is a deep, unspoken conflict within them—an instinctual knowing that their time is near, yet a profound love that makes them want to stay. That tug-of-war between the soul's agreement to move on and the powerful bond you share can be felt on both sides. Now, the moment has arrived to fulfill the sacred *soul contract* you made with each other before this lifetime even began.

Many people ask me, *"Does my pet know how much I loved them?"* The answer is a resounding *yes*. They knew it in life, and they know it now in spirit. Every act of care, every attempt to heal them, every decision made in their best interest was an expression of that love. The story unfolded exactly as it was meant to.

The lessons and experiences you were meant to share have played out according to the contract your souls agreed upon before this incarnation.

And now, a new journey begins—perhaps even another one together, if that is what you both chose before stepping into this lifetime.

The law of cause and effect—also known as the Law of Karma— states that every action has a corresponding reaction, creating a ripple effect across time and space. This universal law applies to all beings, including animals, as they transition from physical form back into spirit.

## HOW THE LAW OF CAUSE AND EFFECT RELATES TO A PET'S ASCENSION

1.  **Energetic Imprint and Completion of Purpose**

    Every soul, including animals, enters an incarnation with a purpose, whether it's to teach unconditional love, patience, healing, or companionship. When a pet passes, their energetic imprint—everything they gave and received—remains. Their actions, love, and experiences continue to influence their human companions and the world around them. The energy they shared does not vanish; it reverberates, fulfilling its karmic purpose.

2. **Healing and Reflection in Spirit Form**

   When an animal crosses over, they do not carry human-like karmic burdens, as their souls operate on a purer vibrational level. However, if they have endured trauma, suffering, or a difficult passing, they may enter a healing phase in the spirit realm. This is not a punishment but rather an energetic rebalancing, allowing them to integrate their experience before deciding on their next steps.

3. **Soul Contracts and Continuing the Journey**

   The bond between an animal and their human is often a sacred contract that extends beyond a single lifetime. If a pet's departure leaves an open lesson or an unresolved emotional connection, they may choose to reincarnate to continue that journey. This aligns with cause and effect: their presence in your life was a cause, and their return—whether in spirit form or through reincarnation—is the effect.

4. **Choosing the Next Path**

   An animal's soul, like all souls, has free will within the framework of divine order. They may choose to rest in the spirit realm, guiding their loved ones energetically, or they may feel a pull to return to physical form based on unfinished lessons or a continued mission. Their reincarnation is not random, but a direct result of the love, energy, and karmic connections they created in their previous life.

## UNDERSTANDING THROUGH A HIGHER LENS

Unlike humans, animals do not accumulate karma in the same way because they exist in a state of presence and purity. However; the energy they share, the love they give, and the lessons they bring, all create ripples in the grand design of the universe. Their ascension back into spirit is not an end—it is simply the next step in their eternal journey, guided by the laws that govern all existence.

## THE LAW OF CAUSE AND EFFECT
## IN A PET'S ASCENSION

The **Law of Cause and Effect**—also known as **Karma**—governs all energy in the universe, ensuring that every action creates a ripple of consequences. This universal law applies to all beings, including animals, as they transition from physical form back into spirit. Their passing is not an endpoint, but a shift in energy, guided by the very love and purpose they embodied in life.

### 1. The Completion of Purpose

Every soul, including that of an animal, enters an incarnation with a purpose—whether it is to teach unconditional love, offer companionship, or help their human guardian heal. When a pet transitions, their **energetic imprint remains**—a vibration of love, lessons, and shared experiences that continues to influence the world they left behind. Their presence was the **cause**, and the profound impact they had on your life is the **effect**.

While many animals incarnate to support the healing and growth of their human companions, it's essential to recognize that not all soul-pets come solely for our benefit. Some arrive with their own higher self assignments—to resolve karmic patterns, to gain experiences that elevate their soul's understanding, or to serve the collective energetic balance of Earth. These beings choose the animal form because it allows them to embody unconditional presence, humility, and service—lessons that support their soul's ascension in subtle yet profound ways.

In such cases, the guardian may play a supportive role in their evolution. Whether through the environment they provide, the love they offer, or even the challenges they unknowingly present, the relationship becomes mutually transformative. These pets may not stay long, or they may reincarnate multiple times to complete their work. But make no mistake—their journey is not a passive one. They are evolving, too—fulfilling divine assignments that may one day allow them to transition into new forms of consciousness or service beyond the animal kingdom.

## 2. Healing and Reflection in the Spirit Realm

Unlike humans, animals do not accumulate **karmic debt** in the same way, as they live in the present moment without attachment to ego or moral conflict. However, if a pet has endured trauma, illness, or a difficult passing, they may **enter a phase of healing** in the spirit realm. This is not punishment, but rather an **energetic rebalancing**, allowing their soul to integrate the experience and restore harmony before deciding their next steps.

During this healing phase in the spirit realm—often referred to as a "light chamber" or resting dimension—an animal's soul is gently supported by benevolent guides and higher vibrational beings. In this space, they are surrounded by frequencies of unconditional love, safety, and restoration. Here, the emotional and physical imprints of their most recent incarnation are lovingly dissolved. Their essence is held in a field of pure intelligence where they are able to review their journey, not with judgment, but with clarity and peace.

For soul-pets who have taken on heavy emotions from their guardians, this period is especially important—it allows them to release what they absorbed out of love and loyalty, preparing them for their next soul assignment, whether that be a return to Earth or a new plane of service within the spirit world.

## 3. Soul Contracts and Continuing the Journey

The deep, unbreakable bond between a pet and their human is often part of a **soul contract**—an agreement made before incarnation to walk together in this lifetime. If a pet's departure leaves an unresolved lesson or an unfulfilled connection, they may choose to reincarnate to continue that journey. **Their return is not random; it is the natural effect of the love, devotion, and energy shared between souls.**

Sometimes, before we are even born, our souls make promises to each other. These promises are called soul contracts. A pet's soul might say, "I will come into your life to help you feel loved," and your soul might say, "I will take care of you and help you feel safe." These special agreements are made out of love and trust, so when your pet finds you, it's like two pieces of a puzzle coming back together.

If a pet's time on Earth ends but their heart still feels connected to yours, they might decide to come back again in a new body. This is called reincarnation. Their fur might be a different color, or they might be bigger or smaller—but inside, they are still the same loving soul. When they return, it's because your story together isn't finished yet. They come back to keep the promise they made long ago—to love you, grow with you, and be by your side, just like they always were.

## 4. Choosing the Next Path: Spirit Guide or Reincarnation

Once an animal has transitioned, their soul has **free will** within the divine framework of universal law. Some may choose to remain in the spirit realm, watching over and guiding their humans from beyond, while others feel the pull to return in physical form. Whether they reincarnate in a similar body or take on a new form depends on the **lessons and experiences still to be fulfilled.**

After a pet leaves their body, their soul goes to a peaceful, loving place full of light. There, they get to rest and think about their journey. Just like people, their soul gets to choose what comes next. Some pets decide to stay in the spirit world, where they can become like a little guardian angel. They watch over you, send signs like feathers or dreams, and stay close in a different way—not with paws, but with presence.

Other pets feel a strong wish to come back to Earth. Maybe they want to be with you again, or maybe they have something new to learn or do. If they still have more to grow or more love to give in a body, they might pick a new one—sometimes similar, sometimes totally different. Their heart always remembers you, no matter what form they take. The choice they make is always based on love—and what will help *both* of your souls grow the most.

## 5. A Higher Perspective on Cause and Effect

Animals exist in a state of purity and presence, making their karmic cycle different from that of humans. While they do not create negative karma, their energy continues to ripple outward, shaping the lives of those they touched. Their ascension is not an end, but a shift in form—a movement of energy that aligns with the divine balance of the universe.

In essence, the law of cause and effect ensures that no love is ever lost, no bond is ever broken, and no journey is ever truly over. Your pet's soul continues its path, just as you continue yours, until the time comes to meet again.

### PHYSICALITY AND THE IMMINENT TRANSITIONAL PROCESS

I remember the exact moment Jack was diagnosed. It was a Friday morning. He wouldn't look at me the entire ride to the vet, his gaze fixed straight ahead, as if he already knew. I remember posting on Facebook: *"Can I ever get a break? Buffy last week, Jack this week."* If I had known what was coming, I would have never complained again. *God, if you had just granted me that one last request, I swear I would never have complained again.*

The signs of transition had already begun—I just didn't recognize them at the time. Only as I wrote this book, with the wisdom of hindsight, did I see them clearly. Jack had been sitting by the front door for weeks before his diagnosis. He still responded when I called, but he no longer jumped onto the bed—I had to carry him. And when I said *"Sleepy night-night"* at 9 p.m., as I had for the past 9.5 years, he no longer rushed to his crate. He moved slower, no longer in a hurry for anything. Yet, through it all, he never stopped kissing me. Never stopped snuggling. Right up until the very end.

In those final 24 to 48 hours, you may notice a shift in your pet's eyes—they become **glazed over, dark, like polished marbles.** You look into them, but it feels as if they're not *fully there* anymore. Their aura begins to dim, as if the light inside them is slowly fading. This is the time to hold them close and gently ask, *"Will you be coming back to me?"*

If you hold your pet's paws, you may notice them growing cold—this is a sign that they are already 80 to 90% out of their physical body, preparing for their **pre-scripted journey.**

As the transition continues, their gums pale, their nose and ears chill, and their responses become dulled, their reactions slow. Some will close off completely—this means they are almost fully detached from the physical realm, their soul nearly free.

Not everyone will witness this process. Sometimes, a sudden accident occurs, and your pet transitions without your presence or assistance. If this happens, **please know that it was part of the soul contract you shared.** Their journey is still intact, and they can still find their way back to you in another form.

What many don't realize is that a **soul contract** doesn't just include the joyful moments of meeting, bonding, and growing together—it also gently holds the moment of parting. Sometimes, that parting is peaceful and shared, with you holding your pet as they take their final breath. But other times, it happens when you're not there—while you're away, asleep, or even just in another room. This can be deeply painful, and yet, it is never a mistake. It is part of the sacred agreement your souls made *before* this lifetime began.

In some soul contracts, the moment of passing is meant to be private—chosen for reasons our human hearts may not fully understand. Your pet may not want you to carry the weight of that moment, or they may want you to remember them in strength, not in pain. In other cases, their departure while you are away is part of *your* growth, teaching you about trust, surrender, and the unseen bonds that transcend physical presence. The love between you is not broken by distance—it is honored by it. And even if you weren't physically near, your souls were forever connected in that final moment, just as they were in the first.

My experience with Jack was different. Though I had no more than 48 hours left with him, he *fought* to stay. He showed me in the most intimate ways. He drank water only from my mouth. He laid in my arms for hours, kissing me, as if trying to imprint his love onto my very soul. In his final days, he indulged—he ate pizza, sipped wine, even jumped off the bed for a big bowl of dog food. It was as if he wanted to remind me, *I'm still here, still with you, but this is not the last chapter of our story.*

Then came the moment of surrender. His body dimmed like a TV screen powering down—his responses dulled, his reactions slowed, until there was nothing left to tether him to the physical world. And then, he was gone. **But I knew, deep in my heart, that he was never truly gone.** His journey had simply continued.

### BON VOYAGE, NOT GOODBYE

Honor and respect are what you want to focus on during this time. You want to let your beloved pet know, *"I love, respect, and support your choices."* Insert your pet's name here: _____.

I will not say goodbye, but rather, *see you soon*! I share my heart-centered energy, from the love deep within my heart to the depths of my soul, so that you may carry out your desires during this time. This will help your pet transition, feeling the love in your heart and assisting them, in their weakened state, to cross the lifeline from this earthly plane to the ever-after spirit world.

Your own life force energy can be shared with your pets, and it is greatly appreciated when you understand these concepts and can assist them during this time of need.

Let's revisit "free will." Animals, just like humans, have it. And within the soul contract, there is a predestined "finish line" in the story. Yes, free will allows your pet the choice to stay, heal, and continue their journey on this side—or to move on to the other side and work from there. But please remember, with all illnesses—whether human or animal—there is a point of no return.

We have all had a family member lost to disease or sickness, and we have witnessed the devastating effects of illness. It's a harsh reality, and sometimes, physical renewal is simply impossible.

## SAYING GOODBYE AND GIVING YOUR PET YOUR LIFE FORCE ENERGY

Saying goodbye to a beloved pet is one of the most profound moments in life. It marks the end of one chapter but also the beginning of another—a journey into the spiritual realm. During this time, one of the most powerful gifts you can offer your pet is your life force energy. This is not merely a physical presence, but a deeply spiritual act. By consciously sharing your life force energy with your pet, you are helping them navigate their transition with love, compassion, and peace. You are guiding them with the light of your own soul, providing comfort and reassurance as they move beyond the physical world.

This exchange of energy is not just a symbolic gesture; it is part of the Law of Divine Oneness, which states that all beings—humans, animals, plants, and all forms of life—are interconnected. We are all part of a larger, unified field of existence. Our thoughts, emotions, and energy ripple through this web, affecting the whole. When you offer your life force energy to your pet as they ascend, you are acknowledging this sacred connection, reinforcing the bond that exists between your souls, even beyond the physical world.

As your pet begins the sacred process of transitioning from the physical world to the spirit realm, your **life force energy**—the essence of your love, presence, and intention—becomes one of the most powerful gifts you can offer. This energy is not just physical; it's vibrational. It's the quiet strength in your touch, the steady rhythm of your breath, the love in your voice, and the silent prayer in your heart. When offered with peace, gratitude, and openness, your life force becomes a **bridge**—helping your beloved companion cross with comfort, dignity, and clarity.

Sending them off with your life force does more than ease their passage—it reassures them that all is well. Animals are incredibly sensitive to energy; they feel when we are calm, and they feel when we are afraid. In their final moments, your grounded, loving energy helps them release attachment to their physical body without fear or confusion. It tells them, "You are safe. You are loved. You are free." This energetic blessing follows them into the next realm, surrounding them like a familiar scent or warm light, guiding them gently into the arms of spirit. In this way, you become not just their guardian in life—but their **guide in death**, walking them home, one soul to another.

## THE LAW OF DIVINE ONENESS AND YOUR PET'S ASCENSION

The Law of Divine Oneness is a universal principle that reminds us of our interconnectedness. Everything is linked, from the tiniest particles to the vast universe. In the context of your pet's ascension, this law holds great significance. As your pet prepares to transition, they are not leaving you—they are stepping into another realm where the bond you share remains intact. Your energies are always connected, and your life force continues to influence their journey.

When your pet ascends, they are returning to the Oneness from which they came. This process of ascension is not separate from you, but a part of the greater whole. Just as your pet's soul is one with the divine, so too are you. You may feel sorrow, but it's important to remember that this is not the end—only a transformation. Your soul and your pet's soul are still intertwined, still part of the same divine web of existence.

By offering your life force energy, you assist in the ascension process. This act of love helps your pet transition peacefully, knowing they are supported by your unconditional love. It also provides healing for you, as you begin to understand that this separation is not permanent. The Law of Divine Oneness ensures that no true bond is ever broken. You and your pet remain eternally connected, both within this lifetime and beyond.

## THE SACRED BOND BETWEEN YOU AND YOUR PET

The ascension of your pet is a process of returning to the source—of reuniting with the divine energy that created them. This is the ultimate return to Oneness. While their physical form may no longer be present, their essence, their soul, continues to exist in the eternal flow of energy that binds all living beings.

When you share your life force energy with your pet, you are helping them to make that final transition smoothly and with grace. You are reminding them of the love and bond you share, which transcends space, time, and physicality. This energetic exchange ensures that both you and your pet remain a part of the same spiritual journey. You may feel an emotional loss, but you are not truly losing them. Your pet's ascension is simply another form of evolution, just as their time with you was a chapter in their soul's ongoing story.

Remember, your connection with your pet is never severed—it is eternal. By embracing the Law of Divine Oneness, you can find peace in the knowing that the bond you share will never fade, and that, when the time is right, you will be reunited in spirit.

## THE LAST IMPRINT

A moment will come when your pet creates an unforgettable, bittersweet exit—a moment that will be etched in your heart forever. All animals possess consciousness and awareness, and at this time, your faithful companion will recognize and honor your love and devotion. They will acknowledge the deep bond you've shared, and, in turn, will feel your release as they prepare for their next journey. The greater the number of evolutions an animal undergoes, the higher their level of consciousness.

With this evolution comes a heightened ability to communicate their feelings. At this pivotal exit point, you may realize that this is not your first incarnation together—and perhaps, not your last.

It's important to remain open-minded during this transition. Your pet will communicate with you, not just through their physical eyes, but also through your intuitive energy field. Remember, both of you have consciously chosen this path. There is a profound "knowing" on a soul level—a deep recognition that transcends time and space. This is a knowing that is consciously felt and experienced between you and your pet. Both of you are aware of this, and this awareness exists on a higher level for you both.

As you rub your hands through the fur of your faithful companion, you can feel the energy. The more incarnations your pet has had, the more their soul has evolved. With each life, they accumulate more experience and often form bonds with humans, sometimes with more than one. Although your pet may not speak your language, they are capable of communicating beyond words. The more evolved they become, the better they are at expressing themselves. The healing power and peaceful energy that pets offer is immeasurable to us as humans.

It's essential to remember that a negative environment or negative energy is harmful to a pet. Often, your pet will absorb this negative energy from you, and it can make them ill. This time of transition should be free of negativity. A quiet, peaceful crossing is always the best for both you and your pet. Animals communicate most effectively through their eyes and through our telepathic energy. If you're new to animal communication, it may be helpful to schedule a session with an animal communicator a few days before your pet's transition.

When I faced this moment with Jack, I had countless questions, the biggest one being, "Why?" Why are you leaving me? Why are you going away? Pets feel your sadness, and that's okay. In most instances, while they are "ready" to depart, they, too, struggle with their love for you and the feelings of sadness that arise. At this juncture in your journey, you may experience visions or simply have a deep "knowing" that you've been here before—that this is your soulmate. This is the deepest relationship possible.

Through animal communication, you may come to understand that you and your pet have shared many incarnations together. The depth of the connection and the grief you now feel will start to make sense. The choice to reincarnate is, at this point, entirely comprehensible.

If you don't believe in reincarnation but your pet has the intention to return, the universe will make provisions. One way it may do so is by creating opportunities for you to learn and understand the reincarnation process—perhaps through reading this book. This could open your mind and broaden your perspective. If not, and your soul contract calls for another journey together, rest assured that the opportunity will arise in another lifetime.

### THE LAST IMPRINT AND THE LAW OF INSPIRED ACTION

The **Last Imprint** is the moment when your pet transitions, leaving behind a profound emotional and spiritual mark on your heart and soul. It's a bittersweet, unforgettable moment that lingers long after their physical form has departed. This imprint is not just a memory; it is a powerful energetic mark that carries the essence of your connection, love, and shared experiences. It's in these moments that you might feel a deep sense of "knowing" that goes beyond words or understanding, as if your souls have known each other far beyond this lifetime.

Now, when we introduce the **Law of Inspired Action**, we're talking about the law that dictates that in order to manifest our desires or move forward on a journey, we must take action that is aligned with our highest good. This action is not about force or effort; instead, it's about being attuned to the intuitive nudges, ideas, and inspiration that arise when we are in a state of alignment with our true desires and purpose. Inspired action is the universe guiding us gently toward our goals, but it requires that we trust, listen, and act when the time is right.

How do these two concepts—the **Last Imprint** and the **Law of Inspired Action**—work together?

1. **The Imprint as a Catalyst for Growth:**

   The **Last Imprint** is not just the end; it is also a new beginning. When your pet transitions, they leave behind an energetic imprint that remains with you—an imprint that continues to inspire and guide you on your path. This imprint, especially in the case of a deeply bonded relationship, serves as a powerful catalyst for personal growth and spiritual evolution. The imprint may awaken a new awareness or desire to seek out more knowledge, perhaps around animal communication, reincarnation, or the deeper meaning of life's cycles. This is where **inspired action** begins to play a role.

2. **Inspired Action from the Soul's Deepest Desires:**

   When the loss of a beloved pet occurs, it often brings up feelings of deep sorrow, but also a longing for understanding and connection. This loss can activate a desire within you to better understand the nature of life and death, the eternal bond between souls, or the profound healing energy of animals. The **Law of Inspired Action** kicks in when you act on these inner nudges, such as seeking guidance through books, connecting with an animal communicator, or even opening yourself to the idea of reincarnation and the Universal Laws. This action isn't forced—it's a natural flow, guided by the spiritual insights and inspiration you receive as a result of your pet's transition.

3. **Aligning with Purpose and Connection:**

   The transition and the energy left behind by your pet can be transformative. As you move through the stages of grief and healing, the **Law of Inspired Action** might lead you to new ways to honor your pet's memory—such as starting a new project, sharing your experiences through writing, or offering your understanding and wisdom to others. These actions help fulfill your soul's deeper purpose and honor the bond you shared. The inspired action could manifest as a simple moment of remembering your pet fondly or as profound as launching a new chapter in your life that is dedicated to animal welfare or communication.

4. **Healing and Rebirth:**

   Inspired action is not just about external accomplishments; it's deeply tied to internal healing. As you process the **Last Imprint,** you might feel moved to heal in new ways. The Law of Inspired Action may lead you to certain practices—meditation, journaling, or connecting with others who have experienced similar losses—that assist you in navigating your grief. Through these small, aligned actions, you allow space for healing to occur and prepare for your pet's eventual return, should they choose to reincarnate into your life.

In essence, the **Last Imprint** is a powerful and transformative moment that shapes the course of your journey. When combined with the **Law of Inspired Action**, this imprint guides you toward healing, growth, and deeper understanding. It calls you to action—not out of urgency, but out of love, connection, and an innate knowledge that the next chapter of your life is unfolding, with your beloved companion's energy still very much a part of you.

## ASKING THE AGE-OLD QUESTION: ARE YOU COMING BACK TO ME?

If you're reading this book, then this is the part you've been waiting for! Will my pet return? How will I know? How do I ask? Do I need an animal communicator to help me? Can I miss it? What if they return and someone else gets them?

Stay calm and carry on, as they say. Breathe... You cannot miss it.

To prepare for this sacred moment, you will want to sit quietly, center yourself, and ground your energy. Preparing for communication is essential, whether you are reaching out after your pet's passing or while they are still in their physical body.

One of the greatest obstacles I had to overcome was the traditional way of communicating—speech. We've been speaking since we were babies, but before words ever came to us, there was a gentle, intuitive way we communicated with the world around us. Culturally, we are conditioned to communicate through a series of words that form thoughts. Once we learn to speak, that strong, intuitive or telepathic ability to communicate without words often goes dormant.

We live in an age of nanoseconds, where receiving replies to our requests is as quick as hitting the "open" key. Society has become high-tech, commercialized, and fast-paced—often at the cost of our ability to tune into our inborn gifts of silent communication. We learn not to pay attention to these inner messages. We run through life, most times not really listening to anyone, including ourselves.

But at this moment, as you ask the universe, "Are you coming back to me?" "Why?" it's important to return to that quiet, inner space where the truest communication happens.

Telepathy is not yet a widely accepted form of communication, but the tide is changing, and awareness is steadily coming to the forefront. People like me are passionate about educating others on what is, and what *can* be. When you slow down and tune into yourself, you will be amazed at what you can learn... and hear! When you take the time to find a quiet place and open yourself to receive, you may realize that someone has been speaking to you all along.

Getting ready to communicate with your transitioning pet is simple, but it does require patience and a certain openness. A relaxed state should be your first priority, as it will help you open to your intuitive guidance. Sit quietly and comfortably. You can do this with your pet in the room or not—sometimes, grounding yourself away from them may be beneficial.

One of the best ways to ground your energy is to spend time with a tree. So, if you feel the urge to step outside in the sunshine and stand next to your favorite tree, follow that instinct—it will support your quest to communicate effectively with your pet. Bare feet on the ground can further enhance this connection.

Breathe deeply in and out. Close your eyes and focus on *nothing*—just let go of any distractions. Ask your angels and guides to be present, guiding you to receive everything you're open to. Breath is key to your psyche. In the Greek language, the word for soul, "psyche," literally means "breathe." As you breathe deeply, feel a profound inner peace settling within you. This is the moment when you open your heart center, preparing yourself to connect to your pet. Feel the peacefulness in your being as your mind clears and your heart opens to the profound connection you're about to make. This is the beginning of a beautiful exchange—one that transcends words and connects souls.

When you feel grounded and ready—and remember, there is no time limit here—simply form the questions in your mind and heart, preparing yourself for an awakening. Once you are fully prepared, and not caught in a state of crying or negativity, go to your pet. You can have them sit in your lap, or lay next to them—whatever feels comfortable for both of you. It's important to make some sort of physical connection at this time. You may hold their paw, have them in your lap, or gently lay your hand on their fur. If you're able to look into each other's eyes, you may feel an even deeper connection, but remember, it is not necessary. What truly matters is that you are connecting through each other's heart center and souls. This physical connection helps bridge the space between you and your pet, and creates an opening for the energy to flow. You may feel warmth, tingling, or a calm presence surrounding you both. Just trust the experience, knowing that you are in the perfect moment to receive and share this powerful, sacred connection.

## ASKING THE AGE-OLD QUESTION:
## ARE YOU COMING BACK TO ME?

If you're reading this book, this is likely the part you've been waiting for. *Will my pet return? How will I know? How do I ask? Will I need an animal communicator to help me? Can I miss the signs? What if they return and someone else gets them?*

Take a deep breath... and relax. You **cannot** miss it.

To begin, find a quiet space where you can center and ground yourself. Preparing for communication is essential, whether you are reaching out after your pet has transitioned or while they are still in their physical body. One of the greatest challenges I had to overcome was the way we are traditionally taught to communicate. We rely so much on spoken words—after all, we have been speaking since we were babies. But before we ever uttered a word, we communicated in a more natural, intuitive way.

We are conditioned by society to express ourselves through structured sentences and verbal exchanges. Yet, once we learn to speak, that innate telepathic ability—the silent language of the heart—begins to fade into the background.

We live in an age of instant gratification, where responses are expected at the tap of a screen. Our high-tech, fast-paced, commercialized world has dulled our ability to tune in and truly listen—to others, to ourselves, and to the subtle whispers of the universe. We've been taught to go, go, go—rarely slowing down to notice the quiet messages always surrounding us.

But here's the truth: when you *do* slow down, when you *do* tune in, you will be amazed at what you can hear.

Living in the 4D means dwelling in the realm of **imagination, feeling, and belief**—the space between thought and manifestation. According to Neville Goddard's teachings, imagination is not a fantasy; it is **creation itself.** When you imagine your fur friend returning, when you feel their presence, picture their eyes, or sense their energy curled beside you again, you are not "pretending"—you are **dwelling in the state of the wish fulfilled.** In 4D consciousness, you live from the end, not toward it. You speak to them, you prepare space in your heart and home, because you *know* they are returning. That knowing, felt deeply and held consistently, draws the invisible into the visible.

Do not let outdated paradigms or other people's logic interfere with what you feel to be true in your soul. The 3D world may offer absence, but the 4D world holds reunion. Living in the 4D is claiming your role as a co-creator with the Divine. If what you would truly love to happen is your soul-pet's return, then imagine it boldly and richly—walk them in your dreams, feel their paws again, thank them for coming back. As Neville taught, "Assume the feeling of the wish fulfilled," and persist in that assumption until it hardens into fact. In this realm of imagination, where love leads and belief sustains, **all magic happens—and your beloved companion finds their way home.**

## TELEPATHY: A SILENT LANGUAGE AWAKENING

Telepathy has not always been widely accepted as a legitimate form of communication, but that is changing. Awareness is rising, and people are beginning to recognize the profound connections that exist beyond words. Those of us who understand this language—who feel its truth—are passionate about educating others on what is possible and what can be.

When you slow down, when you quiet the noise of daily life and truly tune into yourself, you may be astonished by what you can learn... and hear.

Preparing to communicate with your transitioning pet is a simple, yet a deeply sacred process. Your first priority should be achieving a relaxed state, as this will open the door to your intuitive guidance. Find a quiet space where you feel at ease—this can be with your pet in the room or in a separate space where you feel more grounded. Trust what feels right.

One of the most powerful ways to ground yourself is by connecting with nature, especially with trees. If you feel drawn to step outside, stand in the sunlight, or rest beside your favorite tree, honor that instinct. It will only enhance your ability to communicate with your pet. If possible, place your bare feet on the earth—this strengthens your connection to the natural world and helps stabilize your energy.

Breathe deeply, in and out. Close your eyes and let go of all distractions. Allow your mind to settle into stillness. Ask your Angels and Guides to be present, to support you, and to guide you toward receiving whatever is meant for you at this moment.

Breathing is not just a physical act—it is the very essence of life. In the Greek language, *psyche* means both "soul" and "breath." As you inhale and exhale, feel a deep inner peace wash over you. This is your soul aligning, preparing to connect with your pet through the purest channel—the heart.

With a clear mind and an open heart, you are ready to receive.

Today, I created an intention between myself and *(insert pet's name here)*.

I am expressing my desire to you, *(pet's name)*, and to my angels and guides, to make it known that I desire another lifetime with *(pet's name)*.

I am open to receiving the answer to my question:

*"Will (pet's name) and I be together again in this lifetime, to live out our days once more?"*

It's important to be calm and grounded for both parties. While you are experiencing pain like never before...

**Your heart will hear the answer!**

Sometimes, when we try to connect for the first time—or even after several attempts—we may not receive a clear answer. Do not give up! You are so accustomed to verbal responses that it may take a few tries before you recognize the message in a different form.

Do whatever it takes to be calm and grounded. Light candles, play a meditation CD, or engage in anything that soothes your inner self.

I promise—you will feel the answer. Some of you will experience it more quickly than others.

Often, the feeling that you haven't accomplished what you set out to do stems from the overwhelming emotions surrounding your pet's imminent transition. If you don't receive an answer before your pet crosses over—some will, some won't—know that you can still connect with your beloved companion in spirit. My reincarnation prayer cards can serve as a bridge to that connection.

Rest assured; you will have even greater access to your pet in spirit than you did during their physical existence. Some pets have a specific soul agenda and choose to reveal their plans only after they have crossed. Sometimes, this is simply part of the soul contract—more will be revealed in divine timing.

## GRIEF LIKE NO OTHER

If you have started this book before your pet's crossing, I want to acknowledge exactly where you are at this moment. You have tried the connection exercises, asked the questions, and for some of you, success has been attained. But for others—nothing. And now, sadness and anger have wrapped themselves around you like a storm.

You've become frustrated by your attempts to connect before your beloved crossed over. And now, when you try—you feel *nothing*.

This is one of the biggest reasons I wrote this book. I went through the worst grief imaginable.

There are two types of grief: *good* grief and *bad* grief. And I can tell you—*bad* grief will block everything you're trying to accomplish. It will cast a heavy shadow over this entire process.

Remember, losing a pet is no different than losing a person you love—sometimes, it's even harder. I know because I've been there. As many of you know, there are five stages of grief. For those unfamiliar, I will explain them briefly, as understanding them is essential to navigating this journey.

## THE PHASES OF GRIEF AND THE
## UNIVERSAL FLOW OF LIFE

### Denial and Isolation

The first reaction to learning of a terminal illness or the death of a cherished loved one is often denial—a rejection of reality. This is the mind's way of rationalizing overwhelming emotions. It is a defense mechanism, cushioning the initial shock and giving us time to process the unthinkable.

We block out words, hide from the facts, and convince ourselves that there must be a mistake. This temporary response carries us through the first wave of pain, allowing our psyche to protect itself before we are ready to fully absorb the truth.

From a universal perspective, the **Law of Relativity** teaches us that nothing is inherently good or bad—it is our perception that gives meaning to our experiences. In denial, we are unknowingly applying this law, comparing our loss to what "should have been" rather than seeing it as part of a greater soul contract.

### Anger

As the protective veil of denial begins to lift, the full weight of reality sets in—and with it, pain. We are not ready. This raw and intense emotion often manifests as anger, deflecting from our vulnerable core and seeking an external target.

We may lash out at inanimate objects, complete strangers, friends, family, or even at our beloved pet for leaving us. This anger may seem irrational, but it is a necessary stage of grief—an emotional response to the deep sense of injustice we feel.

The **Law of Vibration** reminds us that everything is energy, including emotions. Anger is a powerful frequency, often masking deeper feelings of sorrow, helplessness, and fear. Rather than resisting it, allowing the energy of anger to flow through us can prevent it from becoming stagnant or destructive.

## Bargaining

When faced with helplessness and vulnerability, our natural instinct is to regain control. We begin negotiating—sometimes with ourselves, sometimes with God, the Universe, or any higher power we believe in. We make silent pleas, attempting to alter fate:

- *If only we had sought medical attention sooner...*
- *If only we had gotten a second opinion...*
- *If only we had been a better guardian...*

Bargaining is an illusion of control. It is an attempt to rewrite the past and prevent the pain of what is unfolding. The **Law of Cause and Effect** reminds us that every action has consequences, but not everything is within our control. The soul has its own journey, and no amount of bargaining can change what was already agreed upon before incarnation.

**Disenfranchised grief** is the pain of a loss that isn't openly acknowledged, socially validated, or publicly mourned. When it comes to losing a beloved pet, many experience this kind of grief—deep sorrow that others may minimize or fail to understand. Society often fails to honor the profound bond between humans and animals, leaving pet guardians feeling isolated or ashamed of the depth of their heartbreak. Yet this grief is real and sacred. When it goes unrecognized or unspoken, it can complicate the process of saying goodbye. Pets are deeply attuned to our emotions, and unresolved pain can create a subtle energetic tether, making it more difficult for their soul to fully transition with peace and ease.

Bargaining often appears quietly alongside this grief: "If only I had caught the illness sooner," or, "Maybe if I had done one more treatment..." These thoughts come from love and desperation, but they can pull you away from acceptance. It's important to acknowledge this stage—not as weakness, but as part of the soul's attempt to make sense of loss. When you begin to release blame and gently shift into gratitude for your time together, you help free your pet's spirit. In doing so, you allow their crossing to be surrounded not by regret, but by the loving energy that supports both their journey—and your healing.

## Depression

Grief carries a heaviness that is often misunderstood. Depression during mourning comes in two distinct forms:

- **The first type** is a reaction to the practical implications of loss—sadness and regret over what was left undone, worry about how our grief is affecting those around us, and a longing for the comfort of what once was.
- **The second type** is more internal and private—a quiet preparation for the final goodbye. It is a sacred surrender,

allowing the soul to detach from the physical presence of our loved one.

The **Law of Rhythm** teaches us that life moves in cycles—ebb and flow, light and dark, loss and renewal. This phase of grief is a natural descent into stillness, where we are given time to process before we rise again. Sometimes all we need in this moment is a hug—a presence that reassures us we are not alone.

Depression after the loss of your beloved pet can feel like being pulled into a tide you didn't see coming—suddenly, the world is quieter, heavier, colorless. But within this sorrow, the **Law of Rhythm** reminds us that all of life moves in cycles: highs and lows, expansion and contraction, day and night. Just as the tide recedes, it also returns. This universal law gently assures us that even in the depths of grief, the rhythm of healing is already in motion. You may not feel it now, but the swing of the pendulum will shift again. Your sadness is not a failure or a weakness—it is a sacred winter, preparing the soul for spring.

Trust that the stillness you're in is not forever; it is part of love's rhythm, part of your transformation. And in time, your heart—once shattered—will beat again with new light, carrying both your pain and your pet's eternal love in every step forward.

## Acceptance

Reaching acceptance is a gift, but not everyone experiences it in the same way or on the same timeline. If the loss was sudden or unexpected, acceptance may feel impossible. If anger or denial is too strong, it may take much longer to arrive.

This phase is often marked by withdrawal and calm—not happiness, but an understanding that life will continue, even if forever changed.

The **Law of Perpetual Transmutation of Energy** states that everything is constantly shifting, evolving, and transforming. Our grief, too, will transform—what was once unbearable sorrow will one day become a softer ache, and eventually, even gratitude for the love we were privileged to experience.

Grief is deeply personal. No two people will go through it in the same way, and there is no right or wrong timeline. The best thing you can do is allow yourself to *feel*—to surrender to the waves as they come, without resistance. Suppressing grief will only prolong the natural process of healing.

## THE JOURNEY BEYOND LOSS

By now, many of you have realized that grief is an intensely personal experience. It is not linear, nor is it predictable. Some days will feel unbearable, while others will carry a glimmer of hope. Once your emotions begin to *soften*, you may find it easier to revisit the techniques and processes of connecting with your beloved companion.

Remember, do not attempt to connect with expectations. If you release all expectations, there can be no disappointments—only experiences.

The **physical death** of a beloved family member is one of the most profound transitions we experience in this lifetime. But the *good* news—though it may not feel like it yet—is that death is not the end. It is merely the first step toward reunion.

Your fur child is not gone forever. Their journey with you is not over.

Think of it as trading in an old Pierre Cardin suit for a new Hugo Boss one—different in form, but the same essence underneath.

Their love for you remains. Their soul remembers. And when the time is right, they will return to you, ready to continue the journey you both agreed upon long before this lifetime began.

## THE ETERNAL BOND: LOVE NEVER DIES

If you have come this far, you now understand something truly profound—love is not bound by the physical, nor is it confined to time. It is eternal, flowing endlessly between souls, whether they walk on two legs or four, whether they speak in words or in whispers of energy.

Our beloved animals—our companions, our confidants, our soulmates—are sentient beings with vast, ancient wisdom. They, too, have souls. They ascend back into spirit, returning to the conscious collective, where love is the only language, and time does not exist.

It is rare for an animal not to reincarnate. Most of the time, we ask them to return, and they oblige. They do not fear this journey, for they are guided by love and a deep knowing that our story with them is never truly over. Some return quickly, eager to reunite and continue their mission at our side. Others may have completed their divine assignment, having served their higher purpose for both themselves and us. If that is the case, they will remain near, a guiding force in spirit, watching over us with the same unwavering devotion they did in life.

But one thing is certain—**they will never let us miss their return.**

They send signs, gentle nudges, and undeniable synchronicities. You may feel a sudden warmth wash over you, as if wrapped in an invisible embrace. A familiar scent might linger in the air, seemingly out of nowhere. You may hear their paws in the hallway, feel the weight of them beside you in bed, or dream so vividly of them that you wake with tears of joy. These are not coincidences. These are messages from a love so powerful that it transcends the veil between worlds.

And when the time is right, when your hearts align once more, they will find their way back to you.

Energy is never lost; it only transforms. Ice melts into water, water rises as steam, steam returns as rain—such is the divine cycle of existence. Our beloveds, too, shift in form but never in essence. They remain connected to us, always. And when they are ready, when you are ready, they will make their way home.

An animal communicator can help bridge this sacred reunion, offering guidance and reassurance, but trust this: even if you choose to walk this path using only your intuition, your heart will know. You will *feel* them before you see them. And when you do, it will be as if no time has passed at all.

I know this truth deeply because I have lived it.

Jack was the love of my life, my husband in another existence. And now, he is here with me once more. A love so strong could never be severed by death; it could only transform. He was granted another lifetime, longer than the first, a blessing I cherish every single day.

To be chosen by God and spirit to hear the whispers of animals across all species, to speak their language, to witness their journeys beyond the veil and back again—this is my greatest honor.

And my deepest wish is that this book brings you solace, understanding, comfort, and, above all else... **hope**.

Because love never dies.

And neither do they.

They always, always, find their way home.

In Love & Light Susan

# CLIENT TESTIMONIALS

**TRUE STORIES... YES, REALLY!**

This book is a journey into the profound mysteries of reincarnation, and I believe the very first story should come from the one who helped me reach out into the vast, loving universe to bring my precious baby home. Debbie is not just a guide; she is someone who has walked this path herself, shedding tears of love and loss, and experiencing the crossing—and return—of her own beloved pets.

So, without further ado, here is Debbie's deeply moving story of her beloved Sugar Baby. **Grab your tissues**—because this one is sure to tug at your heartstrings. Don't say I didn't warn you.

. . .

# SUGAR BABY'S STORY

To my friends,

Many of you have been asking about the details and the messages that I've received from Little Sugar. They have been so profound and heart-healing, I wanted to share them with each of you. It's just been an amazing expansion experience as well as a wondrous healing experience. I hope you enjoy!

## SO HERE GOES:

As many of you know, my constant companion of nearly thirteen years transitioned on Sunday, August 10, 2008. It was her thirteenth birthday. She was a very special little animal companion and spent almost all her waking time with me, when I was home. So it was a great physical loss, when she chose to transition. It wasn't a surprise, she had been communicating to me that her time was near and she'd be leaving soon, for about two months. I chose to not hear her or to interpret her messages in a different way. But there was a part of me, deep down inside, that very clearly knew what she was telling me. The night before she left us, I clearly heard her tell me that this would be the last night she would be with us. I spent extra time saying goodnight and telling her how much I loved her. I then ignored the big message of what she was trying to tell me.

*Lessons Learned:* Listen to your gut instinct. It's the most accurate information system ever and it's how your intuition/higher self speaks to you. And when a message keeps repeating (over and over and over, like a neon sign flashing in your head), there's a reason. It's an important message. Note to self: Pay Attention! Sugar transitioned very quickly and immediately moved into Spirit. I was able to see her around us carrying a beautiful peachy gold energy/aura; as we said goodbye to her. It was especially traumatic for me as there was an enormous amount of blood involved. I kept seeing this tiny little Pomeranian, covered in blood. I could not remember her in her beautiful glory.

*Lesson Learned:* Don't let a few minutes of drama replace years of love, joy, fun and beauty.

Over the next day or two; Sugar stayed connected and assured me that she was coming back in physical form, right away. She told me that she was tired of being the alpha dog (we had seven female dogs and she kept them all in order) and that she wanted longer legs that worked. She had tiny little legs and had 4 surgeries on them over the course of her life. The first surgery was 2 weeks after we got her, she jumped off the coach and broke her leg. Her little legs were very achy and painful and she decided it was time to get new ones that worked much better.

*Lesson Learned:* This is not new, but has a lot more meaning to me now. We are not physical beings having a spiritual experience. We are spiritual beings having a physical experience. And we chose that experience.

On Monday, David called a breeder named Nancy. We got one of our other Pom's (Gracie) from Nancy. David felt this was where we'd find Sugar's new little physical suit. Interestingly enough, I had kept Nancy's phone number on the refrigerator and almost threw it out a couple of weeks before. A little voice told me to keep it, and so I did. Nancy told David that she had one little girl Pomeranian left, but it was promised to another person. David asked her to call us back if the woman decided not to take her. Nancy also told David that the Pom was four months old and was sweet but very independent. David hung up knowing that Nancy would call back. I was not so sure.

*Lesson Learned:* Trust and Believe. When things seem to be the darkest, trust that everything will work out perfectly. Everything is in divine and perfect order. Even when it doesn't seem possible. Trust and Believe that the Universe wants you to be happy. It's not working against you, but is working for you! On Tuesday, Nancy called and told us that the little Pomeranian was ours, if we wanted her. My mind was spinning. Sugar had just left us, not even three days earlier.

How could she be back this soon? How could she have made arrangements to swap souls that quickly? But a little voice in my head told me to go and look at her. Sugar also told me that I would know for sure it was her, because her birth date would be April 28, our wedding anniversary. Of course, I told no one this. If I don't tell anyone, then if it doesn't work out, nothing will be lost.

Right?

*Lesson Learned:* Trust Yourself. If you can't trust yourself, who can you trust? Trust opens the doorway for all possibilities. Well, we went to Nancy's. We saw the little baby and she wasn't at all what I thought she would look like. I picked her up and I could instantly feel the familiar feeling. My heart felt good again. She snuggled up underneath my chin and just cuddled with me. She didn't want to be put down, she just wanted me to hold her. I kept looking at her. Her nose was long, her legs were long, her ears were long. Sugar had a cute little snub nose, short round little ears and very short little legs. How could this be the same little soul?

I wanted to bond with her, but there was something telling me that this couldn't be Sugar. She was born 4 months earlier and her birthday could not be April 28th. It was too late to turn her back, my broken heart was starting to mend and I had already fallen in love with this little dog. A few minutes later, David brought her paperwork over to me to show me that she had been born on our anniversary. He thought it was a sign. At that moment in time, I knew that it had been a perfectly orchestrated event by a tiny giant of a soul.

*Lesson Learned:* Love comes in all types of packages. It's the gift inside that matters.

Here are a few more synchronicities. If I had worked them into the story, it would have been way too long, but I thought they were worth sharing.

- Nancy called the woman that she had promised the puppy to and told her she didn't think it was going to work out. She then called us.

- As soon as we walked into Nancy's house and saw Sugar Baby, she told us that she was just learning to jump off the coach. This is how Sugar broke her leg the first time around.
- Nancy told us that Sugar Baby was 4 months old, she was actually 3 1/2 months old. The exact age that Sugar was when we first got her.
- Before leaving Nancy's house, Nancy told me: "I don't understand it, she doesn't seem like the same dog. She's so calm and wants to be held".
- When we got home, the new little puppy fell asleep in front of my computer keyboard. This was one of Sugar's favorite places. She was home again.
- She wanted to be called Sugar again. We compromised and are calling her Sugar Baby!

I want to thank each and everyone of you for your prayers, blessings and healing energies. Your words and thoughts helped me to make it through a key point in my life. I could feel each one of you as you thought, prayed and sent energy our way. We are truly blessed to have such wonderful and loving friends. And it feels so good!

I hope that you enjoy our story and that you glean something from it.

— With lots of love,
Debbie

*Thank you, Debbie Johnstone, for all that you do, and for all that you have done for me and Jack, and for sharing your beautiful story.*

# ANGELA'S FAREWELL TO WIDGET AND WELCOME BACK DUTCH

It was like any other day—Thursday, to be exact, a cold and snowy one. The sun was going down as I took Widget out for our evening walk. I noticed this pretty male cardinal perched on an old clothesline that I hadn't had time to take down. I found it odd that he was by the door and not in his nest. It worried me a little because I knew the forecast predicted high winds and more snow.

As the night went on, I noticed he was still by the door, not moving at all. He was perched right above my head, yet he just looked at me and Widget as if to say, *I am here to tell you something.* As the night grew later, the feeling became stronger and stronger—something was about to happen that would break my heart. Something that would shatter me forever.

Morning came, and that little cardinal was still in the same spot. Days passed, and I noticed a change in Widget—he was unsettled and becoming more and more disconnected from me. I called the vet who was treating him for what we thought was the final loss of his eyesight. She felt it was fine and that he was just adjusting to his new medication.

By Sunday, Widget was so very ill that I took him to the emergency vet. It was Sunday, February 3, 2013. He had never been sick a day in his 11.4 years of life. After being examined, we found out he was suffering from pancreatitis, and his blood sugar levels were over 400. The situation was dire, to say the least. The vet recommended I leave him overnight.

OMG, what? Overnight? Widget and I had never spent a night apart. How could I leave my blind baby alone? How could I do this? Well, after some thought, something inside me said, *Leave him. You must leave him. Your time is over.* And in my soul, as I left, I knew he would never return home.

When I got home, I took his mate, Darlene, outside and, of course, looked for the cardinal that had stayed by my door for the past four nights. But he was gone, and again, something inside me said he had come for my Widget to tell us something—to tell us that a change was about to occur.

I ran my hand down his back, and his fur was falling out. I heard a voice in my head say, "It's time for me to go, Mommy. Let me go." At that point, it was all over in 15 minutes. My Widget was gone, gone forever. He fell limp in my arms after the last injection. I laid him down on the table and ran out of the clinic into the parking lot. I screamed at the top of my lungs... All I could do was scream! It was Tuesday, February 5, 2013, 1:38 in the afternoon—the day my soul was crushed forever, never to heal... or so I thought.

The days following Widget's transition to The Rainbow Bridge, my heartbreak worsened, and my will to live started to fade. I would look at my other toy poodle and cry, and cry, and cry more. Then, the most amazing things started to happen. At the time, I thought I was starting to go crazy!

Darlene started to literally be knocked over by something invisible so often that she would refuse to enter certain rooms at times—rooms where Widget would have always been by her side when he was in physical form. I thought she was just going into a deep depression, until one night, it was unmistakable that my Widget was still with us!!!!!

The Poodles and I, from day one, had a bath ritual. When I would draw my evening bath, each poodle would get two treats, and no matter what, when they heard the bathwater start to run, they would come running. Widget first, Darlene second. Well, this particular night, Darlene had entered the bathroom, and I was getting her treats ready when it happened—something ran into her hind end so hard that it knocked her almost over.

Darlene and I became so startled that she ran out of the room and just stared at me from the hallway. I was shaken, inside and out. I kept thinking, what did I just see? I said to myself, as Darlene kept looking at me for reassurance, "Just act normal." I got into my bath and called Darlene back into the bathroom. As I was looking down at her, asking if she was ready for her treat... BOOM, my glass dolphin moved to the edge of the counter and fell! At that point, I became afraid. Then, a thought crossed my mind: "It's my Widget communicating with me." I looked down into the bathwater, and there it was—not my face reflected back at me, but my Widget's face!!!!

So, I started my journey for more answers.

After my bath, I decided to try a method of communicating through pictures that my animal communicator told me to try: "Ask Widget if he wants to be in your pictures, then start taking many pictures in a row as you walk around your house." I did exactly what she said right after my experience in the tub, and BOOM, there it was. In the very first picture, my Widget in spirit was laying on the bed in the spot he had laid in for 11.4 years!

My Widget still shows himself in pictures when I ask him if he wants to be in my pictures. Sometimes, he is just a little orb by his urn, but in times of great sorrow, my baby shows himself in spirit form, as his old body, to bring me comfort.

As the days went on, my animal communicator, Susie, started confirming where to start my search for Widget's new body! She was spot on! She was correct—I found the breeder, not close to home by any means, but my Widget was coming home, and I was excitedly waiting for the birth of the new physical body for my baby to return to me—the new baby Widget!!!! I had found his new Momma, and every day Widget would give me signs that I was indeed correct. "You have found me, Momma! You have found me!" Feathers found in the house where there was no reason to find feathers (lol), songs on the radio, cardinals tapping on my windows. So many signs, it would be impossible for me not to hear him!!! Big neon signs hit me over the head with a bat! "Mommy loves and misses you, what a good, smart boy you are. Hurry home, baby. Hurry home. Mommy is waiting."

I had searched Facebook for some kind of group that would understand my loss and my belief in reincarnation. I found a group called *Pet Loss, Grief Support, Animal Communication, and Reincarnation,* a group started by Susie Paradise. They had experienced the same devastation I had. There were many members with the same loss and "found" stories as me!

As the days passed, Widget would let himself be known to me and other animal communicators in the group, as well as to other grieving fur parents in the group. While on the page talking to others, Susie Paradise connected with my Widget. She said she kept seeing the number 6. We thought it was the number of puppies in the litter, but as it turned out, it would be his birthday—5/1/2013 (5+1=6).

My phone rang, and it was the breeder. Her female had gone into labor. As we talked on the phone, she said, "The first pup is a girl, next was a boy, and the last pups were boys!" Woo hoo! I told her I'd be down in two weeks to see the babies.

Angela Clark became one of my closest friends, she was connected to the "magical farm where she had built her dream home. I watched her as she communicated with the wildlife and mother earth. I would watch the trees embrace her as she softly coaxed them with her words, she was the gentlest most authentic light worker I have ever had the pleasure of meeting. January 7, 2024 you ascended into the conscious collective, home again with Widget, Dutch and Darlene. Angela, I miss you every day and I will adore you until we see each other again.

# A MOTHER'S LOVE: SANTOS RETURNS AS LEMMY

### NAT HEX'S STORY

I wanted a dog, and my dad had found out that my Auntie had a Boston Terrier that was expecting in two months. I started to Google Boston Terriers—they are a very rare breed in Norway. What a precious face! I immediately fell in love.

I went to meet my Santos when he was only eight weeks old. I had only seen pictures of him before. This tiny puppy with a heart-shaped nose was everything I had ever wanted!

Being a Mother doesn't Mean being related to someone by blood. It means loving someone unconditionally and with your

We had a wonderful time together; sadly, it only lasted four years. A few days before his fourth birthday, he suddenly got sick with seizures that frightened me. I thought he was dying.

He had been a healthy dog before he received his kennel cough vaccine, which the vet gave him intranasally. This was sadly the cause of his illness. He was diagnosed with a brain infection, requiring medication five times a day, along with numerous tests and vet visits. He was a brave little soldier, and he gave both me and the vet hope that we could manage this together with medication and frequent visits.

From the day of his diagnosis, we had four and a half months together. He seemed to be getting better day by day, and I had hope. One day, he broke one of his canines and had to have a tooth extracted. After that, he got worse. The seizures came back, and I knew I had to let him go. It was a difficult choice to let him transition to the Rainbow Bridge.

A few days before this, I had a dream. I dreamt that Santos jumped out of the living room window—and we live on the third floor. I screamed, "Don't let him jump!" But we couldn't hold him back. Santos passed away on January 23, 2025.

Shortly after his crossing, I had to travel to see my family, who live 2500 km from me. The day after he passed, I couldn't stay home. When my dad picked me up at the airport, he told me he had heard Santos barking in his home—after he had already crossed over.

While I was visiting my family, our family dog acted very strangely. She normally doesn't like other dogs, but she was behaving as if another dog was in the house the entire time we were there. I know now that this was Santos in spirit. It is said that they are closer and more available in spirit form than in physical form, and well... Santos, in spirit, was with us.

Four weeks later, I was back at my home in Oslo. I was trying to pack up all of his things, but I was so sad. Then suddenly, out of the blue, a TV commercial came on playing a song that I used to sing to Santos. It made me feel better. It was a sign from him.

A few days later, I dreamt of him for the first time. In the dream, he was with my dad, who was eating ice cream. I called for Santos, but he didn't come to me—he was more obsessed with the ice cream! I started to feel more and more certain that he was coming back.

Then, I received a call from my Auntie. She had good news—Panda, Santos' sister, was expecting puppies, and she told me I *must* take one of them. "No doubt," she said. "I can feel that he is coming back to you. Sorry if you think I'm crazy, but his life on earth isn't done."

I got goosebumps and said, "No, I can't do this if it happens again."

A few days later, as I was scrolling through Facebook, I suddenly stopped. Someone had posted a song from YouTube—*Richard Marx*— *Hazard*. I immediately thought, *That song played in the taxi on the way to the vet's office the day Santos crossed over. Wow, I haven't heard it in years.*

Then, my dad called me. He had seen a picture of the newborn puppies. "There are two boys and a girl," he said.

One of the boys was born with a Haggerty spot on his head. The Haggerty spot was named after Vincent Perry, a highly respected international dog show judge and Boston Terrier breeder. In his book *The Boston Terrier*, he referred to the Haggerty spot as *The Kiss of God*.

I feel this was very special—another sign that it was Santos returning to me.

I named him Lemmy. He was born on February 15, 2013.

I waited until he was five weeks old before I visited him. I didn't feel emotionally strong enough to make the trip. *What if it wasn't him?* What if I was wrong? But when the time came, he immediately ran to me. The breeder said, "This isn't normal. The other puppies stayed behind, but he came straight to you and started licking your face—just like he used to."

He didn't want to leave my side.

Then, just two weeks before I was to bring Lemmy home, I had another dream. My boyfriend and I were walking in the park with both Santos and Lemmy. In the dream, Santos was healthy. Suddenly, Lemmy disappeared. We searched and searched, but we couldn't find him anywhere. Yet Santos remained very calm, as if he wasn't worried at all.

That's when I became 100% sure—this new little baby *was* Santos returning as Lemmy.

Meanwhile, I had found Susie, a newly realized animal communicator, on Facebook. She had started a pet loss group and told me many things that were correct. She helped and guided me through all my questions. One of them was about Santos wanting to go to the beach. She also identified that he had a blue fleece blanket at home, along with green and orange-colored balls and other toys—and all of it was true.

I brought Lemmy home when he was eight weeks old. As time passed, I saw more and more of Santos in him. Even though I named him Lemmy—since the name suddenly came to me, and I didn't want to call him Santos again—I knew without a doubt that my little precious saint had returned.

I believe that this time, his life will be much longer with me. He had to exchange his sickly body for a new and healthier one so we could continue our journey together.

Santos was, and still is, a very special dog. He was my shining light, and now he has come back as Lemmy Rockstar to give my life new meaning. Together, we will have adventures that will keep us more bonded than ever.

As always, I still tell him every night and every morning, *"I love you."* I always said those words to him, even when he was visiting the Rainbow Bridge. I always felt him in my heart—that is one thing that never changed.

Physically or spiritually, my boy never left my side. My precious little dog has come back to fill my life with joy and happiness.

Our second journey lasted for 11 years and 10 months. Lemmy was 11 years and 10 months old when he sadly earned his wings. It was late on Friday the 13th when I came home from the nursing home, where I work and noticed something was terribly wrong—his eye had ruptured. He had been dealing with corneal issues for some time, and we had tried eye drops, but nothing improved. The vet said we'd try over the weekend, but by Sunday, it was clear he was not getting better. I called the vet again, and she told me they had reviewed his case—his age, his underlying health issues, including hypothyroidism over the past two years—and said that if he were younger or healthier, they might attempt to remove the eye. But gently, she told me it was time to let him go. And I agreed. It was heavier than the first goodbye. But I told him that if he wanted to return, he could. I wanted him back—healthy, and likely for the last time. I asked for signs. And they came. Through dreams. Through music. And I knew he would return. I just had to find him.

Santos first returned as Lemmy, and now, Lemmy has returned as Sonny. After he passed, I was, of course, heartbroken. But I reminded myself to look for signs instead of drowning in grief. Slowly, things got easier. One day, I reached out to a breeder in southern Norway. She was warm and kind, but the process to get a puppy from her would take months. Then she suggested I contact a nice young woman who had puppies available now. I followed her advice—and there he was. One of the puppies had a little mark on his neck that looked like an "L." I asked, "Is he spoken for?" She said, "No." And I knew instantly—*this is him.*

When he turned eight weeks old, we made travel arrangements to bring him home. But just as we were about to leave, the flight was canceled due to technical issues. We had to wait ten more days. I reminded myself to breathe—maybe he needed to stay with his mom and siblings a bit longer. I trusted Spirit. He wasn't ready to come home just yet. Sonny was born on March 5, 2025. Lemmy had earned his wings on December 14, 2024. This time, I had to wait a little longer. I named him Sonny because that's what it felt like *he* wanted. The night

Lemmy left, I told him what I always had: "Good night. I love you." And I still do—every night.

Sonny is clever and full of energy. Unlike Lemmy, who was quiet, Sonny barks—a lot. It feels like he has so much to tell me now. He has returned to me three times, and I feel Santos, Lemmy, and Sonny all within him. There is no doubt. You can see it. You can feel it. We've only had five weeks together so far, but our bond is strong. I truly hope this third journey lasts even longer. I'm so grateful. We're home again. Together.

SANTO RETURNED AS LEMMY AND
LEMMY RETURNED AS SONNY
HE CAME BACK WITH AN "L" ON HIS BACK
SO MOMMY WOULD KNOW IT WAS HIM.

# SHEREE PELTON AND CHARLIE

CHARLIE PASSED AT THE AGE OF ALMOST 8 YEARS
& JESSE/CHARLIE CAME BACK IN A NEW BODY TO
GIVE ME THE NEXT 6 YEARS CHARLIE COULD NOT

THE MIRACLE OF CHARLIE (AKA "CHUCK")
AUGUST 26, 1996 – OCTOBER 27, 2004

It was the fall of 2004 when, suddenly, my wonderful dog and companion, Charlie (da Chow Chow), was diagnosed with terminal cancer. He had just turned eight years old. The specialists gave him two weeks to two months.

Charlie and I were truly blessed with time to say our goodbyes—for now. The Great Universe gave us almost that full two months. We had special times—home-cooked meals, lots of walks and rides, and heartfelt *one-on-one* chats.

In late October, Charlie let me know it was *time* as I looked into his big brown eyes—the awesome gateway to his soul. When I gave him his medicine that day, I promised him it would be the last medicine he'd ever have to take. I don't know if I could have gone through with it if I hadn't made that promise to him.

Charlie and I went for our last walk *of the season* at the park until he tuckered out. The drive to the vet was about 20 miles but seemed like 10,000. He *wind-surfed* all the way there—he loved to ride!

After the *deed* was done, I stayed with him for about an hour at the vet's office. I talked to him and told him to go to the light—to go visit with his *family* waiting for him. Just as I said that, the lights in the room started flickering. I asked, *"Charlie Bear, did you do that?"* and they flickered again.

As I sat there with his head in my lap, I told Charlie he must make it VERY CLEAR to me which Chow Chow body he would come back to me in. My only stipulation was that he had to be the red-headed female.

When I came home that night, a friend had left a message saying he had bred his female Chow earlier that same day and had *puppies in the oven* for me. (He knew Charlie was sick but had no idea what had happened that day.) He also mentioned that another litter from the same father (different mom, of course) was due two weeks earlier.

As it turned out, the father of both *possible* litters was named *Charlie*, and the man who owned *Charlie* was named *Chuck*. That was a pretty awesome sign that my *boy* was on his way back to me! Then, I found out that Papa *Charlie* was actually my other dog Bubba's littermate from five years ago!

Okay—definitely my boy/girl was on the way back to me!

Then, of course, the committee in my head started: *Oh great—two litters, and they will all be red-headed females!*

I began making a list of possible names for my new arrival. On December 22, I was speaking to my girlfriend when she *politely* told her daughter, *"Jesse, get off the phone!"* And bingo—that was it. Her name would be *Jesse*.

Later that night, the phone rang. *The puppies were born today.* There were three males, two females, and only *one* red-headed girl—the one I had been waiting for. (The second litter never came to be.)

A couple of weeks later, a friend looked up the meaning of the name Jesse—it meant *God's Grace*. Oh yes, God is GREAT!

At 26 days old, I finally got to meet my Jesse girl. What a doll! I whispered to her, *"Charlie Bear, you came back to me."* She put her little nose behind my ear and nuzzled.

"JESSE"
26 DAYS OLD
12.16.04 ~ 8.18.11

*Until One Has Loved An Animal, a Part*
*of One's Soul Remains Unawakened"*

~ANATOLE FRANCE

IN MEMORY OF MY DEAR FRIEND SHEREE
PELTON 2.27.25 & HER AMAZING PETS!

# VICKY AND SEASPRAY

## SEASPRAY'S STORY

Where do I begin? From the moment Seaspray came into my life, I just knew I would never be the same again. The journey we were about to embark on together was unlike anything you could prepare yourself for—one that has changed my life forever, for the better.

A week into owning my beloved boy, disaster struck. My baby had been injured badly in the field. At only three years old, he had been kicked so hard that the impact went right down to the bone, puncturing his middle patella ligament and chipping his tibia. That very day, after only a week together, I was faced with an agonizing decision from the vets.

At this point, Seaspray could only bear weight on three legs—a dire situation for a horse. The vets didn't hold out much hope. They told me that, in the slim chance he recovered, he would almost certainly never be ridden again. At this point, they suggested I put him to sleep.

I was heartbroken. I couldn't just give up on him. I didn't care if I could ever ride him again—even though I had only had him a week, something between us had connected from the moment we set eyes on each other. I asked the vets to give us a chance. I was willing to do anything. After a long discussion, they agreed, and our journey continued together.

## THE JOURNEY OF HEALING

The following months were a blessing in disguise. I was on study leave with my GCSEs looming, which meant I could spend every waking minute with my boy.

Being only three years old, it was hard on him—having to stay in a stable all day, unable to move too much, and with no horses for company. So, I became his companion. Each morning, I would pack up a bag (revision included) and head down to the yard on my little moped.

It was then that I knew something between us was going to be inseparable. Every morning, as I parked up, an admiral butterfly would hover around my moped and stay until I left. At the time, I didn't quite understand why the butterfly appeared or what it meant, but as our story continued, all became clear.

One thing that always warmed my heart was the trust he had in me from the very first day. It was incredible—trust that usually takes years to form.

Each day at exactly 11 a.m., he would look at me with the softest eyes, and my heart would melt. Then, he would lie down in his stable and look at me again. His eyes were so gentle. I would slowly walk over to where he lay, and before I knew it, I was lying next to him, our breaths matching each other's.

It was the best feeling in the world. To me, it was the greatest gift my boy could give me—showing me the unconditional love he had to offer, his way of saying *thank you*.

Six months passed, and the same thing happened each day. But one day, something was different.

## A SIGN FROM ABOVE

It was the day of the vet's visit to check on his progress. I knew something wasn't right—Seaspray seemed a little off-color. When he lay down at 11 a.m. as usual, his eyes were filled with worry. I knelt down in front of him and cradled his head in my lap.

Out of nowhere, the butterfly appeared again—this time *inside* the stable with us.

I whispered in Seaspray's ear, *"I will never leave you. No matter the outcome today, I will not give up on you. If you keep fighting, so will I."*

The moment I finished my sentence; a deep sigh came from Seaspray—it was as if he understood. I looked up, and the butterfly had disappeared.

That afternoon, the vet brought bad news. After six months of stable rest, we had made no improvement. Again, I was faced with the same decision. Again, I gazed into my boy's eyes and refused to give up.

## AGAINST ALL ODDS

Twelve long months passed. Seaspray and I spent every waking moment together. We had so much fun—I created little toys, games, and activities to keep him occupied. As time passed, I could feel his spirit lifting.

The dreaded vet visit came once more, but this time, it didn't feel like the last. Seaspray had a spring in his step. It was as if he were trying to put a smile on my face that whole day.

When the vet finished his examination and delivered the news, I was overwhelmed.

We had beaten all the odds.

A miracle had occurred right in our midst—Seaspray's leg had healed, and it was as strong as ever.

**WE DID IT!**


## A DREAM FULFILLED

A few months passed, and I slowly began to bring Seaspray back into work. He was *incredible*—more than I could ever have dreamed of.

I never saw the butterfly again. Not for a while. Not until the day that broke my heart once more.

Seaspray was in full work and had amazed everyone, including the vets. We decided the time was right—we would enter our first dressage competition!

The odds were stacked against us—we had been placed in the wrong class and were now competing against professionals in top hats and tails. It was our first competition together, but Seaspray was a dream. We did our tests, and when I looked into his eyes, I saw the joy on his face—the unconditional love.

Then a butterfly appeared, just like the ones before. At first, I thought nothing of it.

I had no idea what was about to happen.

## THE UNTHINKABLE

As we packed up to go home, I was leading Seaspray toward the lorry. He *loved* to load, so when he went to jump on, I wasn't shocked—until he slipped.

His back end slid out from under him, and he fell backward, crashing to the ground and hitting his head.

He lay motionless.

For what felt like forever—but was only a minute or so—I stood frozen. The butterfly still hovered around me. I ran to him, stroked him, and whispered, *"It's going to be okay."*

Eventually, he stood up, and we got him onto the lorry.

## THE FIGHT OF A LIFETIME

Once home, things went from bad to worse. Seaspray was rushed to the main vet hospital. He was diagnosed with a fractured skull and a torn nuchal ligament.

The vets had never seen a horse survive such a severe injury before. Even more incredibly, there were *no outward signs* that anything was wrong.

They didn't know what to do for him. The decision, once again, was left to me.

I looked at my boy and said, *"Nope. I will try everything in my power. If he wants to fight, so do I."*

And fight he did.

Eighteen months later, **we did it again!**

Seaspray made a full recovery. Another miracle. And once again, the butterfly left us.

## LIFE WITH MY BOY

Life with my boy had begun again, slowly but surely. As we built up our work, he was loving every moment, and I was beginning to read every movement of his as if it were my own. It was magical. Then, one day, the butterfly appeared again—but this time, I wasn't sure why.

Seaspray seemed a bit off color, but I couldn't put my finger on what was wrong. This continued for a few days until he began to colic. The vets came out and managed to ease his pain, and by the next day, he seemed fine. A week later, it happened again—only worse. He was rushed to the vet to be monitored, and as always, I stayed by his side, reassuring him. When he finally came home, he looked so worn out.

The vets discovered that he had stomach ulcers as well as inflammatory bowel disease. We began treatment, but something still wasn't right. The bond between us was so strong that I could tell he was putting on a brave face, but he was suffering. The treatment continued for months, yet he didn't seem to be getting any better.

## A HEARTBREAKING DECISION

Then disaster struck again—Seaspray had colic once more. The vets treated him, and he settled for the night, only to colic again the next day. I looked into my boy's eyes. He was exhausted—we both were. The vets had no idea what more they could do. I sat with him for hours as the treatment began to ease his pain again.

I asked him for a sign of what to do, but I got nothing. So, I changed my question and asked him if he was ready to go. At that moment, he placed his head in my lap and held it there, breathing softly into me. I burst into tears. It was the answer I had known in my heart, but one I didn't want to accept.

The day turned into night, and the weather grew cold. I stayed with my boy until the early hours of the morning before heading home to get warm. The next day, we awoke to snow. It was now Saturday, and Seaspray was utterly exhausted. He had colic again. The vets came out, but this time, the treatment didn't work as well as it usually did.

I asked my boy once more if he was ready to go, and again, he put his head in my lap. His eyes had changed—they looked so tired and drained. The decision needed to be made.

By Wednesday, he had another severe colic attack, and the treatment no longer helped. He was taken into the vets, and the final decision was made. They allowed him one last day outside on the grass, as he had been confined to a stable for weeks due to his illness. I spent the entire day with him, staying by his side well into the night. Over and over, I asked him the same question, and each time, he gave me the same response. My heart was breaking, but somehow, I found the courage to tell him, "It's going to be okay. You will be able to run free soon." Even though I knew I wouldn't be.

## SAYING GOODBYE

Thursday morning came—February 7, 2013—and to my amazement, the snow had melted completely. There wasn't a sign of it left, and the sun shone brighter than it had in weeks. It had to be a sign. I rushed to the vets to see my boy, bringing apples, carrots, and mint—his favorite treats, which he hadn't been allowed to eat for so long. He loved every mouthful.

Then, the vet came over. "It's time," he said.

I was in pieces. I didn't want this to happen, but I knew it was the only option. I pleaded with the vet to reassure me that I was making the right decision. He told me the choice had to be mine alone. Taking a deep breath, I pulled myself together.

"Okay," I said. "It's time."

I walked my boy over to the grass. I promised him I would never leave him and that everything was going to be okay. I told him how much I loved him and that I was sorry I couldn't fix him.

The vet began to administer the injection. I refused to cry as I held my boy's head, watching as he slowly dropped to the ground. I sank down with him, his eyes changing as his life came to a close. I whispered one final time in his ear:

"Be free, my soulmate. It's okay to go. Run free, pain-free, as you belong. I love you."

As I finished my sentence, I looked into his eyes. He was gone.

The earth stood still. My heart was shattered.

I turned to look behind me. Two doves sat on the path, watching us. Then, suddenly, they flew up to where we lay—only to be joined by a third dove. They soared higher and higher until I could no longer see them.

The doves had come to take my boy's soul to the Rainbow Bridge. I was sure of it.

## SIGNS FROM BEYOND

From that day on, I began to see a single dove when I least expected it, along with the admiral butterfly. I believe this is my boy's way of telling me he is still with me.

After losing Seaspray, I was offered an unborn foal. Without hesitation, I agreed to take him before he was even born. Little did I know that this foal had been conceived on the very day my boy was laid to rest.

Months passed, and my grief for Seaspray remained overwhelming. Then, something extraordinary happened. One day, while working with a friend's horse, I suddenly felt as though I was looking at my boy again.

I began speaking to the horse as if he were Seaspray, and to my amazement, he responded just as Seaspray would—the same movements, the same look in his eye, even the same favorite spots to be scratched. I couldn't believe it. My boy had come to me through my friend's horse, just when I needed him most.

When it was time to say goodbye, it felt just like saying goodbye to Seaspray. I told him I loved him and always would. He watched me walk away, his eyes looking straight into my soul—just as my boy's had.

## A NEW BEGINNING

Not long after, I finally went to meet my new foal, who was now four months old. I spent hours with him and cherished every minute. But something was missing—I didn't feel Seaspray's presence in him.

Then, just as I was leaving, my heart nearly melted. My foal followed me for the first time, all the way to the gate. I turned around and told him I loved him. As I took one more step, I heard it—Seaspray's whinny.

But it wasn't a baby whinny at all—it was Seaspray's exact, distinctive call. I couldn't mistake it in a million years. Stunned, I looked into my foal's eyes. There was something there—not fully, but something.

As I drove home, still in disbelief, I looked out the window. A beautiful rainbow stretched across the sky, even though there had been no rain. Thirty miles later, another rainbow appeared—this time, a double rainbow.

I believe it was my boy's way of telling me he is on his way back. Little by little, the first steps had been made.

I just have to trust.

Seaspray will find his way home again.

*The moment that you died, my heart was torn in two,*
*One side filled with heartache, the other died with you,*
*I often lie awake at night*
*When the world is fast asleep,*
*And take a walk down memory lane*
*With tears upon my cheek.*
*They say memories are golden, well maybe that is true,*
*But I've never wanted memories for I only wanted you,*
*A million times I've needed you a million times I've cried*
*For if love alone could have saved you, you never would have died*
*Remembering you is easy; I do it every day*
*But missing you is heartache that never goes away,*
*If tears could build a staircase and heartache make a lane.*
*I'd walk the path to heaven and bring you home again.*

*Love and miss you more than words can say—*

*Forever in my heart, Seaspray xxxxxxxx*

—VICKY THOMPSON

## SEA-SPRAY RETURNS AS BABY BITZ

Vicky had always believed in the unbreakable bond she shared with her beloved horse, Seaspray. From the moment their souls connected, they moved as one, understanding each other in ways that defied explanation. But fate had other plans. After months of battling illness, Seaspray could fight no longer. As Vicky held his head in her lap, whispering words of love and release, she felt her heart shatter. As he took his final breath, three doves soared into the sky, a silent promise that his spirit would live on.

Grief consumed her in the months that followed. The absence of Seaspray left a void too vast to fill. Then, out of nowhere, she was offered an unborn foal. Without hesitation, she said yes, as if something deep within her knew this was meant to be. It wasn't until later that she discovered an astonishing truth—the foal had been conceived on the very day Seaspray had passed. The realization sent shivers through her. Could this be a sign? Could her beloved Seaspray be finding his way back to her?

The foal, whom she named Bitz, was born into hardship. Neglected and frail, his small body bore the scars of a cruel beginning. No creature should have endured what he had. When Vicky first laid eyes on him, she felt an instant pull—a familiarity she couldn't yet place. She nursed him, fought for him, and loved him with every ounce of her being, just as she had with Seaspray.

As Bitz grew, Vicky began to notice something remarkable. It was in the way he moved, the way he looked at her with knowing eyes. The same quiet wisdom. The same fierce will to survive. Then, one day, as she turned to leave his paddock, something happened that made her heart stop.

A whinny—deep, distinctive, unmistakable.

Vicky froze. Her breath caught in her throat. That was *his* voice. Not the soft, uncertain whinny of a foal, but the strong, familiar call of Seaspray. She spun around, staring at Bitz in disbelief. His eyes met hers, and in that instant, she knew. It *was* him. He had found his way back.

Overwhelmed, she climbed into her car to make the long journey home. As she drove, her mind swirled with emotions—grief, wonder, and an undeniable sense of hope. And then, just as the sun began to dip beyond the horizon, she saw it—a brilliant rainbow stretching across the sky.

No rain. No storm. Just a perfect arc of color.

Tears welled in her eyes as she whispered, *"You're here, aren't you?"*

Thirty miles down the road, another rainbow appeared—this time, a double. The message was clear. He was coming back to her, little by little. She had doubts. She had almost lost hope. But Seaspray had never left her—he had simply been waiting for the right moment to return.

Now, their journey began again. A new life, a new body, but the same unbreakable bond.

This time, they would fight and win—together.

### LUNA RETURNS AS LILY

We had an Italian Greyhound named Bella Mia who was around a year and a half old and had pretty bad separation anxiety, so we decided to get her a sister to help. I started my search for puppies near me and ran across an ad for a litter of eight-week-old puppies about an hour and a half from us. Something inside me told me we had to go get one.

When we arrived, it was terrible. I don't remember how many were in the litter, but they were all being kept in a single large kennel in a hot garage, and they were covered in fleas. My heart broke for them. I wanted to take them all home, but we couldn't afford that. We brought the puppies out into the yard so we could love on and play with them. There was one puppy in particular who seemed so happy and wanted to be right with us the whole time, especially my daughter. She was almost all white except for gray on her face and ears and a big spot at the base of her tail, which was adorable. We fell in love with her; she was coming home with us.

We decided to name her Luna because she was white like the moon. She bonded instantly with her older sister Bella. They were inseparable from then on. We called them yin and yang because their coloring was opposite: Luna was white with gray markings, and Bella was gray with white markings.

Luna was the happiest little dog ever. She would stand on your lap when you were sitting, put her legs on your shoulders to give hugs, and try to lick your ears, nose, and mouth like crazy. We always said she was trying to lick your brain. She would wag her tail so hard and fast that she was constantly spraining it. She liked to be picked up and held toward you like a baby. She trotted everywhere she went and was stuck to us like glue. When you sat down, she'd almost immediately come up and plop down against you, always wanting to be covered by a blanket. She was such a little snuggle bug. She slept under the covers every night between my body and my arm with her head on my shoulder.

Luna loved to play with balls, and her very favorite toy was a little stuffed fox that she'd carry around and lay with sometimes. She started having a lot of buildup on her teeth at a young age and would fight us when we tried to brush them. It was like trying to wrestle a greased pig, so we started annual teeth cleanings by the vet pretty early. Luna was always a very picky eater. Sometimes she would completely skip a meal, and we'd have to try different foods to get her to eat. Early last year, we could barely get her to eat at all. She started losing weight, and she was already skinny, so it was very concerning. Otherwise, she was acting normal. I called and made a vet appointment to see what was going on.

This next part is so very difficult for me to even think about, let alone write. My daughter was in school and couldn't come with me to her appointment to hold her on the car trip like usual. She usually traveled in someone's lap. I buckled her into the seatbelt in a dog bed in the passenger seat next to me. She was nervous in the car, and not being on someone's lap made that worse. She kept trying to stand up and come over to my lap, but that wasn't safe because I was driving. I kept trying to get her to sit down. I was getting frustrated, but I kept trying to pet her to calm her down. She kept whining, pawing at my arm, and licking me. She was begging me to let her come over to my lap; I'll never forget the pleading look in her eyes. I stopped at a stoplight and tried to unbuckle the belt to let her over, but I couldn't get it undone, and the light turned green. How I wish with everything in me that I had just let her ride on my lap—I can't help but feel she wouldn't have gotten as worked up. I was trying to keep her safe but wished so much that I could have comforted her.

We went in for her appointment. I picked her up and held her in my lap for a few minutes until they called us back. We walked back, and I set her on the scale to get her weight like normal. Then, as we started toward the exam room, she stopped and froze right outside the door. Her legs were stiff, and she had a scared look in her eyes. I thought she was having a seizure from all the nerves. She had a seizure at home about a year before this, where she got stiff, fell over on her side, and paddled, but snapped out of it quickly. The vet had just said to watch for any other signs, and her bloodwork had been normal. Both the vet tech and I started getting worried.

I picked her up, and the vet tech took her from my arms and rushed her to the back room when she let out a howl like I had never heard from her before. My heart sank into my stomach. The door closed behind her, and I think I knew deep down that it wasn't a seizure. I sat down and heard the tech call for help from the vet, who was in surgery. I could hear several people rush into the room to help her. I sat there waiting for what seemed like an eternity. Then, the doctor came into the room. I asked if she was okay, and he slowly shook his head, no, and said, "She didn't make it. She had a heart attack, and we weren't able to revive her." I burst into tears and started sobbing. He said, "She must have had a heart defect that she was probably born with that never showed up on any of the tests." I was completely devastated.

He asked if I wanted to hold her, and I said, "Yes." He left the room, and one of the vet techs brought her to me wrapped in a blanket. I sat and held her, hugged her, and petted her while I cried. I asked if I could take her home for my daughter and our other dogs to say goodbye. Unfortunately, my husband was out of town for work, so he wasn't able to be there. I carried her out to the car, placed her in the bed in the passenger seat, and drove home. I brought her in and sat down on the couch, letting the other dogs come over to sniff her and say their goodbyes. Then I handed her to my daughter so she could love on her and say goodbye. I sat on the couch holding her and crying for quite a while before I drove her back to the vet's office and dropped off my baby girl for the last time.

Losing Luna that way was incredibly traumatic for me. I was completely broken and blaming myself for everything—wishing I had made the vet appointment sooner, that someone else could have held her during the drive, or that I had let her onto my lap while driving. I second-guessed and "what-if'd" everything. I was so distraught; I wasn't sleeping, had little appetite, and cried constantly. I couldn't believe my baby girl was gone. It was especially hard going to bed since she always slept with me. I missed her so much and wanted her back so badly. I also had a strong feeling that Luna wanted to come back to us, but it was hard to know if she was really trying to communicate or if it was my grief making me feel that way.

Because I was having such a hard time with the loss and my overwhelming grief, I started searching for pet grief support groups on Facebook. I came across the *Pet Loss, Grief Support & Animal Communication & Reincarnation with Susie* group. I read through many posts and saw Susie's responses. I felt like I needed to know that Luna was okay and wanted to make sure I told her how sorry I was because I felt like I had failed her. I reached out to Susie for an animal communication session. I signed up for a ten-question session. A couple of weeks later, she sent me the responses.

Susie explained that there was no fear, pain, anxiety, or grief where Luna was now. The first thing Luna wanted me to know was not to feel guilty, and that there was nothing I could have done to change what happened. She also said that the reason Luna hadn't come to me in dreams or sent signs was that my guilt and grief were blocking her. Luna asked me to let it go and be open to receiving.

One question we asked was if there was anything Luna wanted us to know. She immediately asked if we were ready for her to come back to us. She said she had been with me four other times—not in this lifetime—and that she and our two other girl dogs had also been together many times over the years. Another question was how to find her and know that it was really her. Susie assured me that we would never miss it. Luna said we would know from her eyes. She always had beautiful eyes, and it felt like you could look right into her soul, and she could do the same. She also said that her personality would shine through.

Vixen, our three-year-old Whippet, had gotten pretty sad after Luna's passing. When Luna was alive, she always wanted to run and play with Vixen outside, but we never could let her because Italian Greyhounds are small and fragile. We decided we were hoping Luna would be happy to come back as another small Whippet like Vixen so she could actually play with her. I worried, though, that a Whippet might be too large since Luna wanted to come back as a small dog.

I searched online for Whippet puppies near me and found a litter of five-week-old puppies not far from us. Four were girls. The breeder allowed visits with the puppies the following weekend, so we made plans to go see them. They were too young to tell from the eyes yet. We had another reading with Susie as the next step in the reincarnation process. Luna said she was excited to come home. Susie said Luna kept repeating "happy baby" and the word "small." She also said Luna mentioned "snug as a bug in a rug" and "color change," showing her a ladybug and hearts. Susie thought maybe Luna was indicating a heart-shaped marking or something special.

We drove up to see the puppies that weekend. The two smallest girls, Dahlia and Lily, were both sweet. Dahlia was spunky and lightly pawed at my face when held, but she seemed more independent than Luna was. She pushed her brother aside to lay against my husband's leg, which Luna used to do. Lily was playful but content to be held or sit next to us. She had a marking on her lower back that looked like the shape of Australia. She was smaller with more delicate features. Their mannerisms were so similar that we couldn't tell which baby was Luna. Both were sweet and gave lots of kisses.

Lily sniffed my phone on the floor intently, and when I picked her up, a small white feather was next to it. I had always heard that spirits sometimes leave feathers as signs. We were leaning toward Lily, but because we couldn't be certain, I contacted Susie. She said she could reach out to Luna that night to confirm. She told us the feather was a sign we were in the right place at the right time. Susie contacted Luna that night and confirmed Lily was the right puppy. We contacted the breeder and sent the deposit right away.

Susie explained that this was the reincarnation of the soul into a new puppy, not the same exact pet coming back. Lily slept in a bed on my lap all the way home. When we arrived, Vixen was so excited to meet her. She wanted to play non-stop.

Lily started out lying above my head in bed or across my neck. Thank goodness she grew out of that! As she got older, we saw more of Luna's mannerisms emerge. Luna loved to play with balls, and so does Lily. She loves to chase squirrels and picked out Luna's favorite toy from the toybox, carrying it like her baby, especially at night. She now snuggles in the same spot between my arm and body under the covers, with her head on my shoulder, exactly like Luna did. She even gets zoomies on the bed at night when it's time for bed. Lily also loves to give hugs, although she's too big for us to pick up and hold like we did Luna. We have to get down to her level or sit on the couch to let her hug us.

We are all incredibly happy to have her back home with us again. It has been an amazing process, and we can't thank Susie enough for everything. We were skeptical at first, but hopeful, and it worked out incredibly well for us all.

# EPILOGUE

As this book reaches your hands, Jack and I are savoring a season of peace and joy along the Jersey Shore. At twelve and a half, he carries the wisdom of his years with grace, softened by the spark of eternal youth. Though he now faces the gentle challenges of age—glaucoma, cataracts, and the stiffness that time can bring—his spirit remains irrepressibly alive. Thanks to the advances of modern care, like Librella, Jack runs across the sand with the same exuberance he had as a puppy. To watch him chase the tide or tilt his face toward the ocean breeze is to be reminded that vitality is not measured in years, but in love.

And as Jack continues to remind me daily of the infinite ways love transcends time and form, I find myself called to the next chapter of my own journey. What began as grief transformed into discovery; what began as a single story has blossomed into a mission: to share the wisdom of Universal Law, to shine light on the mysteries of the afterlife, and to guide others in understanding that our connections are eternal.

Even as this book closes, another begins. My next project, a children's story entitled *Never Good-Bye*, carries forward the same message woven through these pages—that love never ends, that presence extends beyond physical form, and that every goodbye is simply a doorway to a new hello. Whether through a child's eyes or an adult's heart, the truth remains the same: we are never separate from those we love.

This book, born from Jack's journey and my own, is not an ending. It is a beginning. My deepest wish is that as you close this final page, you carry with you not only our story, but the certainty that you, too, are never alone. The Universe holds us, guides us, and reminds us that every soul—whether human or animal—walks beside us still.

Jack and I walk forward together, grateful, joyful, and open to what is yet to come. And as I continue to write, teach, and share, I do so with the conviction that these words will ripple beyond these pages, touching lives far and wide. For this is not simply our story—it is all of ours.

— With infinite love and gratitude,
**Susan & Jack**

# ACKNOWLEDGMENTS

To my mother, who has always encouraged me to share my story and to be proud of my accomplishments—thank you for believing in me even when I doubted myself. Your love has been my strength and your faith in me has been the quiet push behind every word of this book. To my grandmothers, whose spirits live within every page.

To **Grandma Mary**, whose intuitive wisdom I carry within me— thank you for spiritually shaping my gift of animal communication and for showing me that the unseen world is just as real as the one before our eyes.

To **Grandma Dotty**, thank you for always opening your home and heart—to me, and to every hamster, bird, and furry friend I brought with me. Your kindness and acceptance helped nurture the little girl who would one day speak for animals.

And to **Jack**, my soulmate through countless lifetimes—thank you for reminding me that love never dies. Our bond is eternal, and your story now brings hope to others who have lost their soul-pet. I am forever grateful for the lessons, the laughter, and the light you continue to bring into my life.

# ABOUT THE AUTHOR

**SUSAN MARANO** is an empathic animal intuitive and lifelong advocate for the sacred bond between humans and their animal companions. A registered nurse for twenty-five years, including service on the front lines of the COVID-19 pandemic, Susan devoted much of her life to caring for others in their most vulnerable moments.

Yet her deepest calling revealed itself in 2011, when her beloved dog Jack crossed over and, in doing so, awakened the psychic gift passed down from her maternal grandmother, Mary. Jack's journey became the inspiration for this story, which aims to open hearts and bring comfort to those who have ever had to say goodbye to a four-legged best friend. As a child, she found joy in caring for all creatures. Today, she continues that path with compassion and grace.

Certified as a Pet Loss Grief Counselor, she gently supports those moving through grief, guiding them to see that love never dies—it only transforms. In addition to her spiritual work, Susan is currently helping her son, Jerry Marano, grow his new venture Cold Noze Creameri—a Colorado-grown, eco-friendly dog ice cream brand dedicated to giving pets healthier, happier treats.

SCAN HERE TO LEARN
MORE ABOUT

*Scan to reach*

**WHISPERS OF THE SOUL:
ANIMAL COMMUNICATION
& THE 12 UNIVERSAL LAWS**